The Princess Story

MODERN
AMERICAN
LITERATURE
New Approaches

Yoshinobu Hakutani
General Editor

Vol. 63

PETER LANG
New York • Washington, D.C./Baltimore • Bern
Frankfurt • Berlin • Brussels • Vienna • Oxford

Sarah Rothschild

The Princess Story

Modeling the Feminine in Twentieth-Century American Fiction and Film

PETER LANG
New York • Washington, D.C./Baltimore • Bern
Frankfurt • Berlin • Brussels • Vienna • Oxford

Library of Congress Cataloging-in-Publication Data

Rothschild, Sarah.
The princess story: modeling the feminine in twentieth-century
American fiction and film / Sarah Rothschild.
p. cm. — (Modern American literature: new approaches; v. 63)
Includes bibliographical references and index.
1. American fiction—20th century—History and criticism.
2. Princesses in literature. 3. Disney characters.
4. Walt Disney Company. 5. Feminist literary criticism. I. Title.
PS374.P646R68   813'.509—dc23   2012014093
ISBN 978-1-4331-1952-1 (hardcover)
978-1-4539-0894-5 (e-book)
ISSN 1078-0521

Bibliographic information published by **Die Deutsche Nationalbibliothek.**
Die Deutsche Nationalbibliothek lists this publication in the "Deutsche
Nationalbibliografie"; detailed bibliographic data is available
on the Internet at http://dnb.d-nb.de/.

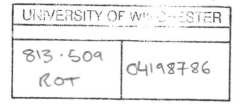
The paper in this book meets the guidelines for permanence and durability
of the Committee on Production Guidelines for Book Longevity
of the Council of Library Resources.

© 2013 Peter Lang Publishing, Inc., New York
29 Broadway, 18th floor, New York, NY 10006
www.peterlang.com

Printed in Germany

For my daughters,
OLIVIA and JULIA,
Who inspired this project
Even though they're not in a princess phase at the moment

For my grandfather,
BENJAMIN MILLER,
Who insisted I be allowed to read
Even when dinner was ready

&

For my husband,
GREG,
Who encouraged me to finish

❖ CONTENTS ❖

❖ INTRODUCTION ❖

What Is a Princess Story?

WHEN I first began considering princesses and the role their stories play in the lives of girls and women, I was the mother of two young girls. My daughters were deeply into pink, and princesses, and wearing dresses—basically being as girly as possible. As their mother and a feminist, I wrestled with this: What was I allowing American culture (and Disney in particular) to teach them? Would they outgrow this phase? Would their future life decisions be impacted by their princess play? Should I dress them in twenty-first century Garanimals, or should I let them express themselves through their clothing as they pleased? Would it be more harmful to allow them to be happy little princesses, or to forbid it?

As my daughters were obsessed, I became obsessed. I began to pay more attention to the princess stories my daughters were consuming and the ways they replicated those stories in their play. I began to read—not just the princess stories and their source material, but the many strands of thought and fields of study that would eventually make their way into this book: folklore studies, feminist studies, studies in children's literature, Disney studies, psychology, sociology, and theories of child development. And I began to recognize that princess stories are different from fairy tales, meaningful in ways that intentionally send messages to girls and women. As this book will demonstrate, princess stories should be considered their own subgenre, worthy of examination. Princess stories have been a part of American popular culture for years, and they will undoubtedly continue to influence and educate American girls and women for many years to come. They should be understood.

In order to understand how my own personal experiences with princesses became the subject for this book, some foundation is needed. The character of the princess, as found in literature and film, has long been a model for emulation and explication. As the embodiment of extreme femininity, the princess character both reflects and inculcates socially desirable behavior and beliefs in and about girls and women in the culture that produces her. A princess story defines the princess in a way that is meaningful both to its audience and to its author, and it teaches its audience how to become a princess through modeling, through commentary, and often through actual princess lessons. America produced a number of "princess stories" in the twentieth and into the twenty-first century. Each of these stories reflected the cultural expectations and anxieties about the roles and responsibilities of girls and women in the period in which it was fashioned. My primary goal in this study is to set out princess stories as a subgenre worthy of examination, much as Mary Cadogan and Patricia Craig's *You're a Brick, Angela!* (1976) did for girls' fiction in general and as Sally Mitchell's *The New Girl* (1995) did for New Girl fiction. Princess stories are a previously undefined subset of fairy tales, which have themselves long been marginalized. Yet fairy tales are important; their enduring popularity for both children and adults speaks to their power. Princess stories are the fairy tales which speak most strongly to many girls, not just in childhood but throughout their lives. It becomes more imperative, then, to examine them.

In tracing the princess story in twentieth and early twenty-first century America, I find the figure of the princess has five primary incarnations from five different eras, three belonging to feminists of different waves and two belonging to Disney Studios, whose patriarchal princess stories serve as counterpoint and resistance to the feminist creations. Frances Hodgson Burnett's first-wave feminist novel, *A Little Princess* (1905), serves as the prototypical princess story; here the princess is envisioned as a thoughtful, self-sacrificing yet self-defining girl whose ultimate reward is to be restored to a loving home. The second iteration of the princess story can be found in Disney's early princess films, *Snow White* (1937), *Cinderella* (1950), and *Sleeping Beauty* (1959), in which the princesses are beautiful and passive, rewarded for their submission by romance and rescue. The third version of the princess story comes from the second wave of feminism; the princess morphs into a girl who is unwavering in her determination to "stand on her own two feet." These independent, anti-romance princesses were soon countered by Disney's second batch of princess stories, the fourth group under examination: *The Little Mermaid* (1989), *Beauty and the Beast* (1992), *Pocahontas* (1995) and *Mulan* (1998). In them, Disney Studios changed the source material to valorize romance, and their allegedly feminist princesses are only superficially different from their mid-century colleagues. Finally, the turn of the century princess stories for young adults offer heroines who combine their independence and achievement with only a secondary interest in romance.

I have two goals in this study beyond identifying the princess story as a subgenre. First, I seek to link the changes in the American princess story to those sought and wrought by the three waves of feminism. The princess is an extremely female role; the character of the princess, the stories she lives, and her social inculcation are all emblematic of and educative for the American girls and women who are the princess stories' primary audience. Princess stories often include a heavy dose of princess lessons, which teach the reading audience as well as the fictional princess how best to become this ultimate girl. While not the only means of inculcating proper ideas of femininity, princess stories, which can both change quickly with their times and which last long beyond their eras, are one powerful, fluid means of doing so. If "the meaning of being female, girl or woman, is constantly subject to change and revision" (Greene 11), then princess stories' plasticity makes them an easy tool in the education of girls and women. The princess story reflects, reinforces, or resists the culture's changing meanings of femininity, as demonstrated by this study's analysis of the American princess story in print and on film.

Second, I use the princess story to examine the dialogic nature of feminism and patriarchy, forces for progress and forces for tradition. As mentioned previously, these forces are embodied by the first, second and third wave feminist princess stories on the one hand and by Disney Studios' princess stories on the other. Furthermore, consumers and creators of princess stories are influenced both by them and by the feminist or antifeminist thought in their society. Traditional (Disney) princess stories were consumed by the girls who became second-wave feminists; as the girls matured, they rewrote the princess stories in ways that reflected and (they hoped) furthered their ideological goals. Disney Studios seemed to accept these changes to the definition of princesses and incorporated them (at least superficially) into their princess story animated films of the 1990s, but there remained some resistance to the ideals espoused by the second-wave feminist stories. The turn-of-the-century princess stories are among the most interesting, tensely balancing romantic desires with feminist expectations. While the field of Disney studies, particularly Jack Zipes' work, has addressed the way Disney has taken possession of and codified traditional fairytales, very few Disney princess stories have been analyzed in terms of their potential impact on female self-image, and none of these analyses have contemplated the princesses specifically, as Disney has branded and marketed them (and as my daughters wanted to own and emulate them).

Early second-wave feminist critics argued three points as they considered fairytales: fairytales discouraged women from realizing their potential; fairy tales highlighted the problems of passive heroines awaiting Prince Charming; and fairy tales assumed men and women are separate but potentially equal (Stone). Traditional princess stories, written in a manner that supports patriarchal values, demonstrate the same qualities feminists identified in the broader category of fairy tales. The points concerning princesses' passivity and their potential are the most important for this study, both because they highlight the ways girls are directed into certain roles through the princess story and because they support the notion of the fictional princess as an object of examination.

Princess stories as fairy tales and as teen novels are important in terms of the effect of reading on the development of identity, just as other teen novels' importance has been well-established (Pecora 49). Yet unlike the identity lessons gleaned from other reading, the lessons in princess stories have often been intentionally, even blatantly, inserted. As girls read princess stories, they internalize the stories' lessons and develop in ways the stories direct. Princess stories are a subgenre of fairy tales, and "fairy tales are among our most powerful socializing narratives. They contain enduring rules for understanding who we are and how we should behave" (Orenstein 10). Traditional princess stories set the traditional fairy tale goal for girls: marriage. According to Orenstein, readers of fairy tales "learn the social and psychological lessons that must be absorbed to reach adulthood" (11). Princess stories take these social and psychological lessons even further than regular fairy tales. They address this socialization directly, by providing not just role models but commentary and lessons for the would-be princess.

Princesses are clearly an important part of girls' popular culture; the roles princesses play and the ramifications of their importance should be addressed. Other artifacts of popular culture have been studied in an effort to "examine the messages mainstream culture gives girls about how to make sense of romance, sexuality, life experiences, body image, as well as gender and culture identity, and the ways girls themselves negotiate these messages" (Odom and Pecora 3). The princess story, as the repository of many cultural expectations, needs similar examination—which this study provides. Deborah O'Keefe has argued that the reading of traditional girls' books is damaging to the reader and to her developing identity. She believes that girls' literature teaches girls to be permanently girlish, not to grow into strong, independent women. Feminist authors who revised princess stories were clearly motivated by many of O'Keefe's concerns: That girls' reading teaches them that females "are the bystanders and the comforters and the sufferers" (13), that they should "deny hostility and avoid confrontation" (13) and that positive feminine qualities, such as sensitivity and helpfulness are "inevitably interwoven" with "submissiveness and self-denial" (14). Princess stories, consumed by an almost entirely female audience, should be examined with an eye toward their inherent lessons and possible effects, especially as these effects may last into adulthood.

Women who contemplate their own reading of fairy tales (princess stories included) can see the stories' influence on their lives. One small psychological study disturbingly suggests that reading fairy tales featuring passive princesses may condition girls to be dominated in future relationships. Susan Darker-Smith suggests that princess stories can be quite powerful, with real-world ramifications, and that authors who intentionally develop their own visions of princesses are correct in thinking that these characters might have significant social impact. Less direly, the essays in *Mirror, Mirror on the Wall: Women Writers Explore Their Favorite Fairy Tales* (2002), edited by Kate Bernheimer, examine the ways in which fairy tales affected the authors' thinking about "emotion, gender, culture and self" (xxiii). Although some women learned the power of narrative as a means of escape, the majority of their impressions tend toward the negative: disbelieving their own attractiveness, or being taught to be silent in the face of abuse, or that the realm of the feminine is trivial. Bernheimer writes that "The exaggerated characters and plots in fairy tales provide interesting mirrors to complex cultural ideas about women" (xxvi). Princess stories, fairy tales about the ur-feminine, can serve as that mirror quite well. Elizabeth Wanning Harries builds on Bernheimer's work as she considers the connection between fairy tales and autobiography, concluding that fairy tales serve as "stories to think with, stories that do not necessarily determine lives but can give children (and adults) a way to read and to understand them" (124). If, as Harries posits, in autobiography there is "no single story of individual growth and development, but rather a tangle of stories caught up...in cultural currents and political realities," then the multi-layered fairy tale fragments, the many princess stories absorbed and unconsciously remembered, give us a way to think about our life stories.

Some might dismiss princess stories as simplistic or archaic, but they are often a form of romance, another often-ignored or maligned genre. Yet romance can be empowering to its readers (Radway), and princess stories can be similarly empowering. One of the key attributes of romances and of princess stories is the readers' ability to identify with the heroine and feel her emotions and, in the case of princess stories, to learn her lessons. Because "most people construct, adapt and use romance narratives at some point in their lives....It is crucial to move beyond condemning romance narratives, to understand their diversity, their uses and how they might be subject to transformation" (Hollows 87). The hundred-plus years of princess stories examined in this study demonstrate their diversity and the ways they were transformed for political and educational purposes; they are far from irrelevant.

It is impossible to consider princess stories without considering gender, as princess stories appeal almost exclusively to girls and women. Gender is not the same as biological sex; it "is constructed, or learned, from the particular conditions, experiences, and contingencies that a culture systematically, and differentially, pairs with human femaleness and maleness, and is a major social category used by most societies as a basis for socialization and for the ascription of social status" (Lott and Maluso 99). A brief discussion of the developmental psychology of gender will demonstrate the importance of princess stories, which both construct and reflect gender concepts. Developmental psychology, particularly concerning gender, offers an interesting theory which is relevant to the different phases of girls' love of princesses and princess stories. People go through different phases of learning gender roles, but not in a linear fashion and not stopping at any particular age. At transitional points in development, such as toddlerhood and early adolescence, children seem particularly sensitive to gender lessons. These are the stages when boys become consumed by war games or football, and little girls become pink-obsessed or princess-happy. Moreover, gender role development, especially for females, continues into adolescence and adulthood, reoccurring at periods of "gender intensification" (Marmion) such as weddings or early motherhood. Interest in princess stories seems to coincide with periods of "gender intensification," stages in life when the person is more aware of and influenced by traditional gender stereotypes.

Gender constancy is a developmental concept with two components, gender consistency (the knowledge that one's gender remains constant throughout a lifetime) and gender stability (the knowledge that gender remains the same despite adopting non-stereotypical behavior or appearance). These usually develop by six or seven years of age, and they impact a person's behavior for a time. "Children who have developed either component of gender constancy (stability or consistency) are generally very motivated to adopt gender-role behaviors, avoiding those associated with the other gender" (Marmion 14). Boys play boy games, such as fireman or football, and girls play girl games, such as house or princess. As children grow through this stage, however, they become much less interested in gender and their play becomes less gender-role specific. Girls outgrow princess play and princess stories; their wardrobes grow to include colors other than pink, and they become less obsessed with being girly-girls.

But childhood is not the only time when gender intensification occurs, nor is it the only time princess stories are popular. Early adolescence is another time of gender intensification and interest in princess stories. Sheila Greene, whose work considers "the psychological significance of the developing body, the changing and mortal body which is both home to the psyche and is intimately involved in making it what it is" (76) explains:

> ...the gendering of subjectivity is liable to wax and wane according to the salience of gender in any particular context and at any particular time. For example, early adolescence has been identified in US culture as a time of 'gender intensification', implying increased gender stereotyping of behavior...One would predict that being a girl and being feminine form central preoccupations for the adolescent female. (Greene 110)

Studies have found this to be the case. As female adolescents' bodies change, so does their preoccupation with gender-stereotypical behavior and interests; they "may increase their gender-stereotypical behavior in order to enhance their appeal to the other sex" (Marmion 15). In some cases, this is detrimental to girls' psychological health; eating disorders develop at this time, and girls begin to show signs of depression and anxiety at higher rates than their male peers (Marmion 15). The reemergence of an interest in princess stories, as evidenced by the plethora of young adult princess story novels, may be one indication of early adolescent girls' gender intensification.

Gender intensification comes at other times in the female life cycle as well. One's wedding may create feelings of gender intensification, and it is no coincidence that Disney has recently created a line of princess-inspired wedding gowns for women who want to feel like princesses on their wedding days. The tagline on the Disney Bridal website makes the connection clear: "Your Fairy Tale Awaits." Kirstie Kelly, first designer of Disney's wedding gown line, uses laymen's language but is clearly discussing gender intensification and the allure of princesses:

The average woman, I don't think on a daily basis, says, 'I want to be a princess
when I get married'...the second she gets engaged, she starts thinking about love,
the idea of a wedding. 'How do I want to feel?' She'll walk into a salon and say, 'I
just want to feel like Cinderella.' That's how they base their decision. 'Do I feel like
a princess in this gown?' (qtd. in Chmielewski)

According to copy on the Disney Bridal website, the dresses "reflect the style
and sensibility of Disney's iconic princesses." Most grown women do not
want to feel like princesses—probably do not even think about princesses—
on a regular basis. But for many women, the gender intensification of their
weddings causes them to reach for the psychological comfort of princess
stories.

Motherhood can cause a similar shift of focus onto gender, particularly
during the "time around the arrival of the first child, when those who have
had a reasonably egalitarian relationship with their male partner may
suddenly find themselves conforming to the traditional female role as mother
and housekeeper" (Greene 110). This phenomenon, the adopting of "traditional gender role norms of the female nurturer and the male provider" is
called "the parental imperative, although there is no evidence that successful
child rearing is related to men and women adopting stereotypical gender
roles" (Marmion 16). Women who read the princess stories available for
adults, usually found in the genres of romance (which has an almost entirely
female audience) and science fiction, may be doing so in part as a reflection
of their gender intensification. Mothers who enjoy seeing their pink-obsessed
little girls playing princesses may not just be observing their daughters'
gender intensification; as relatively new mothers, they may be experiencing
their own in parallel. This may also be one reason that newer incarnations of
the princess story do not simply supersede older versions: women and girls
experiencing gender intensification reach for the most traditional gender-
stereotypical roles.

Gender role development, a complicated, lifelong process, involves
modeling or imitating the behavior of others, which "is related to the availability, likeability, and power of the model" (Lott and Maluso 101). The
overwhelming availability of the Disney Princess merchandise, which has
been much discussed of late[1], creates its own success (it "has currently
generated $3.4 *billion* dollars, with over 25,000 items for sale in 90 coun-
tries" [Goodman]). Girls look for princess models, ultra-feminine, traditionally gender-stereotypical standards, and Disney products are readily
available. Some have dismissed the pink-and-princess years as "a develop-

mental phase of no great consequence, notable only for its commonality" (Goodman). Yet the near-monopoly Disney holds on the market of all merchandise "Princess" is cause for concern. Playing princess might be developmentally healthy, but playing Disney-specific princess is not necessarily salutary. According to Lyn Mikel Brown, "When one thing is so dominant, then it's no longer a choice: it's a mandate, cannibalizing all other forms of play" (qtd. in P. Orenstein). While much has been written recently about the value of purchasing and playing "princess," examining Disney's incredibly popular merchandizing line, not as much attention has been paid to either the Disney princesses within their stories[2] or to non-Disney princess.

Playing princess and reading princess stories also speak to the power of archetypes, to our most powerful cultural and psychological myths. The princess is an easily recognizable character, a variation of the damsel in distress archetype. Archetypal criticism in folklore and fairytale studies recognizes the importance of such archetypes, recurring characters, plot patterns or motifs found in tales around the world and across time. Marie-Louise Von Franz uses Jung's theories to explain how fairy tales from around the world provide insight into humans' archetypal experiences. Archetypal images in fairy tales, according to Von Franz, "afford us the best clues to the understanding of the processes going on in the collective psyche" (1). Archetypes encourage the audience, the readers or viewers of princess stories, to "participate ritualistically in basic beliefs, fears, and anxieties of their age. These archetypal features … tap into a level of desires and anxieties of humankind" (Delahoyde). Examining the changes to this archetype in American fiction through the twentieth century and into the twenty-first will show the changing "beliefs, fears, and anxieties" of their ages, and the ages' desires as well.

Romance writer Tami Cowden has identified and labeled eight female archetypes; her definition of the waif (into which category she places pretty, passive princesses and damsels in distress) has "child-like innocence [which] evokes a protective urge in the beastliest of heroes" (Cowden). This waif archetype is the character presented by Disney's first group of princesses, Snow White and Cinderella and Sleeping Beauty; her strength, according to Cowden, is her ability to endure. "These women are pure at heart, at times a little too trusting, and also insecure. They seem to be untouched by the world, patient and adaptable to any situation. They carry on, looking for the day when they are free of their travails, but taking little action to bring that day closer" (Cowden). But this waif should not be the only princess given to girls to emulate, and feminists of all three waves offered variants that are less passive and pure. Many of the princess stories I examine go beyond using the princess/damsel in distress/waif archetype. They promote it, or deny it, or try to find a version appropriate for their era. How is this archetype used as protagonist or foil, what commentary is offered, and how do authors seek to change it in hopes of changing their audience?

Each chapter in this book illustrates the ways princesses and princess stories reinforce and shape the culture that produced them. Chapter One, "*A Little Princess*: A First-Wave Feminist Girl," examines Frances Hodgson Burnett's life as a first-wave feminist and the ways *A Little Princess*'s Sara Crewe embodies Burnett's feminist beliefs. Although Burnett never publically declared herself a feminist, and she is not generally ranked among those of the first wave, her life and the issues she raised in her work certainly belie the absence of that feminist label. Sara Crewe, whose personal project is to become princess-like even in the face of hardship, is the prototypical modern princess. She transforms herself into a princess through intentionally cultivated qualities of character and through her strong sense of identity. She is a character worth emulating, both within and without the world of her book. For readers to learn from and emulate the heroine is one of the primary goals of the princess stories, and Sara Crewe is the prototypical princess.

A Little Princess is enduringly popular; dozens of versions, from picture books to unabridged, scholarly annotated editions, are currently available. Her story was thrice adapted by Hollywood during the twentieth century, in Mary Pickford's 1917 silent film, in Shirley Temple's barely-recognizable version of 1939, and in director Alfonso Cuarón's 1995's production. Each of these adaptations reflect the changes in society at the time they were produced, and what each one does with Sara's character illuminates the ways this princess story was modified to make it more palatable to its period. Interestingly, the most recent filmic adaptation most undermines Sara's story, rendering her least powerful of the three.

Chapter Two, "Disney's First Princess Stories," explores the ways Disney's first three princess stories, *Snow White* (1937), *Cinderella* (1950), and *Sleeping Beauty* (1959), ignore the progress made by first-wave feminists in favor of a retrogressive view. For millions of Americans, the Disney version of these princess stories is the definitive one, but Disney himself had a very conservative worldview; these films combine elements from traditional fairy tales with mid-twentieth century American mores to perpetuate his old-fashioned outlook. These are the princess stories which give princesses a bad name, each valorizing its heroine's domestic qualities: her joy and competence in tending house and patient acceptance in awaiting her prince. The princesses are passive, with two of them in magical comas for part of their stories and the third sobbing at home until magical intervention grants her desire. Archaic as their outlook is, these princess stories remain current in American culture, their films available for home viewing and their merchandise heavily marketed. The lessons these stories teach young girls and the ways in which they serve as a foil for second-wave feminists are the focuses of this chapter.

Chapter Three, "Second-Wave Feminism and Ideologically Intent Princess Stories," highlights the largely forgotten ways that feminists in the 1970s and 1980s adapted the princess story for their ideological purposes. Second-wave feminist critics in academe examined the traditional princess stories, decrying the cultural imperatives dictated by the stories and absorbed by their readers. Traditional (Disney) princesses, to whom most American feminist critics had been exposed as children, were taken to task for their passivity and their exclusive goal of marriage. Simultaneously, second-wave feminists revised those stories in ways that would better reflect their feminist beliefs.

This chapter is divided in half. The first half, divided into three sections, focuses on the work of the Ms. Foundation: Gloria Steinem's appropriation of Wonder Woman, the Amazon Princess; the *Free to be...You and Me* project, a record album, book and television special which featured the princess story "Atalanta"; and *Stories for Free Children*, which was both a regular feature of *Ms. Magazine* and a stand-alone collection. The second half examines second wave feminist princess stories not affiliated with the Ms. Foundation. These include some of the few successful second-wave feminist princess stories, *The Paper Bag Princess* and *The Ordinary Princess* (both first published in 1980 and both still in print) foremost among them. Finally, the question of why so few second-wave feminist princess stories reached cultural saturation is examined; while princess stories from every other era still survive, layered into popular culture, these second-wave feminist princess stories are not generally known today. Ironically, the success of the women's movement in America may be one reason for their stories' unusually ephemeral nature. As artifacts of an important moment in feminist history, they are worthy of examination; moreover, as Catherine Orenstein noted in an interview with *Ms. Magazine*, "the women's movement so changed the fabric of society that you see all our myths being reinvented all the time as a result" (qtd. in Cupaiuolo). These second-wave feminist stories paved the way for widespread revisions such as those seen in Disney productions and, more convincingly, in the third-wave feminist princess stories.

Chapter Four, "Disney's 'Feminist' Princess Stories," examines in depth Disney Studios' late twentieth century princess stories. Disney's depiction of princesses changed in response to a changing society; in an America that had adapted many feminist precepts, Disney needed to create more modern, more independent princess stories. The new group of stories, *The Little Mermaid* (1989), *Beauty and the Beast* (1991), *Pocahontas* (1995) and *Mulan* (1998), purportedly offer feminist-friendly protagonists. Yet the alterations are largely superficial, and a close examination of these end-of-the-century princess stories reveals a disturbing, distinctly anti-feminist undercurrent. These Disney tales leave their heroines' feminist mindsets unsupported by the world in which they live; at the end of the twentieth century, the studio had yet to create a feminist heroine operating in a world that lent any support to her beliefs and values.

Chapter Five, "The Third-Wave Princess Story: A Redefinition," explores early twenty-first century princess story in novels for young adults and in Disney adaptations of two of them. The princesses in these novels neither passively await their princes nor eschew romance altogether. They have personal goals and desires, and romance is but a delightful addition to their busy lives. The girls consuming these stories live in a culture that recognizes the demands of feminism and the desire for the feminine; in the terminology of Jennifer Baumgardner and Amy Richards, these princess stories are within the realm of the girlie, at the intersection of the feminine and the feminist (*Manifesta* 136). These princess stories play against the traditional vision of the princess, deploring her blond passivity, yet they do not denigrate the idea of princesses in general. Instead, they seek to redefine the princess and retell the princess story in a way that makes sense in modern America.

Meg Cabot's *The Princess Diaries* series (begun in 2000) is an interesting example of third-wave feminist princess stories, and Cabot intentionally embedded lessons for her readers as well as for her protagonist. Disney's two *Princess Stories* films render this three-dimensional princess sitcomishly flat, with few goals or adventures outside the romantic. Disney's alterations went even further in Gail Carson Levine's *Ella Enchanted*, taking a strongly feminist character engaged in independent adventures and diluting her strength, deleting her independence and making her curse of obedience humorous rather than psychologically torturous. These filmic versions of young adult princess stories are the ones more widely disseminated, yet frustratingly, they are the ones more likely to compromise the heroine's integrity.

When contemplating the changes made by feminists to American culture, no one figure is as worth examining as the fictional princess. An ultra-female character, she serves as a paragon of femininity. The princess' various creators define her differently, in light of their disparate views on females and female roles, views which changed with the times. There is no one depiction or idea of the princess in American fiction over time; as Peggy Orenstein has said, "the myths that we tell and the social and cultural narratives that we replicate every generation, every year, are powerful driving forces but they are not static. They are constantly evolving. They are timeless because they are so historical and adaptable" (qtd. in Cupaiuolo). So it is with the princess. The character and the lessons her stories teach, both implicit and explicit, demonstrate what it was to be female through the twentieth and into the twenty-first century in America. They also serve as markers of social upheaval, artifacts of times when American culture was under stress. Orenstein writes that "princess mania is a response to a newly dangerous world." She quotes historian Miriam Forman-Brunell as saying "Historically, princess worship has emerged during periods of uncertainty and profound social change" (Orenstein). Thus examination of princess stories can shed light on American culture as a whole in addition to girl culture.

More than that, though, Sara Crewe and Disney's *Cinderella* are still in current circulation, existing side-by-side with more modern princesses; to ignore them or to assume that they have been usurped is to ignore works that remain hugely influential. As Christina Bacchilega, postmodern transformations of the fairy tale are "doubling and double: both affirming and questioning" (22). Princess stories, a strain of fairy tale, have this doubling and doubled effect. The telling and retelling of princess stories is powerful, retelling (as Bacchilega writes of fairy tales) "history, values and gendered figurations" (24). Princess stories do not go out of currency; they become layered, one new incarnation on top of and next to the previous one. Tracing the princess story in twentieth and early twenty-first century America demonstrates the various iterations of feminist thought during the same period and the multiplicity of female expectations and experience. This book will trace the changing definitions of the princess and examine the ways princess stories have been used by different forces in society, feminists and traditionalists, as a means of social progress or resistance to that progress.

❖ CHAPTER ONE ❖

A Little Princess:
A First-Wave Feminist Girl

FRANCES HODGSON BURNETT'S 1905 novel, *A Little Princess*, serves as the prototypical princess story for the purposes of this study. It has long and repeatedly been described as a Cinderella story (sometimes favorably, sometimes deridingly), and there certainly are elements of a fairy tale in the story of rich Sara Crewe's fall into abuse and penury and her later restoration to love and wealth. But the defining element of a princess story is the educative quality of the material: princess stories include a heavy dose of princess lessons, which teach the reading audience as well as the fictional princess how best to become this exemplary girl. For the purposes of this discussion, and certainly for the examination of the prototypical princess story *A Little Princess*, a princess story is defined as a story in which the protagonist either is a princess or is attempting to become one (either through marriage or through character development). There is always an element of the transformative in these stories: the heroine transforms into or becomes identified with a princess through marriage or through discovered identity, or both—and the girls reading about her are encouraged to do the same.

A Little Princess is a princess story with biographical overtones from its author's life, but more than that it is a work that exemplifies the ways first-wave feminist thought permeated American culture. So while some may dismiss *A Little Princess* as a Cinderella story, far more important are the ways in which Sara Crewe is not like Cinderella: her strong sense of identity and her intentionally cultivated qualities of character and imaginative power make her a princess worth emulating, both within and without the world of her book. This chapter, which examines *A Little Princess* as the defining princess story, has three goals. First, as Frances Hodgson Burnett is not generally ranked among the first-wave feminists, some background into her life is required to set the stage for *A Little Princess* as the work of a feminist. Next, *A Little Princess* will be examined as the ultimate "princess story," serving as a model and comparison for those explored in later chapters. Finally, I will analyze how Hollywood film adaptations changed the story to suit the needs of audiences throughout the 20th century.

Frances Hodgson Burnett:
Representative of the Woman Movement

AS Ann Thwaite, Frances Hodgson Burnett's biographer, writes, "I have always been amazed that the women's movement didn't take Frances Hodgson Burnett up earlier because she was the most extraordinary figure in her time" ("Biographer" 18). Frances Hodgson Burnett, whom I shall call "Frances"[1] in this section, lived from 1849 to 1924, almost exactly the years of what we now consider the first wave of feminism. Hers was a fascinating, troubled life, one which could, superficially, be called a Cinderella story—but which was decidedly not one. Shortly after her death, her son Vivian said people would be surprised to know "the fact that her life was not a happy one" (qtd. in Gerzina xvi). She was a woman "who worked within and against the restrictions of Victorian life to develop her own code of spiritual and moral behavior; who wrote love stories but ardently believed in a woman's right to independence" (Gerzina xvii). She was the wealthiest woman writer of her time, British or American, and yet she toiled relentlessly, even after fame and fortune came to her; she would often fall ill from financial pressure and the ceaseless writing with which she staved it off. She suffered deeply with the loss of her beloved son Lionel. She struggled, as women have always done, to combine work and family—and she began this struggle young. Although never a declared feminist, Frances Hodgson Burnett certainly lived and wrote as one.

Frances experienced two failed marriages. She married both times under duress, emotionally blackmailed the first time (afraid that Swan Burnett would harm himself if she refused him) and financially blackmailed the second (Stephen Townesend threatened to ruin her reputation). Neither marriage provided her support or pleasure, and in each she was the main breadwinner, even to the detriment of her health. Her experiences as a wife would provide both autobiographical and philosophical fodder for her work.

Her first marriage came at the end of a seven-year courtship, for Frances "reveled in her freedom and seemed in no hurry to marry" (Gerzina 40). Swan Burnett was more intense about the relationship, more seriously involved; although "both felt equal ambition for their careers" (Gerzina 40), being married was more in line with a working man's future than a working woman's. In the largely autobiographical *Dolly* (1877), Frances describes the heroine's love interest as far more interested in her than she was in him, and this certainly seems the case between Swan and Frances as well. This novel also valorizes freedom and unconventionality, both of which Frances values more as she ages. Frances resisted marriage, although she would eventually, reluctantly acquiesce, and the two were married in 1873. Her distinct lack of enthusiasm for the union would determine the course of their relationship.

According to Thwaite, an 1876 trip to Manchester illustrates the stress that Frances felt in her dual roles of wife and breadwinner. One new acquaintance recorded their meeting in a letter, describing himself as surprised that Frances was an author; she had seemed "much like many thousands of other young English wives and mothers" (qtd. in Thwaite 52) and a "fond unpretentious wife" (Gerzina 63) in her attention to her young children and in her support of her husband's interests. Thwaite, however, finds this image of Frances as the ideal nineteenth century woman a false front. A wife "was supposed to be submissive, quiet, gentle, to identify herself with her husband's will and interest, bear his children and keep his house. Frances was already well aware that her nature did not her for this, but that any other path was likely to be a thorny one" (52). The combination of life as both a financially successful author and a dutiful wife, and the stresses of the juxtaposition, irritated Frances and eroded her marital relationship.

Frances traveled alone frequently throughout her marriage to Swan, developing exciting new friendships. "[S]he began to associate with women who held advanced social ideas, women who wrote and edited, and who regularly moved in the stimulating atmosphere of books and women's rights" (Gerzina 87). Her circle of friends would widen and become increasingly important to Frances, and her friends' influence would be seen both in her work and in her lifestyle. She was befriended by Mary Mapes Dodge and Louisa May Alcott; she had a great deal in common with both. She spent the summer of 1880 at Nook Farm, "a warm and familial community of writers, professionals, and activists" (Gerzina 91), invited there by Isabella Beecher Hooker, a women's rights activist. Harriet Beecher Stowe and Mary Hooker Burton, Isabella Hooker's married daughter, were also there. Through her relationships with these women, Frances found not only the peace and productivity she had been looking for, but a new recognition of her own social beliefs. At Nook Farm,

> ... she found her complicated feelings about domestic life ratified: women could be
> both devoted mothers and ambitious authors. They could stand for what they believe
> and expect the support of their husbands. In theory at least they could find a way to
> achieve what they wanted on both the family front and the public one. She worked
> some of this different kind of feminine view into her fiction beginning that summer.
> (Gerzina 95)

Indeed, her views on marriage and women would become more progressive and be more frequently and plainly evidenced in her work.

She befriended other free thinking women during her marriage to Swan, besides those she met at Nook Farm. In 1885, Frances met Gertrude ("Kitty") Hall and her sisters, Gigi and Daisy. Their friendship drew Frances away from home and into a wider world. In 1893, she developed a friendship in London with Ella Hepworth Dixon, editor of the *Englishwoman Magazine*, and author of *The Story of a Modern Woman*, a book considered shocking by some for its feminist viewpoint. "Frances, however, was glad to meet another woman and writer who dared to question rules governing 'proper' female behavior" (Carpenter 87). Her circle of friends and her work would make her feminist views more public and more solid.

By 1884, "it seems certain that their marriage had already ended in every real sense" (Thwaite 89), although Frances made no open break from Swan for another fourteen years. She stayed, according to Thwaite, for their two sons, and because divorce was so unconventional. She traveled extensively, crossing the Atlantic a remarkable thirty-three times in her life (Gerzina xiii), but "Frances's prolonged absences from home put a strain on a marriage that she was clearly beginning to question" (Gerzina 107). She was obviously willing to put this strain on her marriage, preferring her independence to the relationship. After one eighteen-month trip to Europe, she suddenly "bought 'a lovely house for myself' at 1770 Massachusetts Avenue.... There was no mention of Swan, and the sale was in her name" (Gerzina 126). The legal question of who had the right to take out a mortgage on this house would eventually sound the death knell for the marriage. By the time she and Swan filed for divorce in 1896, using the charges of desertion and failure to support, "her friends believed her to be divorced already" (Gerzina 196) and encouraged the decision; according to the *New York Herald*, "Friends, knowing that their differences could never be reconciled, have frequently advised that a divorce be secured" (Thwaite 177). Friends, in fact, "were stunned not by the news but by the fact it hadn't occurred years before"

(Gerzina 203). Frances seemed about to live the life of freedom she had long wanted.

It is odd that Frances married again given the destruction of her first marriage, to say nothing of her statements against marriage in general and the female friends who would have lauded her for remaining unmarried. She had long been linked publically and professionally with Stephen Townesend, a doctor turned actor who served as Frances' business manager. They had met in (or shortly before) the summer of 1889, when he was "a handsome young man of 29 (she was 39)" (Carpenter 70). They were linked romantically in the press, and perhaps their relationship crossed boundaries of propriety. Frances took him under her wing, writing parts for him and allowing him to be recognized as her co-author. He handled her business dealings and secretarial work, but as "she wrote to Vivian, she seemed to do more in the way of taking care of him than the other way around" (Gerzina 153). It was a strangely co-dependent relationship.

His temperament was difficult, and "his moods and neediness wore her down" (Gerzina 154). Yet even with these difficulties, evident from the first, she married him. They had a "terrifying and terrible relationship…he had bullied and blackmailed her into marriage, and she feared he was mad" (Gerzina 217). Stephen's behavior, both before and during their marriage, follows a pattern easily recognizable today. His mood swings, his jealous outbursts, the way he isolated her from her friends and family, his apologies and protestations of love all constitute a psychologically abusive relationship, even if it never progressed to physical violence. "Vivian wrote later that Stephen took a position of 'domineering ownership'" (Carpenter 97), another hallmark of abuse.

She married him to protect herself and her reputation, but she could not predict the ways he would try "to drain into himself everything she represented: fame, financial freedom, even power" (Gerzina 220). She wrote about the situation in a letter to Vivian:

> Why in heavens name should I – free, able to support myself – with an enviable position, surrounded by friends, holding as my most fixed creed that *not* to be married was Paradise – why should *I* marry any man -- & of all men one who was penniless, horrible in temper & more impudently tenacious & exacting than any creature ever beheld –besides seeming at times not to have any taste or thought in common with me…I cannot imagine myself *willingly* marrying any man. (qtd. in Gerzina 222)

Thwaite concludes "that he had literally blackmailed her into it and that the reason he did so was her money. He needed her financial support and her patronage, but he was sick of being an underdog. As her husband, he would have rights" (Thwaite 191). Considering her fame and financial freedom, it is surprising today that she agreed to marry Stephen, but as a woman who (most likely) had a bit of a past, and whose reputation as an author was by then based largely on children's books, she felt she had to protect herself.

Frances managed to keep Stephen from acquiring control over her money, although he pressed her for it repeatedly. She also, despite her fears to the contrary, survived the relationship. After a complete physical collapse in the spring of 1902, Frances entered a New York sanitarium; she gathered her strength, summoned her husband, and ended their relationship. He seems to have agreed without a fight, and he never followed through on his supposed threats to blackmail her (Carpenter 100), although Thwaite believes it likely that Frances did pay him off (203). They did not divorce, but Stephen was quickly off her mind and out of her life. Frances soon resumed the freedom and social life that she had enjoyed prior to their marriage.

The views Frances developed as a result of her financial self-sufficiency and her unfulfilling and unhappy marital relationships found expression in her work for adults, in which she develops her positions on marriage and women. These views did not go unnoticed. In 1895, she was honored as 'the Woman of the Moment' by London's Vagabond Club. She was becoming recognized as a New Woman, although she never claimed that label. Even married to Swan, she lived as a New Woman, challenging traditional gender roles and claiming her own public and intellectual life. "Frances, at forty-six, was older than the young women whom the term generally covered, but in other ways she could serve as a model for them. She had forged an independent life for herself in literature and, although married, no longer seemed bound by its traditional restraints" (Gerzina 184). Both the freedom she claimed in her first marriage and her doubts concerning that relationship were evidenced in her work from that time; the philosophical and political beliefs which resulted from her disastrous second marriage are central in her later work.

Through One Administration (1883) "examines a failed marriage, the consequences of marrying the wrong person" (Thwaite 74). In it, Frances "grappled with the fact that 'she married the man who loved her' rather than following her own heart, that she gave in to her worries that he would do himself harm and fall into misery if she refused" (Gerzina 96); in fact, she had delayed marrying Swan as long as possible because, as she confessed in later years, "she never wanted to marry anyone—marriage was too confining, especially for a woman as independent as she" (Gerzina 40). The book, reflecting her personal experience, was "about a loveless marriage held together primarily for the sake of the children" (Gerzina 102). The novel contains a love triangle, but the element of interest in this for Frances was the lack of love between husband and wife rather than the romance. There is also an astonishing admission: the heroine, who is generally taken to represent Frances herself, admits that she is less fond of her husband and children than people might expect.

A Lady of Quality (1896) explores the question of what woman was. It tells the story of a girl raised like a boy until, at fifteen, she decides to turn back into a girl in order to make a good marriage. Frances found this character, Clorinda Wildairs, "a wonderful creature....a beautiful virago renowned for her splendid build & strength & nerves of steel" (Gerzina 179). Clorinda shared "Frances' determination to remake herself and her future, her maternal instincts, and her ability to keep damning secrets" (Gerzina 179). More than that, Frances wrote to a friend,

> Clorinda is not at all a departure for me ....That 'Lass o' Lowrie's' was Clorinda in disguise – so were Rachel Ffrench and Christian Murdoch in 'Haworth's.' So was Bertha Amory, who laughed and wore tinkling ornaments and brilliant symphonies in red when she was passing through the gates of hell—so was little Sara Crewe when she starved in her garret and was a princess disdaining speech. Oh, she is not a new departure. She represents what I have cared for all my life. (qtd. in Gerzina 179)

Although Frances had declared that she was not interested in examining the Woman question, the character of Clorinda casts doubt upon that statement.

The Making of a Marchioness (1901) returns to the question of marriage "as a financial and social arrangement rather than as a love match" (Gerzina "Life and Legacy" 13). It is, writes Gerzina, "an unflinching commentary on marriage... she pulls no punches when she talks about the Victorian and Edwardian marriage state" (225). One character recommends "If people will marry, they should choose the person least likely to interfere with them" (qtd. in Thwaite 76); here Frances wrote from experience, as lack of interference was one benefit of her first marriage. In *The Making of a Marchioness,* love "is not necessary for marriage; money is" (Lurie 88). The social burdens placed upon women abound: the burden to marry well, and the competition for a good husband; the threats of illness and poverty and little education.

The heroines, who are granted a happy ending, know exactly how lucky they are.

By the time Frances published *The Shuttle* (1907), she had suffered not just one but two failed marriages: the first, irritating and pointless; the second, abusive. Begun while married to Stephen, "the book offers many insights into their relationship" (Carpenter 98). Based as it was on Frances's marital troubles and the conclusions she drew from them, "*The Shuttle* signals a more explicit feminism, as Frances confronted social double standards and a legal system that did not necessarily support women" (Gerzina 249). Rosalie, the heroine, "quickly learns that her marriage is 'one of those nightmare[2] things in which you suddenly find yourself married to someone you cannot bear and you don't know how it happened, because you yourself have had nothing to do with the matter'" (Lurie 101). Frances herself had learned that even bowing to a husband's unreasonable demands could not improve an abusive marriage; the heroine of *The Shuttle* learns the same.

As Frances's growing feminism is evidenced in her novels, it was also evidenced in her public statements. She had achieved an enviable state of financial and personal freedom, with enough money for comfort and no demanding husband to interfere. Interviews with her indicate hope for marital happiness—for others. "Women today are freer than ever before from the awful necessity of acquiring the first man in sight" (qtd. in Gerzina 265). The marriages in her books were "about strong women finding their equals" (265). More overtly,

> ...in 1909 she, along with other major writers, signed a petition by the National American Woman Suffrage Association supporting a constitutional amendment granting women the right to vote. As the women's suffrage movement gained force in New York and rallies were held in Manhattan in 1910, the Equal Suffrage league received a message from Frances saying 'she was also a suffragist.' In her later years, when asked to join in marches, she agreed, but when her poor health kept her in bed she sent in donations and added her name to lists of supporters of the cause. (Gerzina 265)

It took many years and two failed marriages, but Frances did eventually take her beliefs about women public.

Frances's feminism can perhaps best be considered through the shifting, overlapping facets of the Woman Movement as described by Susan Cruea, who sees True Womanhood, Real Womanhood, Public Womanhood and New Womanhood as "overlapping parts of a long-term change in cultural attitudes toward gender, a gradual shifting of power away from its patriarchal basis, and a steady movement for women toward twentieth-century feminism" (1). Upon the death of Frances' father, her middle-class, domestic mother abruptly learned that True Womanhood, the female role "bound by kitchen and nursery" would not put food on the table; she was forced to work. Frances's childhood was, as a result, freer and less bound by middle-class conventions than it might otherwise have been. She was ripe for the beliefs of Real Womanhood, which encompassed new attitudes toward health, education, marriage, and employment. Real Womanhood encouraged "healthy exercise and activity, permitted women a minor degree of independence, and stressed economic self-sufficiency as a means of survival" (Cruea 3); it also considered spinsterhood preferable to an unhappy or abusive marriage. The third phase of the Woman Movement, Public Womanhood, "allowed women to be engaged in the cultural realm"—as Frances, a professional writer, surely was. The cultural impact of 1884's *Little Lord Fauntleroy* alone was tremendous (if derided by some), sparking a fashion craze and Fauntleroy souvenirs including playing cards, writing paper, toys and chocolate (Carpenter 50). More than that, she challenged lax copyright laws and won, in a precedent-setting case. Her impact on the culture in this matter was lauded by The Society of British Authors (Carpenter 65) and benefitted authors on both sides of the Atlantic.

The final stage of the Woman Movement, with which Gerzina identifies Frances, is New Womanhood. The New Woman rejected marriage and motherhood "and turned to a career for emotional and intellectual fulfillment" (Cruea 9), which is only partially true for Frances (although perhaps more true for her than she thought). She certainly did reject marriage, resisting the marital state as long as she could, and ultimately escaping both of her two marriages. As for rejecting motherhood—that is harder to evaluate. According to Gerzina, "her work excited her just as much, needed just as much protection, and took just as much effort as the raising of her children" (76). On the one hand, she spent a tremendous amount of time away from her children, leading professional and social lives which did not include them. On the other hand, she wrote them long, sentimental, whimsical letters, and seems to have thought those letters an acceptable substitute for herself. She also suffered deeply, cruelly, with the death of her first-born, Lionel; it is hard to conclude that she rejected motherhood.

Another belief shared by the majority of women involved in the New Woman movement was "that sexual identity and behavior should not be linked with public respectability. Sexual activity should not destroy a woman's reputation" (Cruea 9). This, Frances did not adhere to—although certainly it would have been better for her had she been able to do so. She was blackmailed into her terrible second marriage because Stephen Townesend had "threatened to go public with stories about their relationship, to tell people she had pursued him from the moment she saw him and that he had been able to kiss her within only two weeks of meeting her" (Gerzina 218). Certainly, her life would have been better without the power of these threats; but as Frances was never quite a New Woman, she could not open the intimate details of her life to public scrutiny and judgment. Frances travelled far down the path of the Woman Movement; if she did not fully embrace the ideals of the New Woman, she was not alone. "Though nineteenth-century culture was not ready for the New Woman, for many women, she represented the promise of a future where, someday, independent, intellectual women would be accepted. Without these alternative ideals, the feminist movement might never have occurred" (Cruea 10). Frances' importance, and the importance of others who stopped short of the Cult of True Womanhood, cannot be overstated. From her determination to support herself through writing, to the marriages she left, to her life as an ocean-crossing benefactress of friends, relatives and strangers, Frances Hodgson Burnett lived as a feminist.

A Feminist Princess Story: *A Little Princess*

Burnett's *A Little Princess* has withstood the test of time; it is still in print in various editions, abridged for younger readers, and made into coloring books and movies. First serialized in *Saint Nicholas Magazine* as "Sara Crewe; or, What Happened at Miss Minchin's" in 1888, it was published that year both in a stand-alone edition and in a hardcover collection by Scribner's. Burnett later reworked the story into a play. Titled *A Little Un-Fairy Princess* for its London December, 1902 opening and retitled *The Little Princess* for New York the following January, this play introduced many characters not included in the original story. Scribner's later encouraged Burnett to revise her novella, incorporating the new characters and episodes from the play; she did so, and *A Little Princess*, with a new introduction by the author explaining how this was now "the whole of the story" was published in 1905. The story's basic premise remained unchanged through these permutations: rich Sara Crewe is orphaned, impoverished, and abused before being restored to family, wealth and love. Burnett wrote many stories with a Cinderella theme, and this is surely one of them; but the Cinderella aspects of this tale are not what make Sara Crewe and *A Little Princess* of enduring interest.

A Little Princess, Burnett's final version of Sara Crewe's tale, is an excellent example of what I call a princess story: it has the structural underpinnings of a traditional fairy tale, with a girl protagonist; and it has a preoccupation with the transformation into princess-hood. For although some critics would argue that Sara is a princess from the start of her story, the truth is that she is not. Phyllis Bixler, for instance, argues that "Burnett's stories do not emphasize a change within the main character but rather in the recognition of that character's true nature" ("Tradition" 193). She sees Sara's challenge as that of maintaining "the charitable nature and even temper of a princess" (194). Yet Sara changes over the course of her story; she learns to control her temper through her princess play, and she learns consideration for others as well. While other characters call Sara a "princess", some with a smile and some with a sneer, Sara does not adopt the title herself until later; when she does claim princess status, it has nothing to do with the material wealth on which others previously based their assessments.

Most importantly, *A Little Princess* is a princess story in that it is educative; the character learns how to be a princess, and as she learns, the reader learns as well. Although "it has been read as a Cinderella story, it is actually the story of maturation and self-discovery" (Keyser 241); it is also the story of the heroine's discovery of others, of understanding and relating to those around her. Defining herself and self-identifying as a princess are Sara's ways of both improving herself and becoming less self-centered. As Roderick McGillis writes, these lessons transcend the world of the book:

> In fact, we might say that the power of story in *A Little Princess* takes both Sara and the reader beyond story. By internalizing her sense of what a princess is from her reading of books, Sara turns to act in the real world by feeding the populace. The final gesture of the book is also an encouragement to the reader to go beyond the book and act in the reader's real world. (71)

Burnett's *A Little Princess* not only teaches and transforms its heroine into a princess; it provides a model for its readers so that they might do the same to themselves.

Although each of Burnett's versions retains the same basic story, it took three iterations for Sara Crewe's story to evolve from a Cinderella tale of redemption to a true princess story. None of the critics examining the development of "Sara Crewe" into *A Little Princess* have discussed the growing importance of the princess concept to Sara, but this concept is the key to her character development and the key to her position as a role model. In "Sara Crewe," being a princess was one of several "pretends" that Sara enjoyed. It does become a repeated metaphor towards the end of the story, but it is not nearly as important as it will be in the novel. In the stage version, some of the other girls, jealous of her wealth, snidely refer to Sara as a princess; Miss Minchin seems to take this as a sign of respect and uses the appellation as well. While there is some discussion of the value of playing princess, the needs of stagecraft limit the pretend play in favor of interaction with others. In *A Little Princess*, the meaning of being or becoming a princess is enmeshed with the condition of creating one's own life. Burnett thus created a heroine who can serve as a role model both for those fictional characters around her and for her readers. Sara is restricted in her beliefs and behavior by her time, it is true, and restricted as well by her youth, but she develops into a strong and independent princess nonetheless. As the story developed from novella to play to novel, it became more princess-centric, deeper and more educative.

The story is replete with lessons, both having to do with being a princess and having to do with being a strong female. Sara-the-princess is not, as McGillis would have it, "obedient, agreeable, [and] dutiful" (17). Deborah Druley and I disagree with McGillis's depiction, because "although Sara upholds many Victorian feminine values, she also violates and challenges them through her exercise of agency and free thought" (Druley 58). McGillis's description of a princess has little to do with the qualities that make Sara special. She acts more from her sense of ethics than from blind duty; she has a "fine, hot little temper" (Burnett 21) that is often aroused when she sees injustice. She draws others to her both with her power of invention (and her storytelling) and with her disinclination to be disagreeable. But Sara as a character draws readers to her as well, not because she is always agreeable but because we see her struggle with the negative elements of her personality. Moreover, her story offers "crucial knowledge…that we truly are who we feel ourselves to be, that we can trust this inner certainty regardless of how others perceive us, or what they wish us to become" (Schwartz 224). Sara's struggle to improve herself and to hold on to her personal identity links the concept of being a princess to inner strength, and as she schools herself she also schools her readers.

The Value of Female Community

One of Sara's first lessons is to respect and value other girls. In Chapter I, we are told that Sara "did not care very much for other little girls, but if she had plenty of books she could console herself" (Burnett 7). She comes to school expecting to avoid the other little girls by losing herself in books. Yet Chapters III, IV and V are all about her interactions with other girls: Ermengarde, Lottie, and Becky. These chapters, each of which demonstrates a key element about Sara's personality (that she has a sense of justice, that she is motherly, that she is egalitarian), also establish the girl-friendships which will become important to her when her fortune is gone. These girls, whom Sara befriends at the height of her wealth and power, and from various positions of superiority in relation to them, will sustain her when she is in need. Their relationships will grow and change, nourishing her in different ways.

Becky the scullery-maid is the first of Sara's diminished-status friends. In the first weeks following Sara's plummet into poverty, Sara "was far too proud to try to continue to be intimate with girls who evidently felt rather awkward and uncertain around her" (Burnett 73), but as Becky shares her penury there is no social barrier between them. They initially become friends when then-wealthy Sara comes across Becky asleep in her sitting-room. She allows Becky to rest and feeds her cake, and Sara comes to the realization that "we are just the same—I am only a little girl like you. It's just an accident that I am not you, and you are not me!" (41). Sara is willing to cross class lines to befriend a girl who clearly needs a friend, and she stands up to Lavinia, the school bully, to do so.

Most importantly, it is Becky who gives Sara the idea to pretend to be a princess. Seeing Sara in her dancing-frock inspires Becky to tell her about the time she saw a real princess ("I called her to mind the minnit I see you...You looked like her" [42]). Sara's response is immediate: "I've often thought...that I should like to be a princess; I wonder what it feels like. I believe I will begin pretending to be one" (42). She and Becky spend a few more minutes together, with Sara feeding Becky cake and promising to tell her stories. The two have changed each other in this initial interaction. Becky "had been fed and warmed, but not only by cake and fire. Something else had warmed and fed her, and the something else was Sara" (43). Sara, in turn, has been inspired to start the pretend play that will lead to personal growth, and as Becky leaves, Sara muses "If I was a princess—a real princess...I could scatter largess to the populace. But even if I am only a pretend princess, I can invent little things to do for people. Things like this. She was just as happy as if it was largess. I'll pretend that to do things people like is scattering largess" (43). This idea of being a princess, suggested to her by Becky, will comfort and sustain Sara through the travails to come.

Simply knowing Becky prepares Sara for the horrors of her new life of hardship; she's heard all about the rats in the attic, where Becky sleeps (Becky once told her, "You gets used to the noise the makes scuttling about. I've got so I don't mind 'em s'long as they don't run over my piller ....I'd rather have rats than cockroaches" [49]). After the death of Sara's father, Becky and Sara become much closer. They live in adjoining garret rooms; they share days of toil and nights of cold and fatigue. Sara helps Becky by inviting her to pretend they're in the Bastille together and by sharing what food she has. Sara is twice rescued from this misery, and she brings Becky along. When Ram Dass secretly brings material comforts to the attic, Sara shares her fire and food with Becky, and Becky gets Sara's old mattress to add to hers. Later, when Sara's identity is discovered and she is removed to Mr. Carrisford's home, she brings Becky along as her maid.

Sara's second friend in poverty is the one she met first: Ermengarde, "the monumental dunce of the school" (22). Sara pities Ermengarde when their classmates laugh at her, and this pity is the basis of their friendship. Ermengarde is fat and dull, but she admires Sara and loves her devotedly. They are not equals when Sara lives in luxury; Ermengarde "clung to Sara in a simple, helpless way; she brought her lessons to her that she might be helped; she listened to her every word and besieged her with requests for stories" (75). When Sara's father dies, Ermengarde has been so insignificant to her that Sara forgets about her for a time.

But Ermengarde, who does not forget Sara, will teach her the value of friendship. Ermengarde suffers sorely with Sara's change in status, but cannot think of an effective way to bridge the financial gap between them. Sara lashes out at her for an awkward attempt at intimacy, but she later repents: "she realizes that if her wretchedness had not made her forget things, she would have known that poor, dull Ermengarde was not to be blamed for her unready, awkward ways" (76). Sara, however, initially misinterprets this awkwardness and further avoids Ermengarde—until Ermengarde takes matters into her own hands, creeping to the attic to visit and clear the air. Sara takes comfort in this visit: "It must be confessed that Sara's small black head lay for some minutes on the shoulder covered by the red shawl" (78).

Sara concludes, "Adversity tries people, and mine has tried you and proved how nice you are" (79). Sara tutors Ermengarde in French, and Ermengarde provides Sara with books; the dullest student in the school is thus responsible for Sara's continued education and mental stimulation. In a crossing of boundaries similar to the one she experienced first with Becky, Sara, who "always felt very tender of Ermengarde, and tried not to let her feel too strongly the difference between being able to learn anything at once, and not being able to learn anything at all" crosses the boundary between clever and not. Through Ermengarde she comes to appreciate that "to be able to learn things quickly isn't everything. To be kind is worth a great deal to other people" (134). Sara and Ermengarde and Becky together cross economic and educational barriers to break bread and play together in the attic.

Sara's third friend in her reduced state is Lottie, first introduced as "a very appalling little creature" (30) of four years old, throwing a tantrum about being motherless in order to manipulate those around her. Sara bonds with Lottie by telling her that she, too, is motherless, but that she will be Lottie's new "mamma." Lottie, as the youngest of Sara's friends, might be expected to bring her the least. While theirs is quite an uneven relationship while Sara is wealthy—Sara defends Lottie against bullying, kisses away her pains, and generally babies the younger girl—Lottie brings Sara unexpected gifts after Sara's fall. Lottie, too young to understand Sara's plight, seeks her out one afternoon. Sara cuddles her, finding "a sort of comfort in the warmth of the plump, childish body" (81). Physical affection is a human need, and Lottie provides that to Sara. More than that, as they look out the skylight, they throw some crumbs from Lottie's pocket to sparrows; Sara will use the largest of these crumbs later that day as she begins to tame the rat that will become her pet. Lottie thus provides Sara two kinds of affection, small but crucial comfort to someone in Sara's circumstances.

There is another girl important to Sara, although she is not to be found at Miss Minchin's. When Sara was wealthy, surrounded by servants and with "toys and pets and an ayah who worshipped her…she had gradually learned that people who were rich had these things" (6). Sara does not, however, understand poverty at the start of the story. She learns this through her own experiences and through her interactions with Anne, the beggar-girl, a "little figure not much more than a bundle of rags" (119). Sara's "princess pretend" reminds her that this girl is "one of the populace." One extremely hungry day Sara purchases six buns but gives five of them to Anne, rationalizing to herself that "if I'm a princess—when they were poor and driven from their thrones—they always shared—with the populace—if they met one poorer and hungrier than themselves" (120). This, according to Marian E. Brown, illustrates "the novel's real theme, which is that it's no use pretending you are a princess unless you behave like one when the occasion arises" (204). Seeing Sara's generosity moves the baker-woman to invite Anne into the shop; Sara has saved Anne from starving not just for a day, but permanently.

Sara does not forget this girl or her own days of hunger, and once she has been restored to wealth, she conceives a plan: "I was wondering if I could go to the bun-woman, and tell her that if, when hungry children—particularly on those dreadful days—come and sit on the steps, or look in at the window, she would just call them in and give them something to eat, she might send the bills to me" (185). When Sara revisits the shop, she learns that Anne is still there. Sara asks her if she would like to distribute the buns to hungry children herself. The girls converse little, but "Sara took her hand out of her muff and held it out across the counter, and Anne took it, and they looked straight into each other's eyes….And, somehow, Sara felt as if she understood her" (187). These relationships between Anne and Sara, Sara and the baker-woman, and the baker-woman and Anne, speak to how each female helps the other and raises her out of herself and her own miseries. "Almost despite her deep-seated class consciousness, Burnett has created a true female support group that includes members from both ends of the social spectrum" (McGillis 86). Indeed, the mutuality of their gaze and the communication that passes between them suggests an equal relationship. Sara, who had no use for girls when she first came to London, has been buttressed and comforted by the friendships she has made, and for all her seeming superiority, each girl has taught her a valuable lesson.

Sara's positive relationships with each of these disparate girls—the scullery-maid-turned-mentor, the dullard-turned-source of stimulation, the brat-turned-comfort, and the beggar-turned-colleague in largess—mitigate the negative relationships which develop with Miss Minchin and Lavinia. They keep Sara from forgetting who she is, bolstering her identity. As Knoepflmacher notes, "the characters of Ermengarde, Lottie, Becky, and the street child Anne act as relational outlets in Sara's dramatic struggles to avoid self-fragmentation and death" (xiv). They serve as her foils and mirrors, reminding her who she is and what she values. They also, according to Reimer, offer a 'writing beyond the ending' hope "that a remnant of female community can exist within the patriarchy" (128). If *A Little Princess* were merely a Cinderella tale, as it has so often been dismissed[3], Sara would not have made these friendships; she would have been adrift in a world of stepmother and stepsisters, here represented by Miss Minchin and Lavinia. Instead, according to Janice Kirkland, the story's message is that "we must not let the malice of the Miss Minchins of the world make us malicious; instead we must make kindness contagious" (193). The sympathetic and supportive female characters far outweigh the antipathetic and antagonistic ones; Sara learns, and we readers learn with her, that girls can help girls, and that a female community can be sustaining through hard times.

Self-Perception

There is no getting around the princess elements in *A Little Princess*, and it is true that this story, like many others Burnett wrote, is set on what has been categorized as a Cinderella framework. Indeed, Cinderella stories were very popular at the time the permutations of Sara Crewe's story were written. Yet this one is different:

> Burnett's Cinderella demonstrates some significant advances over her predecessors: Sara's fortunes are not restored by marriage, nor is her endurance either mute or passive....Sara also plays an active role in her redemption; not, however, through 'longing and plotting' but through imaginative invention and sympathy. (Gruner 168)

Sara is thus a strong character, not the passive one generally associated with Cinderella. She teaches herself to be the sort of princess she admires, one like her vision of Marie Antoinette: a "noble and determined woman, a model of fortitude and resistance" (Gruner 169). The sort of princess Sara decides to become is not determined by her appearance. She is in control of those things she can control, she is kind, and she is generous.

Others apply the appellation of "princess" to Sara long before she does. Shopgirls suppose she must be "at least some foreign princess—perhaps the little daughter of an Indian rajah" (11). Miss Minchin, less impressed, finds her luxurious clothing "perfectly ridiculous" and notes that "she has been provided for as if she were a little princess" (13). (Miss Minchin also immediately plans to put Sara and her "ridiculous" finery at the front of the line of school-children when the walk to church, so while the clothing may be inappropriate, it is not unappreciated.) Sara's maid, pleased with her position, remarks to herself, "Elle a l'air d'une princesse, cette petite" (16). But these princess remarks are made neither to Sara nor by her; they are based on outer trappings and not on the character of the girl herself. As such, they do not impact Sara; she is unaware of them. These comments are based on appearances, and Sara considers herself unattractive; she would dismiss such comments as irrelevant and inapplicable and absurd. She likes princess stories, as evidenced both by the tales she tells her schoolmates and by her reaction upon first finding Becky asleep in her room (she is reminded of Sleeping Beauty), but she does not yet identify with princesses herself[4].

Not until the end of Chapter V, nearly a third of the way through the novel, does it occur to Sara to play princess. From then on, it becomes one of her "pretends," but not the only one. Sometimes she pretends to be a soldier, her first play-role; sometimes, in her poverty, she is a prisoner in the Bastille. The most effort, however, goes into being a princess—in part because the lessons of being a princess are harder than those of being a soldier or a prisoner, and in part because it is harder to hold onto princess values in poverty. Princess play gives her strength and self-control, and serves not simply as an escapist fantasy but as a method of self-preservation. When others were cruel, Sara imagined their reactions to her princess identity; "she found comfort in [the idea] and it was a good thing for her. While the thought held possession of her, she could not be made rude and malicious by the rudeness and maliciousness of those around her" (109). Sara holds her tongue, saving herself a beating on at least one occasion, by imagining she is a princess; this inner persona improves her situation both psychologically and materially. And of course, princess is a more desirable role for little girls than that of soldier or prisoner.

Sara shares this imaginary play with her friends, which is revealed in giggling, mocking conversation between Lavinia and Jessie, her best friend.

> "One of [Sara's] 'pretends' is that she is a princess. She plays it all the time –
> even in school. She says it makes her learn her lessons better. She wants Ermen-
> garde to be one, too, but Ermengarde says she is too fat."
> "She is too fat," said Lavinia. "And Sara is too thin."
> Naturally, Jessie giggled again.
> "She says it has nothing to do with what you look like, or what you have. It has
> only to do with what you *think* of, and what you *do*." (45)

This conversation highlights several crucial elements in Sara's conception of a princess. The first is that a princess values education, or perhaps she values work—either way, if being a princess helps Sara learn better, then being a princess is active. No one learns her lessons better by sitting passively. Secondly, being a princess has nothing to do with appearance or material possessions; Sara urges Ermengarde to play princess even though Ermengarde is fat (and later will encourage herself to be a princess in "rags and tatters"). The only requirements for being a princess, according to Sara, are what you think and what you do—in other words, your beliefs and your actions determine your identity. Your surface, the "you" that others see, is irrelevant. Fat or thin, rich or poor; anyone can be royal, if she's willing to school her thoughts and behaviors.

Denying the value of appearance is quite powerful. Throughout the story, Sara will maintain her control and her identity by not acceding to others' perceptions of her. She is powerful in the sense of the subject-object problem: she is always the subject in her own story, not the object. She is always powerful, always active, because she is always the subject; she sees the world around her and uses her imagination to make perceptual changes in the world. One of the first things we learn about Sara is that she is observant; she has a "queer old-fashioned thoughtfulness in her big eyes" (Burnett 5). Sara quickly and correctly assesses both the school and Miss Minchin upon first meeting, and she will correctly assess the things she sees throughout the novel. As Marian E. Brown writes, "[Sara] is observant, the first step in being in control" (201). But Sara's gaze is more than merely observational; she uses her perceptions of those around her to maintain control of herself and of the situations in which she finds herself, situations in which she would otherwise be powerless. The ways she looks at herself makes her powerful in a Lacanian ideal-ego sense; others looking at her have no power to change who she is.

The fact that Sara is so often looking at others (and either seeing them clearly for who they are, as she does with Miss Minchin and Lavinia, or inventing stories about them, as she does with the Large family) establishes her in a position of power. "Gaze" is more than simply looking at something; according to Jonathan Schroeder, "it signifies a psychological relationship of power, in which the gazer is superior to the object of the gaze" (qtd. in Chandler). The gaze, then, characterizes the relationships between the subjects by looking—and as Sara is almost always the one looking, she is almost always the one in the position of power. Her superiority through gazing is often remarked upon in the novel, especially after her fall into reduced circumstances; she loses her material superiority, but she maintains her inter-relational, psychological superiority. As Sara becomes more and more impoverished and the students have begun to feel "as if, when they spoke to her, they were addressing an under-servant" (74), jealous, bullying Lavinia remarks on Sara's gaze:

> "...I can't bear that way she has now of looking at people without speaking—
> just as if she was finding them out."
>
> "I am," said Sara promptly, when she heard of this. "That's what I look at some
> people for. I like to know about them. I think them over afterward."
>
> The truth was that she had saved herself annoyance several times by keeping an
> eye on Lavinia, who was quite ready to make mischief, and would have been rather
> pleased to have made it for the ex-show pupil. (74)

Sara knows all about Lavinia and refuses to be victimized. This may be seen
as a defensive act, but Sara's gaze is a pre-emptive strike and as such shows
Sara on the offensive. She renders Lavinia powerless by her gaze.

The domineering Miss Minchin also finds Sara's gaze particularly unsettling, both when Sara looks at her—almost into her—and when she cannot
disturb Sara enough to change the expression in her eyes. "Sometimes, when
she was in the midst of some harsh, domineering speech, Miss Minchin
would find the still, unchildish eyes fixed upon her with something like a
proud smile in them" (106). The fixity of Sara's gaze is disconcerting to
Miss Minchin, especially when Miss Minchin knows she has been cruel to
the girl. Sara gazes at Miss Minchin one final time, when Miss Minchin,
understanding that none of Sara's restored wealth would be coming to her
seminary, appeals to her to return to school. Miss Minchin first tries to
manipulate Sara by evoking her dead father; she then lies outright (choking
on her words a bit):

> "And—ahem! —I have always been fond of you."
>
> Sara's green-gray eyes fixed themselves on her with the quiet, clear look Miss
> Minchin particularly disliked....
>
> She looked Miss Minchin steadily in the face.
>
> "You know why I will not go home with you, Miss Minchin," she said; "you
> know quite well."
>
> A hot flush showed itself on Miss Minchin's hard, angry face (177).

Her sister, Miss Amelia, elaborates with misery: "She saw through us both.
She saw that you were a hard-hearted, worldly woman, and that I was a weak
fool, and that we were both of us vulgar and mean enough to grovel on our
knees before her money, and behave ill to her because it was taken from her"
(179). Sara's powers of observation allow her to retain some semblance of
control in the face of those who would do her wrong, and they bring her
wrongers to despair in self-awareness.

Sara also deflects the gaze of those who would cast her in a role different
from that which she chooses to play; she refuses to be the subject of an-

other's gaze when that subjectivity would be detrimental to her self-identity, her ego-ideal, her princess pretend. Running errands in the evenings, Sara develops the game of inventing stories about her neighbors. Her favorite is "the Large family," a household with many children whom she watches fondly and gives fanciful, romantic names. One night, however, in an actual encounter with some of them, Sara's outer appearance and her inner identity clash. The five-year-old boy sees Sara, who has paused to watch the family enter a carriage, evidently on the way to a Christmas party. The family had been reading stories about giving charity, and the young boy "burned with the desire to find such a poor child and give her a certain sixpence he possessed, and thus provide for her for life" (92). He sees Sara watching him, and he misinterprets her hungry eyes: "He did not know that they looked so because she was hungry for the warm, merry life his home held and his rosy face spoke of, and that she had a hungry wish to snatch him in her arms and kiss him" (92). He offers her a coin. Startled, Sara begins to decline his offer. She recognizes that she would be at the other end of the same encounter she had had so many times when she was wealthy, and she does not want to be the receiver in this exchange. Seeing his face fall, however, she reconsiders:

> There was something so honest and kind in his face, and he looked so likely to be heartbrokenly disappointed if she did not take it, so Sara knew she must not refuse him. To be as proud as that would be a cruel thing. So she actually put her pride in her pocket, though it must be admitted her face burned.
> "Thank you," she said. "You are a kind, kind little darling thing." (93)

He goes away proud of himself, and Sara goes away surprised that she might be mistaken for a beggar.

Keyser reads this incident as evidence that "Sara's habit of viewing herself and others as fictional characters has begun to trap her in the roles others would have her play—such roles as princess, prisoner, pauper" (236). But this, I believe, is a misreading. The older children of the Large family recognize that Sara is not what she first appeared to be; they become interested in her and call her "The-little-girl-who-is-not-a-beggar" (94). Even more importantly, although Sara graciously allowed the boy to give her his sixpence, she does not accept it as offered, as money. Instead, she bores a hole in it and wears it on a ribbon around her neck. It so completely becomes not-money, not-charity, that she does not spend it even at her nadir. According to Kirkland, "Being a princess means, to Sara, being in control not of her surroundings but of her own perceptions of them and her reactions to them"

(196). Even more than having control of her perceptions of her surroundings, Sara holds onto her perception of herself. She refuses to accept the young boy's perception of her; she refuses to be the object he perceives her to be. Her grace and kindness toward him and her talisman-like treatment of what would be charity in a different situation show that she retains her position as subject, not object.

Self-Control and Reliance

Another lesson, besides those of valuing female community and maintaining a position of psychological power, is that of controlling one's anger. Sara, we are told, occasionally demonstrates "a fine bit of unheavenly temper" (37). Her father declares that if Sara had been a boy, "she would have gone about the country with her sword drawn, rescuing and defending every one in distress. She always wants to fight when she sees people in trouble" (21). This characterization of Sara having a temper when others are in need is charming, prince-like, but not necessarily the whole truth—although her father, never having seen her in any situation to be angry on her own behalf, would not know his error. She is irritated by commonplace things as well as seeing others suffer injustice; for instance, "never did she find anything so difficult as to keep herself from losing her temper when she was suddenly disturbed while absorbed in a book" (46). She goes to great lengths to keep control of her temper; it is a struggle, but she usually succeeds by recalling her inner princess identity. Lavinia brings out the worst in her when she threatens to slap Lottie.

> "Well," [Sara] said, with some fire, "I should like to slap you, —but I don't want to slap you!" restraining herself. "At least I both want to slap you—and I should like to slap you, —but I won't slap you. We are not little gutter children. We are both old enough to know better."
>
> ....Sara...looked as if she were going to box her ears. Perhaps she was.... She felt the blood rush up into her face and tingle in her ears. She only just saved herself. If you were a princess, you did not fly into rages.....When she spoke it was in a quiet, steady voice; she held her head up, and everybody listened to her.
>
> "It's true," she said. "Sometimes I do pretend I am a princess... so that I can try and behave like one." (47-48)

This scene combines Sara's control of her temper with her gaze; after her final comment, she "stood quite still, and stared at [Lavinia] steadily" (48), until Lavinia turned away. Both her control and her gaze serve as effective weapons against her enemies.

Miss Minchin, of course, has more opportunity to harm Sara, and thus Miss Minchin falls prey to Sara's self-control more often. Sara's self-control defies Miss Minchin's cruelty, and Miss Minchin feels this defiance. "When she was scolded she stood still and listened politely with a grave face; when she was punished she performed her extra tasks or went without her meals, making no complaint or outward sign of rebellion. The very fact that she never made an impudent answer seemed to Miss Minchin a kind of impudence in itself" (154). It's not that Sara isn't angry; she's furious. She admits that "I've thought perhaps I might do something wicked, —I might suddenly fly into a rage and kill Miss Minchin, you know, when she was ill-treating me" (133). But ultimately expressing this rage would hurt Sara far more than Miss Minchin, and by controlling herself, by maintaining her dignity and outward appearance of calm, she irritates Miss Minchin far more than she could by crying or raging. She does this with great self-awareness:

> I never answer when I can help it. When people are insulting you, there is nothing so good for them as to not say a word—just to look at them and *think*. Miss Minchin turns pale with rage when I do it, and Miss Amelia looks frightened, and so do the girls. When you will not fly into a passion people know you are stronger than they are, because you are strong enough to hold in your rage, and they are not, and they say stupid things they wish they hadn't said afterward. There's nothing so strong as rage, except what makes you hold it in—that's stronger. It's a good thing not to answer your enemies. I scarcely ever do. (95)[5]

Being a princess helps Sara stay strong in the face of her enemies and thus defeat them.

Sara also defies Miss Minchin in other small ways. We first see her defiance immediately after Captain Crewe's death, when Miss Minchin orders her to put down her doll. Her refusal highlights the true relationship she and Miss Minchin have: "She had always made Miss Minchin feel secretly uncomfortable, and she did so now. She did not speak with rudeness so much as with a cold steadiness with which Miss Minchin felt it difficult to cope— perhaps because she knew she was doing a heartless and inhuman thing" (66). Again, Sara's control of her emotions grants her the upper hand. She, bereaved, has the emotional strength not to comply with an unreasonable demand, and Miss Minchin is left feeling ill at ease. At the end of this first post-poverty interview, Sara does lose control a bit, but although "her thin little chest heaved up and down," she simply "spoke in a strange, unchildishly fierce way" (68). She does not, as requested, thank Miss Minchin for her kindness in giving her a home; instead, she declares "You are *not* kind, and it is *not* a home" (68). Miss Minchin can do nothing but "stare after her with stony anger" (68).

Sara refuses to kowtow in the face of Miss Minchin's fury. One memorable day Miss Minchin startles Sara out of a reverie. Sara, thinking of various royal personages in disguise, wonders what Miss Minchin would say if she knew that Sara herself was a princess. "The look in her eyes was exactly the look Miss Minchin most disliked. She would not have it; she was quite near and was so enraged that she actually flew at her and boxed her ears" (107). Sara, startled, laughs. She explains that she was thinking, and when Miss Minchin demands she beg her pardon at once, Sara refuses. "I will beg your pardon for laughing, if it was rude...but I won't beg your pardon for thinking" (107). Sara's response, then as always, was to "say something queer" and "not seem the least bit frightened" (107). She explains that she was imagining being a princess, and what Miss Minchin's reaction to the discovery would be; every girl in the schoolroom stared, wide-eyed, enthralled. When Miss Minchin breathlessly sent her away, "Sara made a little bow. 'Excuse me for laughing, if it was impolite,' she said...leaving Miss Minchin struggling with her rage, and the girls whispering over their books" (108). This quiet defiance, a combination of emotional control and daring to stand up for herself, undermines Miss Minchin's authority and leaves Miss Minchin buffeted by her anger. Sara wins this confrontation by being polite, dignified, and unafraid to assert herself.

Sara also defies Miss Minchin by maintaining her relationships with Lottie and Ermengarde. Miss Minchin is quite adamant in her desire for Sara to lose contact with the students: "I will not have her forming intimacies and talking to the other children.... It is better that she should live a separate life—one suited to her circumstances" (73). But Ermengarde and Lottie each sneak to Sara's room, and Sara defies Miss Minchin in more ways than one. Not only do the girls continue to be her friends, but Sara tutors them in their lessons. Ermengarde's much-improved French is a source of mystery to Miss Minchin; similarly, "[s]he doesn't understand why Lottie is doing her sums so well...but it is because she creeps up here, too" (135). Undermining Miss Minchin's low expectations of her least-favorite students affords Sara and Ermengarde a laugh at Miss Minchin's expense. Laughter is part of Sara's nature (her very name, besides "princess" means "she who laughs"), and it is an act of defiance.

Pretending to be a princess also becomes an act of defiance for Sara. Many times Miss Minchin characterizes the look on Sara's face or her refusal to be beaten down as "defiance"—and these are brought to her by her princess pretend.

> "There is something very disagreeable in seeing that sort of thing in a child of her age," said Miss Minchin, with haughty vagueness.
> "What—sort of thing?" Miss Amelia ventured.
> "It might almost be called defiance," answered Miss Minchin, feeling annoyed because she knew the thing she resented was nothing like defiance, and she did not know what other unpleasant term to use. "The spirit and will of any other child would have been entirely humbled and broken by—by the changes she has had to submit to. But, upon my word, she seems as little subdued as if—as if she were a princess." (158)

Miss Minchin clearly sees her own thwarted desire to break Sara's spirit—she stumbles when naming the element that should have broken Sara's spirit, settling on "changes" but really meaning herself. She also very clearly remembers, although she denies it, the day that Sara wondered about her reaction to finding out her true princess identity. But deny it though she does, Miss Minchin herself likens Sara to a princess. Sara defies Miss Minchin by being her best self, playing her princess pretend.

Sara learns to value female community, to control her anger, and to defy those who would harm her. "One thing might ring from these pages: a girl is not helpless, silent, entirely dependent, and necessarily subservient. Girls can survive on their own merits and using their own wits" (McGillis 40). Sara's gift of storytelling, of changing her perceptions and those of people around her, is one of her great strengths. Other strengths include her recognition of the value of work (see Connell), her ability to mother those around her (see Gruner), and her generosity. Some of these are inherent in her character, and some come to her over time as she develops her princess identity.

Other Feminist Issues

Burnett declared some of her feminist beliefs through Sara; others she let ring through the supporting characters. The wide range of female characters, for instance, offers many opportunities to look at women in the world. Miss Minchin herself is an excellent example of a sharp businesswoman; she is mean-spirited but also smart, as Captain Crewe's solicitor notes: "he knew that Miss Minchin was a business woman, and would be shrewd enough to see the truth. She could not afford to do a thing which would make people speak of her as cruel and cold-hearted" (61). Miss Minchin recognizes the money Sara could save her, too, when she was old enough to become a full teacher. Similarly, at the end of the novel Mr. Carmichael explains Sara's changed situation "and all its legal significance, which was a thing Miss Minchin understood as a businesswoman, and did not enjoy" (175). She is cruel; she is narrow-minded; but she is an educated businesswoman. Miss Amelia, on the other hand, is "the better-natured of the two, but she never disobeyed Miss Minchin" (13). She is often portrayed as kind but ineffectual, with a sort of innocent insight that Miss Minchin lacks. "Pretty, comfortable Mrs. Carmichael" (172), the mother of the "Large" family, is loving and happy, sympathetic to Sara's plight and tender in trying to counter the years of privation. "She felt as if [Sara] ought to be kissed very often because she had not been kissed for so long" (172). She is a stay-at-home mother, not a woman working outside the home, but she is not the only kind adult female model; the baker-woman, too, is both kind and employed, and she mothers Anne. This wide range of adult female roles speaks against essentialist beliefs about what women should do and be.

The story ends with Sara restored to wealth, living with her father's best friend, and surrounded by loving friends and caregivers. She is restored to her own childhood. Her story most emphatically does not, as Gruner has pointed out, end in marriage, as many princess tales do. Nor does it end in death, the other common ending for novels of the time. She has the powerful, valued position of mother without the powerless position of the romantic beloved: "Nurturing poor children with food and the wealthier children of the Large family with her imaginative tales, Sara exercises a maternal function without the intermediate steps of courtship and marriage which so often occupy center stage in the Cinderella story" (Gruner 178). *A Little Princess* demonstrates that there is no need of a romantic love interest in a successful princess story, although many later princess stories will indeed have romantic love at their center.

McGillis would argue that "Burnett's position is ostensibly conservative. She champions the female as nurturer, a dispenser of largess and a person willing to sacrifice for others, especially for men" (1). I disagree. Sara's princess pretend does lead her to dispense largess toward other girls, but only those she perceives as needing it more than she; self-sacrifice is not her defining characteristic. She ultimately gives away nothing she cannot afford: imagination to her schoolmates and buns to Anne. Nor do I see her dispensing largess to men; there are few men in the novel, and those who are there are rarely in the same chapter as Sara. When she does interact with them, she is usually the receiver of largess: Ram Dass conceives of and facilitates the "magic" gifts Sara receives in her garret, and Mr. Carrisford spends his money planning "many charming things" (184) for Sara. The relationships she develops are mostly mutual; Sara is not the sole source of love and comfort in her world, as McGillis suggests.

Two elements of *A Little Princess* are especially problematic for today's readers: colonialism and class relations. While Burnett intentionally embedded princess lessons into *A Little Princess*, she also unconsciously imbued the novel with her beliefs on colonialism and class, and these are less appropriate for modern readers. Ram Dass is first seen emerging from the neighboring attic-window, and his "picturesque white-swathed form and dark-faced, gleaming-eyed, white-turbaned head of a native Indian man-servant" tells Sara he is "a Lascar" (102). In responding to her smile, he loses his grip on the monkey he had been cradling, and Sara asks him in Hindustani if the monkey will let her catch it. His response to her fluency in his native tongue is remarkable:

> The truth was the poor fellow felt as if his gods had intervened, and the kind little voice came from heaven itself. At once Sara saw he had been accustomed to European children. He poured forth a flood of respectful thanks. He was the servant of Missee Sahib....
>
> Ram Dass thanked Sara profoundly. She had seen that his quick native eyes had taken in at a glance all the bare shabbiness of the room, but he spoke to her as if he were speaking to the little daughter of a rajah, and pretended he observed nothing. He did not presume to remain more than a few moments, and those moments were given to further deep and grateful obeisance to her in return for her indulgence...then he salaamed once more and got through the skylight and across the slates again with as much agility as the monkey himself had displayed. (104)

Sara's memory is stirred by this interaction; she remembers the years she spent in India being salaamed by her servants and slaves.

The condescending way Burnett describes Ram Dass, highlighting his "native" quickness and likening his agility to that of a monkey, reeks of colonialist superiority. In a later scene, when Ram Dass and Carrisford's secretary are inspecting her room, Ram Dass discloses the ways he has been observing Sara; he knows her "sadness and her poor joys; her coldness and her hunger" (126). He is intimately knowledgeable about her habits and her needs, and he declares "If she were ill I should know, and I would come and serve her if it might be done" (127). He observes Sara and wishes to serve her—and Ram Dass' scheme to supply her with comfortable accommodations was served up to "the Sahib Carrisford" in order to entertain him and comfort him in his sickness. Ram Dass thus serves two English masters simultaneously, seemingly from love and concern for them both. That this is presented as the natural order of things is problematic for today's readers.

Roderick McGillis sees in *A Little Princess* "Burnett's incorporation and feminine revision of what I think of as the 'Crusoe syndrome'...the imperial enterprise that was all pervasive in late Victorian England" (11). *A Little Princess*, according to McGillis, "accepts the imperial myths while it also promotes the woman's cause" (11). The female Crusoe story had to incorporate the notions of feminine gentleness and passivity into the imperialistic ethos. Burnett offers "a revisionary look at imperialism" (13) in that the colonies are considered to have a weakening effect—Sara's health dictates that she must return to England, and her father's business in India leads directly to his death and Sara's poverty. While Sara's Indian fortunes are returned to her, there is no suggestion that she or Mr. Carrisford will return to India. Thus, while McGillis sees *A Little Princess* as revisionary, "Burnett cannot escape the imperial ethos of her time" (13). In other words, the relations between colonizer and colonized, Sara and Ram Dass, are not ideal—but not nearly as bad as they might have been.

Mavis Reimer examines *A Little Princess* with an eye for "its reproduction of privilege" (112). The princess herself is a figure that can "function rhetorically as a metonym for the British system of rule at home and in the colonies" (114). That others of lower status refer to Sara as a princess from the beginning, based on her evident wealth, suggests to Reimer that "princesses are made by their subjects" (115). She also finds in Sara's relation to Ram Dass, who recognizes her instantly as having the right to rule, that "'the whole story' is as much about an Imperial child coming to power as it is about a powerless child beset by powerful adults is also evident in Burnett's representation of the racialized other" (116). Ram Dass, in speaking to Sara as the daughter of a rajah and in fulfilling her dreams of comfort, demonstrates "the imperial subject's power to command others" (117). Ram Dass "is also the rhetorical figure on which the narrator transacts the relation between the child-adult structure and the Oriental-Occidental structure" (124). Although Sara and Ram Dass are first linked by their homesickness and loneliness, this link is disavowed when Ram Dass places Sara above himself. Ram Dass is also linked to Mr. Carrisford, when he relates the story of the child Sara to him; this link, too, is disavowed when his status as servant and native is brought to the fore ("Without the help of an agile, soft-footed Oriental like Ram Dass...it could not have been done" [169]). As

Reimer notes, "the limit of [Ram Dass's] likeness is set by his racialized identity" (125). Reimer also finds many allusions to the 1857 Indian Mutiny: Ram Dass listening at Sara's skylight raises the specter of "predatory native sexuality" (125); that Sara's mother was French links her to the aristocratic women who died in the French revolution; Captain Crewe's diamond mines are "a metonym for the wealth generated for the homeland by the 'jewel in the Crown'" (126). These images and allusions are not at the fore of *A Little Princess*; rather, "Burnett accedes to the dominant narrative of her culture and reproduces that narrative as the quiescent ideology of her text" (127). It is asking much of an author to expect her to completely transcend her time, and Burnett does not manage to do so.

As issues of race surround Sara's relationship with Ram Dass, issues of class surround her relationships with Becky and Anne. Although Sara encourages Becky to play princess with her, Becky never quite becomes facile with the game. Eileen Connell finds in Becky, and to a lesser extent Ram Dass, the Victorian coding of gender and class. *A Little Princess* "shows that the production and maintenance of English domestic life depends upon the hierarchies of class and race....Burnett's representation of a princess who is forced to be a maid both reveals and conceals the physical, dirty work swept under the rug in most fictions about household romances" (151). According to Connell, although Sara performs the same tasks as Becky, Sara is really only playing house; her imagination elevates her above her work, and her eventual restoration to wealth assures the reader that she was never really like Becky, no matter what the text itself says. Indeed, Becky does continue to consider Sara a princess, and she helps her with the buttons on her dress. When Sara is identified and resumes a life of luxury, she brings Becky along as her personal maid. She is later seen "in the character of delighted attendant, [who] always accompanied her young mistress to her carriage, carrying wraps and belongings" (Burnett 185). Connell declares that "*A Little Princess*'s magic appears to be available to all who wish for it hard enough, but it visits only the princess, and not the lower-class 'ugly Sleeping Beauty' in the 'adjoining cell'" (Burnett 164). This is, of course, true: only Sara ends her story wealthy. But it is also impossible to deny that Becky's lot is significantly improved by her association with Sara; this "delighted attendant" develops "a pink, round face" (Burnett 185) as Sara's personal maid that she never had as Miss Minchin's scullery. She is better fed, dressed warmly, happy in her new situation— thanks to Sara.

Anne's case is similar to Becky's. Connell notes "[i]ronically, Sara's punishment resembles Anne's reward" (165). But that is too negative a reading. There is a tremendous difference between Anne the beggar-girl, so hungry and cold that Sara feels faint just looking at her and Anne, warm, well-fed, clean, clothed, and adopted. Yes, she has to work, as does her adoptive mother. But she is in no danger of freezing or starving, and she is no longer alone in the world. Sara's punishment was much worse than the state in which Anne is left at the end of the story—deprived of love, deprived of food, ill-clothed, and ill-housed, Sara's lot was better than Anne's life begging but significantly worse than Anne's new life, living and working in a bakery. It is difficult for the modern reader to entirely ignore the issues of race and class inherent in *A Little Princess*, but it would also be a mistake to dismiss the story because of them. Burnett created a society of girls that crossed class lines; that they are not perfectly equal is unfortunate but perhaps inevitable, given her era, and in fact is more realistic than not.

A Little Princess in Hollywood

Frances Hodgson Burnett, who adapted many of her stories for the theater, was not initially interested in film. On a trip to Austria, however, she became convinced of the power of the new medium (Carpenter 111); she sold the film rights to the first two films made from her work, *The Dawn of a Tomorrow* and *Esmerelda*, in 1913 (Thwaite 231). The rights to four more films were sold soon thereafter; among them were the rights to *A Little Princess*. *A Little Princess* has been translated to film several times in the ensuing years, with each version using the basic framework of the story but changing the details to reflect its time. Although non-American versions have been made (noteworthy are the Japanese animated television series of 1985, for its oddness, and the BBC-TV version of 1986, for its faithfulness to the novel), as this is an examination of the princess story in American fiction, I will confine myself to a discussion of the Hollywood feature film versions. Each utilizes and discards different elements of the original story, reflecting its creators' interests and beliefs. Ironically, as women and girls in the audience become freer and more independent, with more life choices, each film version of Sara Crewe's story becomes progressively weaker, less feminist and less a true princess story.

Mary Pickford, "America's sweetheart," starred in the 1917 silent version of *The Little Princess*. The story is actually fairly faithful to the book in critical ways that the later versions were not: the film highlights Sara's imagination and how attractive the other children find it. Sara's father dies of a combination of jungle fever and distress. Sara is adopted by Mr. Carrisford, her father's best friend. And the final scene shows Sara dispensing Christmas presents to underprivileged children. However, while the plot is faithful to the novel, much of the tone is not. This can be attributed both to "the aura of the star who played the central role, and the audience demands of an unsettled time" (Kirkland 196). The audience needed lighthearted escape, and although *A Little Princess* quite sentimental—and not at all funny—it becomes the lighthearted piece of escapism the audience desired.

Released a scant six months after the US entered World War I, Pickford's *The Little Princess* uses the character of Becky (played by comedienne ZaSu Pitts) much less as sympathetic foil and much more as comic relief. Becky (identified on a card as "the drudge of the school, Becky-of-All-Work") is first seen stealing cake the schoolgirls have abandoned. When Sara comes across her, she declares, "T'warn't me touched a crumb, 'onest!" Sara laughs, but then she realizes that it's only an accident that each girl is who she is (screenwriter Frances Marion did an excellent job of incorporating many lines from the novel into the film). Becky is also seen hitting her head under a bed, where she has hidden to hear Sara's stories: "Me 'ead bumps into slats, miss, when you talk of murdering the 'ole fambly!" She flippantly interrupts Sara in one of her 'pretends' to ask, "Pardon me, miss, but was you ever dropped on your 'ead w'en you was little?" The novel's Becky was far too much in awe of Sara to entertain such a notion, but such irreverence does relieve the film's sentimental, fanciful quality before it becomes too cloying. Becky's comic nature also gives Sara a chance to be a regular girl in the film; the penultimate shot is Becky on the floor, where she has landed after Sara surprised her with a jack-in-the-box. The playful quality, while not faithful to the novel, does lighten the mood of the piece.

The film also deviates from the source material to highlight the qualities for which Mary Pickford was known. She specialized in playing young girls; in 1917, at 23 years old, she played the title characters in *The Poor Little Rich Girl* and *Rebecca of Sunnybrook Farm* in addition to *The Little Princess* to critical acclaim ("for a ...woman to transform herself into an eleven-year-old child was no mean achievement" [Tibbetts]). She was a comedienne, with a light touch and naturalistic expressions onscreen; her films "were almost always comedies, the light episodes being laced with genuine pathos and much excitement. They were sentimental, but seldom mawkish" (Brownlow). She looks nothing like the novel's Sara Crewe, of course, and the first scene shows her jumping out of a vase and running around, having a bit of a temper tantrum; she does not have the stoic control that the novel's Sara usually maintains. Sara's imagination is highlighted in the film in a way that detracts from the story but which showcases Pickford's talents. Sara tells her schoolmates a very long story about Ali Baba and his love, the slave-girl Morgiana, played by Pickford herself. Thus the film is invested with romance not present in the novel, and Pickford is shown in a variety of attractive ways: her diaphanous veils establish her sexuality, her lover's courtship establishes her romantic and marital worth, and her quick dispatch of the villain (she takes him unawares, leaping on him and stabbing him to death) establishes her spunk.

As one contemporary review put it, "Only an extremist in pessimism could avoid being captivated by this charming characterization of hers" (*Photoplay*). While there are some odd differences between the novel and this first film adaptation, overall, the film is about as faithful to the novel as can be hoped, given the era in which it was released, the state of the art and the complexity of the novel. Sara clearly plays pretend, alluding to being a soldier when her father leaves and reminding Becky, as they slave in the kitchen, that "we are both princesses—inside!" The audience is even exhorted to emulate Sara in a final card:

> So friends in parting, just a word:
> Keep faith, and aye 'dream true':
> Your prayers will never go unheard
> You'll be—like Sara Crewe.

While Kirkland dismisses this version as "an old fairy tale with a happy ending" (197), I think that characterization is not entirely fair. Pickford herself discussed the weeks of preparation and the re-readings of the play and novel that went into the film (McKelvie); that preparation and desire to be faithful to the source material does indeed come through onscreen.

The second Hollywood adaptation of *The Little Princess* came in 1939, when the country suffered both pre-war jitters and economic depression; "the screenwriters apparently wanted to create a happy film to offset the bleakness of reality" (Kirkland 197). It was Shirley Temple's heyday, and she was tapped to play Sara Crewe[6]. This version of the story strays far from the source material—again, in service of audience desires and the strengths (and weaknesses) of its star. The deviations are many, but among the most glaring are the fact that Captain Crewe does not actually die, and that "Shirley of the curls and dimples and easy weeping...is a far cry from Burnett's original conception of Sara as a complex, intelligent, independent girl" (Kirkland 197). Mary Pickford had proven that looking like Sara Crewe was not required to play her; Shirley Temple's version goes even further and posits that it is unnecessary to act like Sara to play her. Temple's Sara has no gift for storytelling, no references to drawing on the inner strength of a princess, and no largess toward those less fortunate than she. What she does do, of course, is cry (although Burnett's Sara "seldom cried" [69]), and sing, and dance, and enable romance. The set pieces of Temple dancing with Arthur Treacher (playing Miss Minchin's brother, Hubert, replacing Miss Amelia) are to be expected; this was a Shirley Temple star vehicle, and Shirley Temple would sing and dance. While she has few scenes actually interacting with her schoolmates, Temple's Sara does interact with her teachers, two of whom are in love with each other. She facilitates their romance and marriage by allowing them to meet in her room, and a dream sequence (which she has while actually asleep) shows Sara as a princess, encouraging them to kiss. This element of romance, only hinted at in Pickford's version and absent altogether from Burnett's, is disturbing. Temple's Sara is precociously interested in such things, and the collusion of the adult teachers is unsettling.

The other strange element—strange in relation to the novel, that is—in this version is the heavy preoccupation with war. Captain Crewe goes off to fight in the Boer War ("when you get there you'll stop them, won't you Daddy?"), and the victory at Mafeking has a prominent position in the film. Sara's father is "killed" in battle, although he really only suffers amnesia; Sara visits the hospital whenever she can, convinced that he is alive (and entertaining the troops with Hubert Minchin, who has run away from his sister, joined the army, and been stationed at the hospital). Sara does find her father, with the intervention of Queen Victoria, and her tears cure his amnesia. The final scene is of Sara (well, just plain Shirley Temple) saluting the queen while strains of "God Save the Queen" play in the background. This, of course, is the same tune as "My Country 'Tis of Thee" and as such is a very patriotic American song. Combined with the close-up on the round, grinning face of Shirley Temple, about whom President Franklin Delano Roosevelt proclaimed "as long as our country has Shirley Temple, we will be all right" ("Biography"), the scene is practically a call to arms.

Reviews of the 1995 production, directed by Alfonso Cuarón, were almost entirely positive: it is "a bright, beautiful and enchantingly childlike vision….stirringly lovely" (Maslein); it "casts the type of spell most family films can only dream about" (Turan); "it restores the heart and defies the gravity of the world" (Kamiya); "you just may want to clap with pleasure" (Schwartzbaum). Any critical reservations were slight, concerned with the loss of the darker side of the novel, the "realism" half of "magical realism." But when examining this film in relation to its source material and on its own, some serious and disturbing issues come to light. The role of the father and other men, the portrayal of the adult women, and Sara's lack of development all detract from this film, undermining its source material's strong princess story.

The role of the father, Captain Crewe, is particularly disconcerting in this film. The director and the producer both see this as a father-daughter relationship story, which is a major difference from the Burnett version. With that in mind, the father does not die at the end; as in the 1939 film, he survives but with amnesia. But, as Kirkland writes, "Let it be noted here that Burnett not only made Sara's father die, but made it clear that his financial improvidence was responsible for her subsequent desperate situation" (199). Burnett's Captain Crewe is beloved but flawed. More than that, if he hadn't tried to spoil Sara with riches to make up for his absence, Sara would not have incurred such debt and been so totally resented by Miss Minchin. The film's other male characters include Mr. Randolph, Miss Minchin' neighbor, an elderly gentleman whose son also goes off to fight (and who turns out to have been in Captain Crewe's regiment); Ram Dass, who has a strong, mystical persona and influences his master and cures, by force of mind, Captain Crewe's amnesia when Sara's cries have failed to do so; and Sara's Indian playmate in the film's opening scene. There is also the story of Prince Rama, which Sara tells her classmates, which is intercut throughout the movie. This male emphasis, with the father at the center (his story is intercut with Sara's throughout), undercuts what had been a female-centric story: "the result has been to devalue and diminish not only Sara's character but the female supporting cast as well" (Kirkland 200). The titular princess has a much-diminished role, as do the friends who were to help her.

There is no loving Mrs. Carmichael in this version of the story to comfort Sara and help her ease her way back to privilege; there is no working-class baker-woman to take in poor Anne. The women who do remain, Miss Minchin and her sister Amelia, are presented as caricatures: evil Miss Minchin has a Bride-of-Frankenstein stripe in her hair and, especially highlighted in her first scene, a mole on her neck where a bolt should be.

Miss Amelia is fat and ineffectual, played for laughs, and so unsophisticated and credulous that she takes romantic advice from Sara. The characters of these women have also been changed to put the emphasis on the men in their lives. Miss Minchin, so heartless, has an implied back-story—one which suggests that she is as she is because her father didn't value her. Miss Amelia loses her one moment of triumph from the novel (telling Miss Minchin off when Sara's identity is discovered) in exchange for an elopement. The man next door takes over Miss Minchin's school in the end, and Miss Minchin ends her days answering to a chimney-sweep—a young boy.

Most disturbingly, Sara's father has appropriated the princess pretend. Sara has heard from her ayah that "all girls are princesses," and when she asks her father, he validates the notion: "I believe that you are, and always will be, my little princess." From then on, he calls her "princess," replacing the nickname Burnett used ("little missus"). Burnett's nickname speaks to the fact that Sara was mature beyond her years; the film's nickname speaks to the fact that Sara's father has made her his princess. Sara repeats the conviction that all girls are princesses to her schoolmates at her birthday, when Lavinia and Lottie are arguing: "Not just me. All girls are princesses. Even snotty, two-faced bullies like you, Lavinia." It is taken as a given that Sara is, indeed, a princess; her daddy told her she was, and the other girls address her—not merely refer to her—that way. The most telling princess-related scene is between Sara and Miss Minchin, at the end of the film. Miss Minchin has burst into Sara's room and found her wearing the locket her father had given her (and which Miss Minchin had confiscated, and the other girls stolen back for Sara in a comic scene):

> "Don't tell me you still fancy yourself a princess! Good God, child, look around you! Or better yet, look in the mirror."
> "I am a princess. All girls are. Even if they live in tiny old attics. Even if they dress in rags. Even if they aren't pretty or smart or young. They're still princesses. All of us. Didn't your father ever tell you that? Didn't he?"

Miss Minchin tears up; apparently her father didn't tell her, and that is why she's so spiteful. But this scene illustrates the ways that Sara's father, any father, now has the power to grant or deny princess-hood. Sara's father told her she is one, so she is; Miss Minchin's father did not, so she is not.

Sara herself moves back and forth from being a princess to being a prince; she tells the story of Prince Rama and Princess Sita, in which her father plays the prince. Sara, then, is waiting for him to rescue her. But on her first night in the attic, she draws a protective circle around herself, as Prince Rama does in her story. This, according to Reimer, gives Sara active power, and "speaks to the aspirations and experiences of contemporary girls and women…. But this active power is found in imitating the father and is dependent on the authorization of the father….the assertion of patriarchal control is extensive in the 1995 version of Sara's story" (Reimer 131). Again, just as the father has the power to make a girl a princess, in order for that girl to become powerful she must emulate the father. Unfortunately, in discussing Sara's power we are confined to discussing what little power Sara has; instead of demonstrating inner strength, Sara's "strength and independence are converted in the film to minor juvenile mischief" (Kirkland 200). She does not maintain her dignity and speak her mind to Miss Minchin; she and Becky giggle together on the roof and pour soot down Miss Minchin's chimney. She does not impress and disconcert Lavinia and Jessie with her poise in the face of adversity; she jumps around and "puts a curse" on Lavinia's hair[7].

This film contains no element of emulation. Because a girl is granted princess-hood by her father (or not), there is no "becoming" a princess, no transformation. Sara thus learns nothing; she has nothing to learn. The girls and women around her also learn nothing, and neither does the audience. Several extremely strong moments from the novel are morphed into one significantly weaker episode in the film. Sara is given money on the street by a random boy. We see none of Sara's inner struggle, her impulse to give it back and her graciousness in finally accepting it; in the novel, she then wore the coin around her neck as a talisman. In this film, she spends it immediately, going into a bakery. She sits to eat her bun but instead gives it to a family of females: a flower-lady making no sales and her dirty, impoverished daughters. The mother thanks Sara with a flower, saying "for the princess." By giving the beggar-girl a mother, even an ineffectual one, there is no need for the baker to adopt Anne. The baker-woman does not see Sara's act of generosity, and cannot be inspired by it. Additionally, Sara does not remember the flower-woman and her daughters; they never make another appearance, whereas in the book they become the means by which Sara feeds poor children after she herself is restored to wealth. What had been two strong scenes—Sara's acceptance of money but ultimate refusal of the role charity-receiver, and her inspiring others to kindness and generosity—are completely lost. Both mothers in this incident are equally unattractive: the first is miserly, chastising her son for giving away money; the second is wholly incapable of providing for her family. This is quite a contrast to Mrs. Carmichael, who encourages her children to charity, and the baker-woman, who becomes Anne's mother. There are no women worth emulating in this film, and no one emulates Sara.

Sara remains unique in this iteration of her story. She is a princess because her father says so, and while she loses her wealth, she does not lose or gain anything else. She is special in that her father loves her and bestows upon her princess-hood; but she is so special that apparently she has nothing to learn. "She does not reach a new stage of development as does Burnett's original Sara, but merely returns to the condition she had temporarily lost" (Kirkland 200): beloved and wealthy, her father's princess. She scatters some largess, but there is no indication that she learned to do this, and there is no indication that anyone around her learned to do it. If every girl is a princess, as bestowed by loving fathers, then they are all special—and no one has anything to learn.

Conclusion

Burnett's *A Little Princess*, although absolutely a product of its time, remains satisfying on many levels. Moreover, it is a story that can be enjoyed by the same reader at different stages in her life.

> This book has the extraordinary faculty of adapting itself to the mental needs of the reader so it can be enjoyed, at different levels, for a surprising range of years. At about six, the straightforward account of events is both satisfying and moving; at ten, the story has become one a girl can absorb into her imagination as happening to herself; later, the realization that Sara's triumph was as much moral as accidental fulfills the purpose of any good book—the extension of the reader's experience. (Laski 85)

Even later than that, the reader can see that Sara is a nuanced and strong character, the product of a first-wave feminist author.

I hope my reading of *A Little Princess* proves that a story can be both a princess story and a strongly feminist one, and that to be a princess is not to be submissive or weak. As Gruner writes, "to find the [princess] in Sara…is not necessarily to find the passive weepy heroine…earlier feminist critics have feared, but to find a dynamically adaptable heroine whose chief function is to spur the imagination of another generation of readers" (180). Sara is a role model worth emulating, in both her fictional world and in the reader's world: she has a strong female support community, self-control, and a powerful identity that she creates and nurtures herself.

It is not Burnett's fault that Hollywood interpretations of her heroine have changed Sara's character as they have, and it is a seeming contradiction that the most recent—one would have hoped, the most modern and feminist—version of the film has the least-strong, least-self-actualized heroine. All of the filmic adaptations have changed the story to reflect their times and creators. Unfortunately, they have all, to greater and lesser extent, changed the character of Sara and the purposes of the novel from a strong, self-made princess to emulate, to a natural princess whom everyone is both like (in that they are all princesses) and unlike; we need not emulate Cuarón's Sara because we're all princesses, too, and we cannot emulate Cuarón's Sara because she is too special, clearly unique in her magical storytelling.

Kirkland, thinking about the different filmic versions of Sara, raises an intriguing concern, one which informs much of this project:

> The cumulative effect of numerous princesses, many of whom have had their strength of character diluted and undermined, can only be damaging to the self-esteem and potential accomplishment of young female viewers who unconsciously internalize them as role models. (202)

Twentieth-century American fiction produced an abundance of princess stories, which changed as the century progressed. *A Little Princess* is the prototypical princess story, representing to me all that a princess story can be: the story of a bright, capable heroine who learns about herself and about the world around her as she assumes the identity of a princess. The next princess stories to capture American's imagination featured anachronous, retrograde princesses, created and perpetrated by a man yearning for yesteryear: the first group of Disney princesses, which pretended the first wave of feminism had never existed. Their cultural supremacy will color princess stories for the rest of the century, and they will be discussed in the next chapter.

❖ CHAPTER TWO ❖

Disney's First Princess Stories

THE DISNEY-PRODUCED FILMS of the various princess stories have definitively codified the stories for millions of Americans; the values reflected in and reinforced by the Disney versions both reflect the changing American culture and construct it. When feminists deride princesses as weak and passive, imposing an archaic image of femininity on the girls who love them, they are referring to the Disney princesses discussed in this chapter. The Disney versions of these princess stories not only co-opted their particular stories—*Snow White* or *Cinderella* or *Sleeping Beauty*—they have, for many, co-opted the entire idea of princesses. As Jack Zipes writes,

> Walt Disney cast a spell on the fairy tale, and it has been held captive ever since....His technical skills and ideological proclivities were so consummate that his signature has obfuscated the names of Charles Perrault, the Brothers Grimm, Hans Christian Andersen, and Collodi. If children or adults think of the great classical fairy tales today, be it Snow White, Sleeping Beauty, or Cinderella, they will think of Walt Disney. ("Fairy Tale" 72)

Put another way, "one of the most prolific authors of the princess today is the Disney organization which produces her in animation, theme parks, on the stage and in merchandise. Combined with Disney's popular and global profile, this makes the Disney princess in effect 'the princess of all princesses'" (Rozario 1). Despite being created after the first wave of feminism, these Disney princesses present a retrograde image of femininity, undermining the first-wave feminist agenda and ignoring the progress women had made before and during the time of the films' creation. Much of this retrograde/regressive message can be attributed to the personal animus of Walt Disney himself. The changes Disney dictated to the literary and historical source material reflect his ambivalence toward women, and the films' continued popularity arises from similar ambivalence: long-standing cultural anxieties about feminism. These princess stories are fairy tales interpreted and presented to a modern audience—modern both in their day and current in our own—and their continuing impact on American culture makes them impossible to ignore.

Although their heroines are currently marketed en masse, historians of animation generally consider the Disney princess films in two distinct waves[1]. Walt Disney himself directed (indeed, he was involved in almost every frame) the creation of the first group of Disney princess films: *Snow White and the Seven Dwarfs* (1937), *Cinderella* (1950), and *Sleeping Beauty* (1959). After Disney's death and as a result of growing public disenchantment with Disney animation, Disney Studios reinvented itself with the creation of the second group of Disney princess films: *The Little Mermaid* (1989), *Beauty and the Beast* (1991), *Pocahontas* (1995) and *Mulan* (1998), which will be discussed in Chapter Four. Princess Jasmine, the love interest in *Aladdin* (1992), is also marketed with these princesses although hers is not a princess story, as she is not the titular protagonist of her film[2]. The early princess stories, the topic of this chapter, were created by a man with a conservative world view; they combine elements of traditional fairy tales with mid-twentieth century American mores to valorize his conservative agenda. Each story changes, in significant ways, its European source material, Americanizing and suburbanizing it for Disney's tastes and audience—yet each prizes most the old-fashioned, homely qualities of its heroines: her joy and competence in tending house and her patience in awaiting her prince. These early Disney princess films were created in an America that had not yet experienced the shift in expectations precipitated by the feminist second wave.

From Page to Screen

Disney animation is ironic in its juxtaposition of the most modern technology and archaic values. The first to use synchronized sound in animation, the first American to produce a full-color, feature-length animated film, Disney "embraced advanced technology and ideas but paradoxically used them to create visions of the past" (Jackson xii). Each of these early princess films opens with a real-world, live-action scene of a storybook with ornate, gothic covers. The books then flip open, revealing the texts that set the scene for the story to come. Disney invokes the traditional print fairy-tale format to lend the weight of tradition to his version of the stories, although in each case he strays far from the credited source material, both deleting and adding to the traditional fairy tales to create a unique yet cohesive vision.

Disney altered the source material several ways, ways designed both to add to the tales' drama and to increase their humor, both elements crucial to a successful film. The princesses are more isolated from humans in the films than in the source material, but they are given special connections to animals that are meant in part to ease their loneliness. With an eye to the age of the audience, the stories' timeframes are telescoped, the princesses' characters are simplified, and some of the horror of the original is removed. Any one of these changes alters only slightly the message of the films' literary antecedents, but taken in aggregate they begin to shift the fairy tales' original message to the Disney message.

Traditionally, each fairy tale requires the princess to be abandoned to some extent; there would be no story without the princess being exposed to evil. Indeed, literary tradition in fairy tales and beyond often provides isolated, orphaned protagonists, the better to justify their adventures. But the Disney versions of the stories go further than the source material in their heroines' isolation. While the Grimm version of *Snow White* begins with a woman who longs for a daughter but sadly dies in childbirth, the Disney version eliminates the mother altogether. Leonard Maltin suggests that this edit was made in response to censors; perhaps the specter of death in childbirth would be too gruesome.[3] More importantly, removing the mother who yearned for a child creates a two-female dichotomy: innocent Snow White and evil Stepmother, with no possibility of a third female path.

Perrault's *Cinderella*, cited as Disney's source material ("the original classic" in the film credits), explains that Cinderella's father was "a worthy man" who was, unfortunately for Cinderella, "entirely ruled by his [second] wife" (Perrault 67); he was alive, yet his daughter knew he could not be counted on for help. In the film, the father comes to an "untimely death" as the narrator gives the exposition. Cinderella on screen is wholly alone, a young girl at the mercy of her wicked stepmother. Her father may thus be considered unambiguously good in the Disney version, as he abandons Cinderella through death rather than through devotion to another woman; the other males in the film will share in his goodness, in contrast to the evil of the other females.

The situation in *Sleeping Beauty* is somewhat different. In the Perrault version, again credited as the source material although deeply altered, the princess is raised by her loving parents. She loses them during her magical slumber (the practical good fairy does not put the king and queen to sleep with their daughter and courtiers, since they must continue to rule the country), but until her unfortunate, predestined accident and subsequent coma she is her parents' "dear child." In the film, however, Aurora—called Briar Rose—grows up in isolation and ignorance. She is taken from her parents on the day of her christening to be raised in the woods by three fairies. Thus, on her crucial sixteenth birthday when she is returned to the strangers who are her parents and told she must marry the stranger to whom she was betrothed at birth, she is bewildered, alone, and vulnerable. All loving parents have been thoroughly removed in the Disney versions of the stories, and the only authoritative adult women left are evil and powerful, full of resentment or hatred toward the heroines.

With the loving parents completely removed, the princesses (or future princess, in Cinderella's case) need allies. Moreover, Disney needed a feature-film length story; more material needed to be added to the fairly thin source material. The solution to both problems was the addition of small, anthropomorphized animals. These serve as the princesses' helpers and foils, giving the girls an audience for their inner thoughts. Additionally, being a friend to the animals—being able to communicate with them effectively—adds to the princesses' charm, highlighting their natural innocence and increasing the wonder factor of their personalities. The animals also address Disney's target audience, providing necessary comic relief. Snow White first finds the dwarfs' house with the help of the animals, who then help her clean it. Snow White's animal friends are funny and charming, with distinct personalities exhibited through movement—the baby chipmunk sneezing from a noseful of dust, the turtle plodding up each individual stair, the squirrels using their tails to dry dishes. All motion in the cleaning scene is set to the beat of "Just Whistle While You Work," which exaggerates the movements and increases the scene's humor. Although the animals in this film do not speak, they clearly understand Snow White, reacting conversationally to her statements (mammals nod heads; birds whistle in agreement) and responding to her orders ("Now you wash the dishes; you tidy up the room; you clean the fireplace; and I'll use the broom!"). The animals lend so much to the film, the *New York Times* review spent an entire paragraph extolling their contribution (Nugent).

In *Cinderella*, the animals are even more important: they speak, they sing, and they carry major segments of the film both in their own subplot and in helping Cinderella. Roger Ebert's review of the film considers the addition of the animal-helpers "the most valuable and original contribution" to the tale (Ebert *Cinderella*). Fully one-third of the film (eight of the DVD's twenty-four chapters) is strictly animal scenes—and that doesn't take into account the scenes in which Cinderella is onscreen with the animals. Cinderella's bird friends help her tidy her room and herself in the first scene, straightening the blankets and squeezing a sponge to shower Cinderella as she bathes. They are clothed in little dresses, shirts and shoes that Cinderella provides. These animals go further than serving as sounding boards; they express some of Cinderella's unspoken thoughts and complain for her ("Every time she find a minute, that's the time when they begin it: Cinderelly, Cinderelly, Cinderella..."). The audience is thus permitted to commiserate and feel indignant without tainting Cinderella's image of unending patience. The mice and birds are also more proactive on Cinderella's behalf than she is herself ("Hurry, hurry, hurry, hurry, we must help our Cinderelly"). In what is "easily the highlight of the film" (Maltin 95), they sew her first ball gown when one of the mice realizes Cinderella will have no opportunity to do so herself. More importantly, they rescue her when her stepmother has locked her in her room. They are thus directly responsible for Cinderella proving her identity to the Duke. She could not have become a princess without her comic little animal friends.

The animals in *Sleeping Beauty* are responsive, yet they have returned to being mute: while Briar Rose is in the woods, discussing her romantic dreams, the animals listen avidly and respond through their actions and animal sounds. The birds whistle a duet with her, awakening the other animals to come scamper about her feet. They provide a needed respite from the heavy, almost sexually mature romance by working together to give Briar Rose a mock prince with whom to dance. Interestingly, the prince himself has a comic animal foil in his horse, which grimaces, snorts and rolls his eyes in response to Phillip's conversationally spoken thoughts. Phillip pales in comparison to his equine companion, as "Virtually every scene of the Prince...is stolen by his horse, Samson, who is far more amusing than his stoic master" (Maltin 155). *Sleeping Beauty* is the film that did the least well at the box office, and it has the fewest animal-centric scenes. With "no tiny creature for audiences to love or to tell them how to respond to what they were seeing" (Schickel 234), the story is much more strongly focused on Aurora and the prince, and they are not that interesting, particularly for their intended audience.

The Disney films also telescope the timeframe of the original fairytales, especially in *Snow White* and *Sleeping Beauty*, both of which have heroines whose source material indicates they magically slumber for many years. In the Grimm tale, Snow White is only seven years old when the wicked stepmother-queen, jealous of her beauty, decides to have her killed. The huntsman takes her out to the forest and runs her off, confident that she will be eaten by wild animals but relieved not to actually kill her himself. In the film, of course, Snow White is significantly older than seven; her romantic dreams and her physique show her to be in early adolescence. In an early development memo, Disney critiqued one rendition of the character as "really too young for the tempests of love (she must have looked about 8!) and [directed] that they should add a few years to her age" (qtd. in Grant 151). Later, Disney described Snow White as "a Janet Gaynor type—14 years old" (Allan 38). She is the same apparent age, although at least one year older (as indicated by the changing of seasons over her coffin), when the prince ultimately rescues her. There is a greater passage of time in the Grimm tale. After eating the poison apple which puts her in a coma, Snow White "lay a long, long time in the glass coffin" (Owens 195). When she awakens, she is of an age to marry; at her marriage, the stepmother-queen recognizes her even though she has "grown to a charming young woman" (Owens 198). This telescoped timeframe removes the difficulties of character development within the film itself and allows the romantic elements to be forefronted from the first scene.

Disney removed some of the repetitive qualities of the plot in his films, qualities which show the heroines as more complex, less one-dimensionally good. In the Grimm version of *Snow White*, the wicked stepmother-queen thrice tries to kill the princess at the dwarfs' house: with a poison comb, with magically tightened stays, and finally with the apple. Notes on the development discussion surrounding Snow White's demise at the hands of the queen indicate that Disney was aware of the three attempts made in the source material (Kanfer 102). He decided to use just the apple, possibly because being tricked once can be attributed to naivety, but being tricked thrice makes the character seem less than bright. Moreover, luring Snow White to her doom via a decorative hair comb or stays plays on her feminine vanity—rather than on the destruction of innocence implied in the apple imagery. Perrault's version of *Cinderella* has the prince's ball lasting two days, not one, and at each appearance Cinderella finds herself in the limelight. Part of her joy in the ball is that she interacts with her sisters there, "bestow[ing] numberless attentions upon them" (Perrault 72). At home after the ball, her sisters tell her about the "most beautiful princess," Cinderella herself. She is "overjoyed" to hear herself described this way, and begs one of her stepsisters to borrow a dress so that she might also see this beautiful princess. She is of course refused the favor, much to her relief, "for she would have been greatly embarrassed has her sister been willing to lend the dress" (Perrault 74). This version shows Cinderella playing psychological games with her stepsisters; it shows her vanity and her feelings of personal triumph. In other words, it shows her to be much more human than the Disney version. Perrault's Sleeping Beauty grows to be a mother so horrified at the assumed death of her children that she begs to be killed herself. This, too, is much more complex emotionally than anything shown in Disney's version.

Some horrific elements of the source material have also been removed from these three Disney princess stories. The wicked queen, Snow White's stepmother, dies of an act of nature in Disney's version; lightening strikes a craggy mountain and she plummets to her death. In the Grimm version, the queen is full of "rage and terror" to find Snow White the prince's bride. "[T]he slippers she wore were to her as iron bands full of coals of fire, in which she was obliged to dance. And so in the red, glowing shoes she continued to dance till she fell dead on the floor" (Owens 198). M. Thomas Inge finds the Disney death "not only more dramatic but more poetically just in that she was not stricken down by another hand but more appropriately by the forces of nature she had tried to bend to her own wicked ends through witchcraft" (9). But this "poetically just" death is also simpler ethically. Not only would the stepmother falling dead on the floor mar the wedding ceremony, but there is a moral ambiguity to this death: should Snow White try to save her, or should she celebrate her demise? By making the death of the queen an act of nature that occurs while Snow White magically slumbers, Disney granted Snow White complete innocence in the matter.

Although the stated source material for *Cinderella* is the genteel Perrault, the film borrows from the much darker Grimm version. The animal helpers in the Disney version are a Grimm touch, as is the sadism of the stepmother (Allan 207). The length of time spent on the stepsisters' attempt to fit into the glass slipper is another Grimm touch, although the Disney version plays the scene for comic effect. In the Grimm version, one sister cuts off her toes and the other cuts off her heel, each at her mother's dictate; their blood exposes the mutilation and the false fit. The Disney version ends as the happy couple rides away for their honeymoon, providing no closure about the stepsisters' fates. The Grimm version, however, provides retribution for the stepsisters: Cinderella's helper-birds peck out their eyes on the way to and from the wedding.

Sleeping Beauty, too, is much tamer in the Disney version than in Perrault's. An entire story takes place after marriage in the Perrault version: Sleeping Beauty's mother-in-law, an ogress who likes to eat tender human flesh, spirits the princess and her two children away to the woods and commands her steward to kill them and serve them to her. He tricks her, serving her other animals instead, and when the ogress learns of this deception she orders a huge vat filled with horrible creatures. Into this vat she plans to throw her daughter-in-law and grandchildren, plus the steward and his family. The prince (now king), rides into the courtyard at the final moment, and his mother the ogress, "enraged at what confronted her, threw herself head foremost into the vat, and was devoured on the instant by the hideous creatures she had placed in it" (Perrault 20). This ending, in fact the entire second half of the story, is far more complex than that in the film, which ends with a tearful family reunion and a final waltz which signifies the lovers' impending marriage. One of the good fairies says "I love happy endings," assuring the audience that that is what they have seen. Further accenting how happy the ending is, the film closes on a book cover closing on the final page of a story, which (naturally) reads, "And they lived happily ever after." No horrible ogress, no difficult in-laws, no imperiled children exist in the Disney version.

The simplification of character and the excision of bloody mutilations are hallmarks of Disneyfication, and may be attributed to the necessities of creating a film rather than a literary tale. Adding cute, humorous animals and removing scenes of death and terror seem reasonable in light of Disney's young audience. But these changes also foreshadow other changes made in production of the Disney princess stories: the princesses' characters are not merely made simpler; they are made submissive. Male characters will take primacy over the passive, pretty princesses. The films' endings are not merely happy; they are happy in specifically romantic ways. And the powerful female characters are not merely evil; their villainy is tied to their sexuality.

Romance, the Role of Men, and Disney Himself

The short source material, made shorter by Disney's expunging of graphic horror, psychological complexity, and years-long passage of time, required more than animal sidekicks to round out the stories. Disney met the demands of feature-length film by bringing to the fore romance, of minor importance in the source material. The heterosexual romantic pairing is given ultimate importance in the Disney princess stories, even when there was little or none to speak of in the fairy tales of Perrault or Grimm. In addition, the objects of romantic desire and agents of romantic fulfillment—men—are given primacy in these princess stories. Men, real as well as animated, frame the story, serve as primary agents of activity, and are the princesses' rescuers and rewards.

One underlying implication in these early Disney princess stories is so deeply ingrained in early twentieth-century American culture that it seems inevitable. These films are, above all else, stories of American middle-class heterosexual courtship; in Disney's definition, "sex—the love a boy has for a girl—is natural" (Rasky 119). This "natural" image of love is propagated through his films, and the idea has become so widespread that it is nearly invisible. As Sean Griffin writes, "Disney has made this vision of sexuality seem such a given fact of life that most consumers are incapable of consciously acknowledging its construction. Disney consequently posits heterosexual courtship as the only 'true'...method by which individuals may conceive of sexuality" (4). The overwhelming heterosexual message in these princess films, and the way that message excludes or alienates some viewers, goes largely unnoticed by the vast majority of the audience. Often only those excluded or alienated become aware of this message—and if they are young enough, they wonder what is wrong with them. According to Griffin, when a "proto-queer" child watches the overwhelmingly heterosexual message of the Disney princess films, he or she embodies the "countersocial potential" described by Henry Jenkins, potential "feelings of outrage over the expectations imposed upon him or her by the social formation" (qtd. in Griffin 78). Queer and proto-queer individuals, writes Griffin, read the Disney texts differently from the way most viewers read them, either identifying with unexpected characters (such as Meriwether instead of Prince Phillip or Princess Aurora [79]) or rooting for those who would disrupt the heterosexual dominance (such as Maleficent [75]). Because of the centrality of the heterosexual romantic relationship, male dominance in the films also seems "natural."

Disney filmmakers almost entirely invented the romance in *Snow White*; the Grimms' seven-year-old Snow White might dream of rescue, but she is too young to dream of love. In the Disney version, the romance is alluded to again and again. Snow White is "wishing for the one I love to find me" in her opening scene; she longs not just for rescue, but for romance. She tells the dwarfs the story of her romance as their bedtime story, assuring them and herself that "someday my prince will come." When the queen, in her crone disguise, tempts Snow White to eat the poison apple by telling her it's "a wishing apple," Snow White wishes again for true love and rescue. This wish is reprised musically as the prince leads Snow White out of the forest and towards a celestial palace. Romance is Snow White's primary desire throughout the film in all her incarnations: as scullery maid, as mother to the dwarfs, and as victim of the queen-as-crone.

In *Cinderella*, too, romance is crucial. The film's overture has a chorus exhorting "Cinderella, if you give your heart a chance/it will lead you to the kingdom of romance/ there you'll see your dreams unfold...." Cinderella, the film audience is told, dreams of romance; in the Perrault version, her dreams are not mentioned. The ball and the prince's reaction to Cinderella are central to the plot, of course, but the filmic Cinderella is also clearly smitten. Moreover, Disney's Cinderella fell in love with the prince without being aware that he was the prince; her romantic dreams are unsullied by any thought of wealth or social status. The film also ends on a note that is romantically satisfying but that unsatisfactorily leaves loose the resolution of the stepfamily's story: the final scene is the happy couple kissing in their honeymoon carriage, and Cinderella's stepfamily is never mentioned again. On the other hand, both the Perrault and the Grimm versions offer closure on the stepsisters: Perrault's version has Cinderella using her new social position to arrange good marriages for her stepsisters, while the Grimm version has the two stepsisters blinded "for their wickedness and falsehood" (Owen 95). Each of these provides more psychologically satisfying resolutions than that offered by Disney: Perrault demonstrates Cinderella's deep capacity for forgiveness and Grimm provides blood-thirsty revenge. Disney's abrupt "happy ending" proves that the film's main storyline is the romance, and that the heroine's marriage is the most important ending.

The romance in Disney's *Sleeping Beauty* is also the most important element, unlike in the Perrault version. Aurora, as Briar Rose, has been dreaming of romance; when she meets a handsome stranger in the woods on her sixteenth birthday, she recognizes him from her dreams. They dance and duet and fall in love, but when Briar Rose returns to the fairies' cottage she is distressed to learn her true identity: she is a princess, betrothed to a prince, and now she must return to her family and fulfill their expectations. She weeps, preferring her young man to an unknown prince, and she continues to do so even after being restored to the castle. Phillip, too, is determined not to marry the princess to whom he's been betrothed since childhood. None of this falling in love prior to the spell happens in the Perrault version; the princess is in her magical sleep for 100 years, which would preclude someone she knew beforehand coming to her rescue. Moreover, Perrault's prince comes to her rescue for sport, not for love; the story of a sleeping princess seems "so gay an adventure" to the prince that he is inspired to see it through (Perrault 10). Nor does the story end at the marriage, instead continuing with the marital problems caused by the prince's ogress mother. Once again, Disney's choice to end the story at the presumptive marriage, with Aurora and Phillip waltzing into the clouds, emphasizes the romantic elements and downplays all others found in the original.

The films' romantic elements are further emphasized by the importance of kissing, which was of no importance in the films' source materials. Disney's *Snow White* includes a long, frightening scene in which the queen poisons the apple she intends to feed to Snow White. Worried that there may be an antidote, the queen checks her spell-book, and learns that the victim of the sleeping death spell can only by be revived by "love's first kiss." The queen cackles, then declares there's "no fear of that—the Dwarfs will think she's dead. She'll be buried alive! Buried alive!" Ironically, obsessed as she is with her own beauty, she underestimates the power of Snow White's. As Snow White sleeps, the passage of time is indicated, and the screen reads "…so beautiful, even in death, that the dwarfs could not find it in their hearts to bury her…they fashioned a coffin of glass and gold, and kept eternal vigil at her side…the Prince, who had searched far and wide, heard of the maiden who slept in the glass coffin." He sees her, kisses her, and the queen's plot is thwarted.

In the Grimm version of the story, Snow White is awakened by the prince, but this awakening is almost purely accidental. A prince—with whom she had had no prior relationship—sees her sleeping in her glass coffin and offers to purchase her. The dwarfs demur until the prince declares "[M]y heart is drawn towards this beautiful child, and I feel I cannot live without her. If you will let me have her, she shall be treated with the greatest honor and respect as one dearly beloved" (Owens 196). She is awakened by chance when a piece of poisoned apple is jostled from her mouth as the prince's men are lifting her coffin onto a horse to carry it away.[4] While love, or desire, is the motivating factor in the prince's interest in Snow White, chance is the primary agent: the prince, riding, sees Snow White by chance; the poisoned apple, by chance, is jiggled from her mouth. There is no romance, certainly no mutual romance: the prince takes possession of the girl's sleeping body and she awakens very prosaically when the poisoned morsel is dislodged.

In *Sleeping Beauty*, too, the requirement for a kiss to break the spell was a Disney invention. In the Perrault version, the prophecy is that "she shall merely fall into a profound slumber that will last a hundred years. At the end of that time a king's son shall come to awaken her" (5). The arrival of the prince at the end of a set period of time is the princess's cue to awaken; no mention of a kiss is made, neither as the prophecy is cast nor as it reaches fulfillment. According to Perrault, the prince is "trembling with anticipation" as he draws near her bed. He falls on his knees beside the princess: "At the same moment, the hour of disenchantment having come, the princess awoke" (13). No kiss was required, and although the prince and princess do fall in love and marry that evening, that is far from the end of their story. Disney changed this prophecy in two ways: the magical sleep is of an unspecified length, and a kiss is required to awaken the princess. Meriwether the fairy casts her ameliorative spell, diminishing the full force of Maleficent's death-spell: "not in death, but just in sleep the fateful prophesy you'll keep. And from this slumber you shall wake when true love's kiss the spell shall break." A background chorus swells up, singing the phrase "for true love conquers all," explaining the meaning and relevance of the spell to the audience.

Cinderella is different, of course; her adversary is her fairly prosaic wicked stepmother, one without magical capabilities. There is therefore no magical sleep from which to awaken the heroine. She does experience an awakening of sorts at the ball, when she realizes "so this is love." She and the prince nearly kiss then, stopped only by the clock chiming midnight. The fulfillment of her romantic dreams is symbolized by the final animated shot in the film, the close-up image of Cinderella and the prince kissing, framed by the window of the carriage which is taking them to their honeymoon. No kiss can be found either in the Perrault *Cinderella* or in the Grimm. The prince falls deeply in love with Cinderella at the ball, and it certainly behooves her to marry him, but no mention of her amatory desires is made.

In the Disney version, however, the stepmother is inspired to lock Cinderella in her room rather than let her try on the glass slipper because she can clearly see that Cinderella is in love.

The roles of the royal men in the Disney versions of these princess stories take on much greater importance than in the source materials. In *Snow White*, the prince falls in love with Snow White at the wishing well at the start of the film. Later, having sought her for a year, he awakens her with a kiss. Although his time onscreen is minimal, he is crucial to the story, first providing the impetus for the stepmother-queen's murderous jealousy (she sees the two fall in love) and ultimately foiling her plot. Cinderella's story is almost entirely the result of the king, whom we see daydreaming about romping with his future grandchildren. His desire for grandchildren is so great that he arranges the ball, and as he watches his bored son meet girl after girl he exclaims, "I can't understand it! There must be one who would make a suitable mother!" He means, of course, a suitable mother for his much-desired grandchildren; his biological clock initiates the plot. The Grand Duke carries out the prince's command and searches for the girl whose foot fits in the glass slipper; it is the prince's desire that brings the plot to its conclusion. All Cinderella must do is await rescue. In *Sleeping Beauty*, the princess is all but married at the day of her christening; her father is thrilled to be able to join his family to that of his dear friend. When Aurora returns to her familial palace and is told she must marry the prince her father has chosen, she is devastated—and this devastation leads to her physical isolation and vulnerability to Maleficent. Prince Phillip (this prince has a name!) fights and kills Maleficent-turned-dragon, then awakens Aurora with a kiss. He has the most screen time of all the princes, fighting on screen rather than searching or giving commands off-screen. The two king-fathers in Sleeping Beauty, planning and celebrating their families' imminent unification, have more screen time than even *Cinderella*'s king.

These Disney additions—the emphasis on romantic love, "love's first kiss" as the means of awakening the sleeping princesses, the king's desire for grandchildren, the kings' desire to have their families joined—create a much more male-dominated theme than exists in the source materials. Jack Zipes references Sandra Gilbert and Susan Gubar's work in his consideration of the changes Disney made to *Snow White*. He writes:

> The film follows the classic "sexist" narrative about the framing of women's lives
> through a male discourse. Such male framing drives women to frustration and some
> women to the point of madness. It also pits women against women in a competition

for male approval (the mirror) of their beauty that is short-lived. No matter what they may do, women cannot chart their own lives without male manipulation and intervention, and in the Disney film, the prince plays even more of a framing role since he is introduced at the beginning while Snow White is singing...he will also appear at the end as the fulfillment of her dreams. (*Fairy Tale* 89)

Indeed, the opening overture first swells with the tune of "One Love," the prince's solo, introducing the prince and his desires before anything else. Zipes identifies the mirror as the approval-withholding male who drives the queen to madness and murder, but the Disney's prince further compounds the competition: the queen, standing in a turret, watches him declare his love to Snow White.

The issue of female competition for male approval is certainly the central theme of Disney's *Cinderella*. The narrative voiceover in the beginning sets the theme, describing the stepmother as "cold, cruel, and bitterly jealous of Cinderella's charm and beauty, grimly determined to forward the interests of her own two awkward daughters." The ball is designed as a competition, with marriage to the prince the prize. Even the final shoe-fitting is a competition: whoever fits the delicate shoe, wins.

Similar to the prince-as-frame in *Snow White*, Prince Phillip and his actions pertaining to the princess become a frame for *Sleeping Beauty*. Prince Phillip is seen onscreen well before Aurora is; in what is the first scene with any humor, he comes to her cradle and grimaces at the new baby. Nearly all of the film's exciting action happens while Aurora sleeps: Phillip encounters Maleficent, escapes from her dungeon, and finally kills her. From there, of course, he is free to awaken Aurora, ultimately waltzing her into a happy future, one in which she fortuitously gets to fulfill both parental expectations and her own romantic dreams. Within the story, Aurora is blameless, almost entirely inert. Aurora's father caused the curse to befall her when he didn't invite Maleficent to the royal christening. Her identity is hidden, even from herself, for the first sixteen years of her life because of that curse. Once returned to her original identity, back to Aurora from being Briar Rose, she cannot (as Zipes puts it) chart her own life without male manipulation and intervention: she will be returned to her father; she will be married to the prince to whom her father betrothed her on the day of her christening; she will bear the children that embody both kingdoms. One interesting little scene sets up the typical female competition for a man, although Aurora is already asleep and not actively competing. When Maleficent captures Phillip in Briar Rose's cottage, she looks him over leeringly, in a manner both predatory and lascivious. "Well, this is a pleasant surprise. I set my trap for a peasant, and lo! I catch a prince!" She has defeated Aurora and captured Phillip, winning (at least momentarily) the marital competition implied in the phrase "catching a prince." Even more intriguingly, once Maleficent has captured Phillip, the future she outlines for him is this: she will keep him for 100 years. When he goes to wake Aurora with a kiss, he will have aged, but she, in her enchanted sleep, will be as young and beautiful as ever. This is a reversal of the usual intergenerational competition, in which the older woman is supplanted by the younger. Here, neither woman will age—only the prince will become too old for love.

Zipes argues that in the early princess films, Disney perpetuated a "male myth about perseverance, hard work, dedication, loyalty, and justice" (*Fairy Tale* 90). In Zipes' reading, the figure of the prince in *Snow White* stands in for Disney himself: "it is the prince who frames the narrative...During the major action of the film, he, like Disney, is lurking in the background and waiting for the proper time to make himself known. When he does arrive, he takes all the credit as champion of the disenfranchised" (*Fairy Tale* 91). Thus Disney the prince becomes the one without whom there is no story, as without Disney the animator there would be no film. The prince is both Snow White's savior and her reward, and the final scene in the film is all about him and his castle, symbolizing his (and Disney's) goodness and glorifying his (and Disney's) wealth. So, too, is the prince both savior and reward in *Cinderella*, saving her from a life of hardship and loneliness, rewarding her goodness, patience, and beauty. And in *Sleeping Beauty* as well: Phillip saves the country from Maleficent-as-dragon before saving Aurora from the spell. He marries her, and she is rewarded for acquiescing to her father's control by happening to be in love with the husband he chose for her.

I would argue that Disney also inserted himself into *Snow White*, his prototypical first film, in his characterizations of the two most distinctive dwarfs, Grumpy and Dopey. The dwarfs, barely mentioned and not given distinct personalities in the Grimm version, take over a good deal of the Disney film; their sharp characterizations and physical humor provide much-needed comic relief, and they were heavily used to flesh out the slight source material and bring it to feature length. Disney made two changes in his development of the Dwarfs: dwarfs are not traditionally friendly, happy characters, and they are not traditionally given unique personalities. Disney made these Dwarfs miners, as is traditional, but changed their mine into a sparkling, shiny diamond mine. More importantly, these Dwarfs have individual personalities, first indicated when Snow White inspects their bedroom. Each bed is labeled with the name of a Dwarf, and when the Dwarfs come home Snow White is able to identify them from having read these name tags. Each Dwarf's identifying quality is reflected in his name: Grumpy is a grouch, Sneezy sneezes, and so on. Freudian critics took issue with this development of the dwarfs, saying their individuation destroyed the psychological journey that made the Snow White story powerful. As summed up by Bruno Bettelheim, "Giving a dwarf a separate name and a distinctive personality … seriously interferes with the unconscious under-standing that they symbolize an immature pre-individual form of existence which Snow White must transcend" (qtd. in Kanfer 107). Freudians' protest aside, however, the dwarfs are successful comic relief and certainly enter-taining for the children in the audience. They have at least as much screen time and certainly more personality than the heroine and hero. They are, by almost every standard, successfully realized characters and a boon to the film. However, as Disney's own alter egos, they personify the uneasy, almost dichotomous, relationship Disney had with women—an uneasy relationship that informs and permeates the Disney princess stories.

We can see Walt Disney in *Snow White*: the short-tempered man who would later publically stylize himself into the avuncular uncle-host of "The Wonderful World of Disney" first worked a similar transformation on the dwarfs. Rather than the traditional, threatening dwarf figures of folklore and fairy tale, Disney wanted cheerful characters capable of loving Snow White. At his direction, character designers created "pawky little uncles" (Kanfer 103), most of whom embrace the princess at first sight. When the dwarfs find Snow White sleeping across their beds, their reactions are largely uniform. Sneezy declares "She's mighty purty!" Bashful sighs, "She's beautiful, like an angel." Grumpy, however, scoffs, "She's a female, and all females is poison—they're full of wicked wiles." He later cautions the others to maintain their independence, not to be taken in by Snow White: "I'm warning ya—give 'em an inch and they'll walk all over ya!" While Walt Disney may have appreciated female beauty as do the majority of the Dwarfs, it is Grumpy, the most vocal and one of the two most differentiated Dwarfs, who most strongly represents Walt Disney himself, giving strong voice to Disney's personal antipathy toward women.

When the other dwarfs are delighted to have Snow White enter their lives and dictate their new living standards, Grumpy alone resents Snow

White's maternal ministrations. He refuses to wash before dinner; he sulks and scowls and generally lives up to his name. As a boy Walt Disney had associated women, particularly his mother and his grammar school teacher, with warmth and security (Watts 15), but this changed as Disney matured. When he arrived in France to serve in the Red Cross, he was so strongly warned against the dangers of venereal disease that, even forty years later, he would recall "That's when you begin to hate women" (qtd. in Watts 15). He was also jilted by his sweetheart while abroad. Later married and father of two daughters, Disney would jokingly rail against being the lone male in his household, but his complaints "had a serious undertone" (Watts 356). When annoyed about a minor incident at home, Disney would rant against women. His comments in the workplace also "hinted at a deep suspicion, even a resentment, of women" (Watts 357). Women were critical to Disney's success, vital in the lower-status Painting and Inking Department, but they were accorded neither creative credit nor power. As Disney sourly mused that women "influence the world" (Watts 357), so Grumpy is reluctantly co-opted into the cult of Snow White.

The other most memorable dwarf is Dopey, the "half wit, who has never learned to talk, who is forever the drudge of the others, but whose smile when Snow White speaks a kind word is enough to soften the heart of the bitterest human" (Flinn). Dopey is immediately smitten by Snow White, basking in her attention and looking even dopier when she smiles at him. He is the only beardless dwarf, suggesting sexual immaturity, but he is also the only dwarf to come back for seconds and thirds when Snow White is handing out kisses. He is Disney before being jilted by his girlfriend, the Disney who didn't know that associating with women could lead to venereal disease. Dopey is the loving innocent to Grumpy's sexual cynic. Grumpy, however, does finally fall sway to the power of Snow White's kiss; Snow White very flirtatiously declares "Why, Grumpy, you do care!" as Grumpy blushes, sighs, and crashes into a tree. One would have to be a dope to be as trusting and loving as Dopey, but even Grumpy cannot avoid the influence of women. The implication is that trusting and loving women is foolish or a source of resentment, a sour and problematic message in a film directed at girls and women.

Whether Walt Disney imbued the prince or the dwarfs—or both—with himself, men have taken over the action and become much more significant than the princesses themselves. This can be seen, in part, in the changes Disney made to the stories' narrative frames. Each source material fairy tale

emphasizes different themes through its narrative frame. They go satisfy-
ingly whole circle, from one starting point, through the plot, to a final point
which reflects upon the beginning. The framing device in the Grimm version
of *Snow White* is the death of the mother-figure, illustrating the hazards of
female biology. Beginning with the death of the biological mother, the
Grimm story ends with the death of the stepmother-queen, who, enraged to
find Snow White the prince's bride, dances herself to death "a sad example
of envy and jealousy" (Owens 198). The frame sounds an alarm: the next
generation is dangerous to women, either as they are fulfilling their reproductive role, or simply as they age and are replaced as the most beautiful in
the land. These framing scenes are both horrible and cautionary, but women
remain central to the story. The frame in Perrault's *Cinderella* is dual: it
emphasizes the importance of marrying wisely (with Cinderella's father's
disastrous second marriage at the start of the story and the marriages Cinderella arranges for her stepsisters at the end) and the goodness of Cinderella
herself (the way she is like her mother, and the way she forgives her stepsisters). In *Sleeping Beauty*, Perrault emphasizes joy in the creation of family:
the joy at the long-yearned-for birth of the princess in the beginning is
matched by a reflection on the joys of the next generation's birth at the end:
the prince (now king) finds "ample consolations in his beautiful wife and
children" soon after the death of his ogress mother. These tales, as presented
in the source material, offer a variety of life's facets, with women at their
centers.

Not so the Disney adaptations of these princess stories. Changing the
framing in the princess stories changes their emphasis; the titular princesses
all lose centrality to men. The man of primary importance, of course, is Walt
Disney himself. The name "Walt Disney" is both the first and final frame;
each film begins with the words "Walt Disney presents" and ends with "A
Walt Disney Production." The audience is never in doubt as to whose vision
created the film or to whom the story belongs. Just inside the "Walt Disney"
frame are the live-action shots of a leather-clad, gothic-lettered book being
opened and closed. These shots hearken to the tradition that Disney is both
leaning on and subverting. They lend actual weight and solidity to the film,
as the only images of three-dimensional objects instead of two-dimensional
drawings on animation cels. Each film then goes to a shot of a fairy-tale
castle, an alleged illustration from the tome just shown; the final animated
shots in the films also include castles, bringing the stories full circle.

The role of male desire in the films grows in importance and in screen time throughout the films; it, too, can be read as a reflection of Walt Disney himself. In *Snow White*, Disney's first feature-length animated film, the prince is, as Zipes indicates, the frame of the story. Additionally, I would argue that Disney and his ambivalent feelings toward women are reflected in the scene-stealing dwarfs. By 1950, when *Cinderella* was created, Disney had children about the age of his princess (his daughters were 16 and 17 at the time of its release), and he could anticipate his eventual role as grandfather. The king in *Cinderella* conceives of a ball after bemoaning the fact that his son is has grown up and away from him; he looks to having grandchildren. The prince still rescues Cinderella via marriage, but it is his father's desire that initiates the film's action. Almost ten years later, the men have almost completely taken over the action of *Sleeping Beauty*. There are two kings, so important that they are given names (as Disney's name was by then a household term); their interests are dynastic—they want grandchildren not simply for pleasure, as does the king in *Cinderella*, but for the powerful joined legacy those grandchildren imply. Disney himself was building a vast dynasty that would include television and theme parks in addition to feature film. No longer simply the faceless name in the background, Disney himself became a vital part of the show by hosting the weekly anthology program "Disneyland"[5].

These films' plots are driven by male desire; male desire leads to action. The men desire something of a princess—a lover, the mother of his grandchildren, the bearer of a dynasty—and the action begins. Had Snow White remained alone and undesired, simply wishing unseen by the well, it is possible that her stepmother would not have been driven quite to murder; the prince's interest, his desire, is the final straw for the queen. Had the king in Cinderella not desired grandchildren, the ball would never have been arranged; Cinderella would have continued as her stepmother's scullery maid. Had the King not desired a child so much that he celebrated her birth—and had that birth not been such an affair of state, acting as the betrothal celebration as well—Maleficent would not have felt slighted by not having been invited. The girls simply are, and in their state of being they are desired. Their very existence provokes action, although as will be discussed in the next section, they themselves act very little.

Defining the Disney Princess

These early Disney princesses and their stories are strongly similar to each other. Considered en masse, the Disney princess stories unite into one monolithic, repetitive story. The princesses' backgrounds are quite similar: "All three come from western European fairy tales, all three spend their early lives in reduced circumstances, and all three spend their childhood and youth under threat from an evil older woman who holds some kind of authority over them" (Davis 101). But one might reasonably expect that there would be changes in the films that reflect the social changes in America in the twenty-five year period from 1934, when *Snow White* was in its initial planning stages, to 1959, when *Sleeping Beauty* was released. This expectation, however, would not be satisfied; as Davis notes, "any differences between them … are largely superficial, stylistic, and artistic" (Davis 101). Much of this repetition was intentional, of course, seeking financial success by reusing the same pattern. But the repetition creates a unified, dominant message for viewers; the advent of home video, the repetitive nature of children's viewing habits, and the role of imaginative play keep this insidious message current, even seventy years after the films' first releases. The princesses' physical, attitudinal, and behavioral similarities, when combined with their similarly romantic happy endings, teach their audience what it takes to achieve princess-hood and all the benefits that go with that position. The princesses' bodies, their dreams, their motherly natures and their lack of agency all define a princess who is simultaneously socially outdated and culturally pervasive.

One almost-invisible implication found upon examination of the first group of Disney princesses is that of the princesses' ethnic origins[6]. They are white, of European descent, with the implication that whiteness is required to be recognized as a princess. Disney was, of course, going to European versions of fairy tales for his source material, but America was far from all-white during the period these films were made. The culture did, as a whole, value whiteness above all other races, and these films reflect that prejudice.[7]

A Disney princess, as demonstrated in these early films, must have a certain body type. There are some differences in the princesses' appearance, although these differences are slight. Each is designed as a "contemporaneous popular image of feminine beauty and youth" (Bell 109). Snow White, designed in the 1930s, was created with silent film star Janet Gaynor in mind; side-by-side comparisons indicate she has Gaynor's hairstyle, face shape, and coloration. Cinderella is considered a Grace Kelly type, regal even in her work clothes (as *Cinderella*'s opening chorus declares, "Though you're dressed in rags/ You wear an air of queenly grace/Anyone can see a throne/Would be your proper place"). Aurora, designed in the late 1950s, has been likened both to Audrey Hepburn and to the Barbie dolls that were then flying off toy store shelves (I find her slim figure much more Hepburn than Barbie, but her coloration and nose are quite Barbie-esque); her clothing, with its wasp waist and full skirt, is reminiscent of Dior's "New Look." However, these princesses have striking similarities of posture, physique and expression which serve to create a standard of beauty—for emulation and, on the flip side, for exclusion. There is a funny little moment in *Sleeping Beauty* when Phillip, hearing Briar Rose singing in the forest, remarks that there's "something strange about that voice—too beautiful to be real." The same can be said of all the girls' bodies, although paradoxically, ironically, there were real models behind the drawn figures.

The early Disney films relied on the technique of rotoscoping for realistic human characters. Rotoscoping, simply put, is the practice of filming a scene with live characters against a plain background, then tracing over those characters frame by frame to create an animated work. The actors chosen to play the princess roles in these rotoscoped pre-films were professional dancers (Bell 110), which is immediately evident in their posture and foot position: what gives Cinderella her "air of queenly grace" is her incredibly straight posture, even when bending to pick up her mop bucket or kneeling to scrub the floor. Her head positively floats off her neck and shoulders; moreover, as dance physician L.M. Vincent notes, even in street clothes a dancer's walk is "still a dead giveaway. The walking apparatus of the ballet dancer is not mutated; rather the peculiar stride results from external rotation of the hips" (qtd. in Bell 111). Watch Cinderella or Aurora walk across the floor, broom in hand, and note that their feet are always turned out, halfway to one of ballet's primary foot positions.

There is, however, a conflict between the beauty, helplessness and passivity of the girls' roles and the strength and discipline implied by their bodies. Classical ballet requires years of training and both physical and mental strength. To be a proper princess, however, requires submitting to the demands of others and passively waiting for one's prince. According to Bell, the Disney artists "have created a somatic mixed message" (112) by relying on young women whose bodies portray (however unconsciously) character traits which oppose the princesses' personalities. More than that, "the Disney

apparatus buys into and then sells the twofold fantasy of little girls who want
to grow up to be princesses and ballerinas" (Bell 111). This recognition that
there is something special about the bodies of the early Disney princesses is
largely subconscious on the part of the little girls who make up Disney's
primary audience. But the physical requirement serves to exclude the vast
majority of girls who would be one of these princesses; they don't realize the
ways in which their own bodies are inadequate, yet they recognize that they
are. It's as if the princesses have a secret—their body models' years of
training—that makes actually achieving princesshood unattainable for their
little-girl audience. Indeed, not even the ballerina-models could have
achieved the animators' princess look. A side-by-side comparison of the
dancer Helene Stanley (model for Aurora) and Aurora herself show the
princess more svelte, more smooth, even sprightlier than the actual dancer
(photos in Solomon 199). Had the dancers been as slight as the princesses
drawn over them, they would not have had the musculature to dance.

In addition to upholding the majority cultural standards of beauty, in order to be a Disney princess a girl must also be a dreamer, specifically a
dreamer of romance (no dreams of wealth, power, or achievement for these
girls). Dreaming of romance is almost—but not quite—an action, yet it is the
one action that the princesses are most likely to take. Snow White set this
trend, and she is dreamier than the others; perhaps her dreams stand in place
of the others' fairy godmothers. As has been discussed above, Snow White
dreams of romance in almost every scene: at the wishing well, with the
dwarfs, when tempted by the apple. It can safely be assumed that if she
dreams while in her magical coma, those dreams are also of romance.

Cinderella, too, dreams repeatedly through her film. The song over the
opening credits assures her that in the "kingdom of romance" she will "see
[her] dreams unfold." Cinderella is first shown sleeping, dreaming of—
something, "the best dream, a lovely dream." She coyly refuses to reveal her
dream to the birds and mice who have come to awaken her, responding,
"What kind of a dream? Uh-uh, can't tell. Cause if you tell a wish, it won't
come true." The audience, however, has seen her sigh, avert her eyes, and
play with her hair as she contemplates her dream; primed by the opening
song's allusion to romance, her coy behavior indicates to the audience the
romantic nature of Cinderella's dream. In one central scene, Cinderella
scrubs the floor while her stepsisters have a music lesson. They sing (comedically badly) and Cinderella echoes them: "Sing, sweet nightingale."
This is an unusual piece; in his musicals, Disney was interested in moving

the action forward even during the songs (Kanfer 105), yet "Sing, Sweet Nightingale" is a repetitive song mirrored by the repetitive motion of Cinderella scrubbing the floor, motion made even more repetitive by being reflected in soap bubbles floating across the screen. The nightingale is a symbol of love, and Cinderella's beautiful rendition of the song is again suggestive of her preoccupation with romance. When her fairy godmother transforms her rags into a ball gown, Cinderella exclaims, "Why, it's like a dream! A wonderful dream come true." When she does actually meet the prince at the ball, her inner monologue comes in song: "So this is love, so this is love…so this is the miracle that I've been dreaming of…" set to a falling-in-love montage. As she has dreamed of love prior to falling in love, so she becomes even dreamier in the actual event of loving someone. She daydreams after the ball; her dreamy appearance warns her stepmother to prevent Cinderella from trying on the glass slipper.

Virtually every line of Briar Rose/Aurora's dialogue, spoken or sung, concerns romantic dreams in general or, later, of the boy (name unknown) she loves; it is her major character trait. In her first significant verbal passage, she sings the song "I Wonder," in which she wonders "why each little bird /has a someone to sing to" and "if my heart keeps singing /will my song go winging /to someone, someone who'll find me /and bring back a love song to me?" She is dreaming about passively waiting for someone to come to her, bringing the romance she desires. She details both her predicament and her dreams to her nonspeaking animal friends. This passage is her longest in the film, and is central to her character, her interests and her plot. Protesting that Flora, Fauna, and Meriwether still treat her as a child, she monologizes,

> They never want me to meet anyone. But you know something? I've fooled them. I have met someone. [Owl: "Whoo?"] Oh, a prince. Well, he's tall and handsome and — and so romantic. Oh, we walk together, and talk together, and just before we say goodbye, he takes me in his arms, and then — I wake up. Yes, it's only in my dreams. They say if you dream a thing more than once, it's sure to come true. And I've seen him so many times.

The animals understand her plight, of course, and find Phillip's cloak and boots in the forest, bringing them back to "play prince" with Briar Rose. This also leads Phillip to Briar Rose, where he can waltz with her and echo her lyrics to "Once Upon a Dream," the movie's central song.

I know you, I walked with you once upon a dream.
I know you, the gleam in your eyes is so familiar a gleam.
Yet I know it's true that visions are seldom all they seem
But if I know you, I know what you'll do
You'll love me at once, the way you did once upon a dream.

This is a song about recognizing one's true love from one's own dreams; dreaming of love is preparation for the act itself. She spends the final third of the film asleep, urged by the chorus to dream: "Sleeping Beauty fair, /gold of sunshine in your hair, /lips that shame the red, red rose, / dreaming of true love in slumber repose. One day he will come, / riding out of the dawn. /And you'll awaken to love's first kiss. / Till then, Sleeping Beauty, sleep on." The film even ends on a particularly dreamy note, with the castle fading into clouds as the lovers waltz together.

The princesses' dreams of romance are markedly pure and simple; they yearn for love, not for a socio-economically advantageous marriage. As a sign of their chastity and purity, each girl is seen running from her prince during their first meeting. Snow White runs immediately, startled when the prince joins her in song at the wishing well. She reappears on her balcony to hear him declare his love. In response, she chastely sends him a kiss by dove; she kisses the bird which then flies down to blushingly kiss the prince. Cinderella does not run as quickly as Snow White, but then again she has gone to the ball specifically to meet the prince. She spends the evening falling in love with a man whose identity she does not know. When Cinderella, moving toward her first kiss, hears the clock chime midnight, she dashes away, excusing her abrupt departure by claiming, "The prince—why, I haven't even met the prince." Aurora also runs from her prince after their first meeting. She falls in love, but is too modest to give him her name. She does, however, set a date with him for that evening at the cottage, where they can be properly chaperoned. Aurora mourns the loss of the boy in the forest, preferring him to her royal, unknown betrothed.

The princess ideal in the Disney films is chaste, but she has strong maternal tendencies; she is imagined as motherly before she becomes a mother. Snow White's relationship to the dwarfs is oddly variable: she is both a mother figure to them and the object of their schoolboy-like infatuation. As discussed above, all of the dwarfs vie for and react to her kisses; they blush, they walk into things, they come back for seconds. But most of her interaction with them consists of her tending them as if they were children. She tidies their house before she even meets them, and makes dinner for what she assumes is a household of motherless children. She inspects their hands before allowing them to sit for dinner; she tells them a story at bedtime. She has an overall civilizing effect on them. Bidding them goodbye as they go to work the next morning, Snow White resembles a mother sending her children off to school. At the end of the film, as the prince is preparing to remove Snow White to his castle, he lifts up the dwarfs one by one for a final kiss from Snow White (seated on horseback). They are clearly in a childlike position relative to Snow White, getting one last kiss good-bye from their mother figure. This, of course, prefigures the role Snow White is riding off to assume: wife to the prince and mother to their future children.

Cinderella is a motherly little figure, too, making clothes for her mouse and bird friends. She feeds them and generally tends them; the audience sees her tame and civilize the mouse she rescues from a trap in the beginning of the film. Beyond her animal "children", most of Cinderella's mothering is implied for the future. The king has two major scenes, one in which he tells the Duke that he longs to have children in the palace. The ball is the means by which the king hopes to acquire his grandchildren, and he plans it down to the last detail: "soft lights, romantic music, all the trimmings." After the ball, the audience sees the king laughing in his sleep, dreaming of romping on the floor with his blond grandchildren. Their blond hair is telling, since the king is grey-and-bald and the prince's hair is dark brown; Cinderella, the only blond in the film, is clearly the mother of these dream-children. Cinderella therefore must be maternal, since her role will be to provide the king with grandchildren. Her desire for children is assumed, a given within the world of the film.

Whether Aurora is motherly is unknown, so underdeveloped is her personality. But her maternal leanings or their lack are irrelevant; her marriage and children have already been decided by her father and future father-in-law. They planned her marriage specifically with an eye toward the children she would produce as the means of uniting their kingdoms. The audience sees her do nothing motherly, but her future maternity is implied in everything that happens to her. The two kings get even more screen time than Cinderella's king; they plan Aurora's wedding when they are together the day of her christening as well as on her sixteenth birthday, the day she is to return. On this day, Aurora's father goers even further, announcing that he'll have the royal woodworkers start building the royal crib. At the end of the film, it is left for the audience to assume that just as the fathers' plans to marry their children has come to fruition, so too will their plans to unite their kingdoms via their shared grandchildren bear fruit.

Although Disney's first-wave princess stories were created during years leading up to the second feminist wave, and culturally one might expect the girls to have larger and more important parts in their stories as the years passed, the opposite is actually the case. This can be demonstrated in two ways: the amount of screen time the princesses have, and the amount of agency they are permitted[8]. No more than half the screen time is allotted to the princesses. That Snow White's screen time is shared with the dwarfs is not surprising; the film's full title is *Snow White and the Seven Dwarfs* (even more correctly and more tellingly, it's *Walt Disney's Snow White and the Seven Dwarfs*). Fully half of the story is given to the dwarfs; Snow White's domestic scenes are intercut with scenes of the dwarfs mining, singing, and racing to her rescue. Much of *Cinderella* is devoted to her animal friends: birds, mice, a dog, and an evil cat. Each has "unique flavor and personality" (Ebert "Cinderella"). The animals pad out the thin story line, and most of the film's humor comes from the animals—characterized as "Tom and Jerry style cat-and-mouse hijinks" (Greydanus). But not only do the animals contribute to the motion onscreen, not only do they have a running subplot; "the cute Disney sidekicks, always present, here overstep their bounds into the main plot" (Greydanus). These animals are vital to the plot, saving Cinderella from her stepmother and delivering her to the prince. Aurora/Briar Rose has even less screen time than the two earlier princesses. She is not seen at all in the first third of the film, which is given over to narration, the fairies, and the kings. She appears on the day of her sixteenth birthday, just long enough to go into the forest and fall in love (which event, and its retelling, takes about four scenes). She's taken to the palace and ensorcelled (another two scenes), from which point she's out of the picture until the final scenes of Phillip's kiss and their happy ending waltz. The fairies (both good and evil) and the royal men (two kings and the prince) own *Sleeping Beauty*.

With each film, the titular princess has less power, becomes less important, less active and less central to "her" story's plot. Snow White runs into the forest, insinuates herself into the dwarfs' home by making herself indispensible, civilizes the dwarfs and generally takes over their household. Until she is felled by the poisoned apple, she is actually quite active. Cinderella is busy too, but not on her own behalf. She remains in her father's home, a virtual slave to her stepmother and stepsisters. Her first attempt to go to the ball was brought about by her mice friends; her successful attempt was brought about by magic. She returns (as far as she knows) to her former state after the ball, apparently satisfied with one night of fantasy and romance. Locked in her room upon the duke's imminent arrival, Cinderella is again dependent on little household animals for her happy ending—her own banging on the door accomplishes nothing. It takes a combination of magic and mice to free Cinderella from her life of drudgery. Aurora is even more passive. She falls in love, but when she is told she's a princess and she must give up her life and her love and return to the family and fiancé she has never met, she cries—but she obeys. She is quickly bewitched into activating her childhood curse, and she falls into her enchanted sleep. The rest of "her" story, all of the exciting parts, goes on without her. Simply put, "The young women are like helpless ornaments in need of protection, and when it comes to the action of the film, they are omitted" (Zipes *Fairy Tale* 90). These princesses wait, suffering and obedient, seemingly content to let the action go on around them.

The animators' own descriptions and summaries of the princess stories highlight the princesses' inactivity. The summary of *Snow White* reads:

> Jealousy leads a vain queen to threaten the life of a young princess, who flees into the woods where she is befriended by seven dwarfs. When the queen, in disguise, tricks her into eating a poisoned apple, the girl is thought dead and preserved in a glass coffin until a prince awakens her with love's first kiss. (Thomas and Johnson 368)

Grammatically, the only active verb ascribed to Snow White is "flees;" in relation to every other verb in the above description she is passive. The action of the film is done to her, not by her. Bill Peet, longtime Disney story man, describes the plots of the princess stories as "pretty young girl in trouble" (Solomon 188); he explained the plot of *Cinderella* in particular as "the heroine holds the story together while most of the action occurs around her" (Solomon 188). Thomas and Johnson, two of Disney's legendary Nine Old Men, describe Sleeping Beauty as "a story of how these three fairies tried to save a girl from the curse of the evil fairy Maleficent, and lost" (Thomas and Johnson 401). The writers and artists had no desire to make the princesses active heroines; they were designed to stay in place and let action happen around them and to them.

This decision to use the princess as an inactive center point resulted from the Disney animation principle of telling "the story through the broad characters rather than the 'straight' ones" (Thomas and Johnson 375). The princesses are the heroines, but as straight characters they were considered a problem within their stories. One guideline from the animation studio instructs aspiring artists:

> There is no way to animate strong-enough attitudes, feelings or expressions on real-istic characters to get the communication you should have. The more real, the less latitude for clear communication. This is more easily done with the cartoon charac-ters who can carry the story with more interest and spirit anyway. Snow White was told through the animals, the dwarfs, the witch – not through the prince or the queen or the huntsman....The girl herself was a real problem, but she was helped by al-ways working to a sympathetic animal or a broad character. This is the old vaude-ville trick of playing the pretty girl against the buffoon: it helps both characters. (Thomas and Johnson 375)

While referencing vaudeville as the rationale for the princesses' lack of agency and character development seems reasonable, it ignores the "simmer-ing antagonism toward feminine influence in vaudeville" identified by M. Alison Kibler (59). Female characters were secondary, derided when they tried to exert control. Women who took lead roles, resisting second-banana status, had their gender impugned. Disney and his animators not only relied on this tradition, they furthered it, bringing it beyond vaudeville (already passé by the early 1930s) all the way to the end of the twentieth century.

(M)other Women: Villains and Godmothers

Although, as discussed above, the maternal aspects of the princesses in these films are crucial to their characters, there is a distinct lack of actual mothers in these films. Snow White's mother was exised completely from the story, and Cinderella's is never mentioned either—although they both have wicked stepmothers, who will be discussed shortly. Neither prince is shown to have a mother, although Cinderella's future father-in-law has significant screen time and plot significance. Aurora has a mother, the queen, but she is insignificant. The narrator introduces the royal characters as "Good King Stephan and his Queen...and the visitors are King Hubert and Phillip, his son and heir." The three male royals have names; the Queen, however, remains nameless, referred to as an adjunct to and possession of King Stephan (it is "the king and his queen" who watch the fairies remove Aurora). Even the fairies, who presumably have a relationship with the royals, refer to them as "Poor King Stephan—and the queen." While the father-kings have a duet, and a mock-swordfight, and while it is their desire for a marriage that decides their children's future, the royal mother has two lines, both in reaction to Maleficent[9]. It is almost preferable for the mothers to be altogether absent than to be this immaterial.

Being practically motherless does not hinder the princesses' development; as we have seen, they are goodness personified, "so virtuous, so warm and welcoming, so in tune with nature" (Douglass 29). Extremely hardworking, they work uncomplainingly, uncompensated; they sing and dance through their lives of drudgery. They inspire desire in appropriate suitors (their princes) and in all other males coming in contact with them (the dwarfs, the kings[10]). Disney's portrayal of these first-wave princesses "suggests that Walt believed in the over-riding view of women in the 1940s and 1950s as characterized by such traits as emotionalism, domesticity, maternal concerns, an over-all emphasis on beauty and romance (as opposed to more 'practical' concerns)" (Davis 115). This is abundantly evident. Yet according to Zipes, "despite their beauty and charm, Sleeping Beauty, Cinderella, and the other heroines are pale and pathetic compared to the more active and demonic characters" (*Fairy Tale* 90). Most critics agree: the evil women, the villains in these films, are fascinating—both on-screen and in their implications.

The antagonists of these films—*Snow White*'s stepmother-queen, *Cinderella*'s stepmother Lady Tremaine, and *Sleeping Beauty*'s evil fairy Maleficent—are strikingly similar, as closely related a group as the princesses themselves. They share a physical type: tall, powerful-looking, sexual. Their bodies are mature, womanly hourglasses. They dominate the screen with every move; their gestures are grand, their voices commanding. The use of shadow and light in their scenes renders them even more sinister: Snow White's queen is seen against the dark of the magic mirror; Lady Tremaine's eyes glint in a slash of light while the rest of her face is in shadow; Maleficent appears as a black figure in a flash of fire, almost an iris in a bright, evil eye. All other characters pale before them, suffering by comparison; as Marina Warner writes, the artists "concentrate with exuberant glee on the towering, taloned, raven-haired wicked stepmother; all Disney's powers of invention failed to save the princes from featureless banality and his heroines from saccharin sentimentality" (Warner 207). The villains tower over those around them, majestic and frightening.

Their personalities are also the most compelling of any introduced in the films. While the princesses are all sweetness and light, accepting and demure, the wicked women are ... not. Their appearance of physical power is matched by strength of personality and desire to dominate. They are vain, jealous, cruel and domineering.

> Perhaps the most distinguishing feature of the villainesses…is the much higher proportion of agency they show when compared to that of their victims. They change themselves into other things when functioning in their usual form is not working for them. They actively seek to control not just their lives but also their circumstances. They are strong, fearless, and very often creative. They are mature, powerful, and independent. In short, they are everything that their female victims are not. (Davis 107)

The magical women change their appearances, turning themselves into other creatures: a crone, in the case of Snow White's stepmother-queen; a ball of light and a dragon, in the case of Maleficent. Lady Tremaine, with no magic at hand, employs dissimulation and subterfuge: lying about Cinderella's existence, "accidentally" destroying the glass slipper.

The power of these wicked women antagonists is bent toward their own goals; the destruction of their princess victims is almost incidental in service to their vanity. Snow White is in danger because her stepmother's magic mirror no longer declares the queen the fairest in the land. *Variety*'s contemporaneous review of *Snow White* characterized the stepmother/queen as "a vampish brunet, of homicidal instincts" (*Variety* 1937); indeed, her vampishness triggers her murderous rage. Lady Tremaine is described by the narrator as "cold, cruel, and bitterly jealous of Cinderella's charm and beauty, grimly determined to forward the interests of her own two awkward daughters." She is so invested in the superiority of her family that Cinderella is pushed aside, used as a drudge, and ultimately imprisoned in her attic. Maleficent is evil, according to the good fairies, because she knows nothing of "love, or kindness, or the joy of helping others." Maleficent's vanity was injured when King Stephan did not invite her to Aurora's birth celebration; from that slight, all evil in the story follows.

These wicked women have been read in a variety of ways. Elizabeth Bell characterizes them as femmes fatales, citing the animators' use of close-ups (no other characters have them), the connection to predatory animals (Maleficent as a "giant vampire bat," Snow White's stepmother-queen as "a mixture of Lady Macbeth and The Big Bad Wolf"), and an "excess of sexuality and agency [that] is drawn as evil" (117). However, femme fatales use their sexuality to endanger men, which is not these villainesses' primary interest. Furthermore, while their sexuality is certainly part of their characters, it is not they source of their power. The danger these villainesses pose is not directed toward the men (with the possible exception of Maleficent holding Phillip captive), as with classic femme fatales; it is directed toward the girls.

Amy Davis goes to the same era of Hollywood film as Bell for her construction of the antagonists, but she comes to a different conclusion. They are not femmes fatales, according to Davis; they are one-half of the pair created in the Women's Film sub-genre of "female double films" (124). In female double films, two women are tied together as mirror opposites: the good woman (sweet, passive, and virginal) connected to yet opposed to the evil woman (nasty, aggressive, sexual). The Disney paired women are not twins, as is often the case in female double films. Instead, they offer even more avenues of comparison: maturity versus youth; sexual knowledge versus innocence; the power to warp nature versus being one with nature. This diametric opposition is the one seen by Susan Douglass as well; according to her, for the girls watching these movies or acting them out in imaginative play, there are "only two choices: the powerless but beloved masochist or the powerful but detested narcissist" (29). While there are certainly links to be seen between the wicked older antagonists and their innocent younger victims, I do not feel that this pairing is the most useful within the context of these princess stories. The princesses are not nearly strong or active enough to challenge opponents of this caliber.

Sean Griffin has yet another reading of these antagonists, both in their bodies and in their desires. Because their clothing covers their bodies entirely, including their heads and necks, they appear to be hiding something.

> Only the hands and face are exposed, leaving the rest of the body cloaked. Their faces both have highly defined features (etched cheekbones, thin sharp noses, strongly set jaws) in contrast to the softer designs of the heroines, and they also have access to makeup, especially mascara and eye shadow....In other words, these villainesses look like drag queens. (73)

Griffin is reading all those signs usually interpreted as frightening feminine sexuality as camp male interpretations of it. He further substantiates this interpretation by examining these villains' goals: According to Griffin, the fact that the wicked women do not want the princes for themselves as authentic heterosexual villains would, as femmes fatales or dashing rogues would, is one of "a number of signifiers that make it easier for homosexual viewers to read villains not only as 'anti-couple' but specifically as 'queer' figures" (75). This reading opens up identification possibilities for nonheterosexuals alienated from the romantic storyline, but of course, the identification is almost entirely negative. Yes, the wicked women (or "women") get the best lines and most dramatic entrances, but they are all ultimately doomed.

The villains' ultimate damnation is inextricably linked to the power they wield, the primary lesson gleaned from these princess stories' wicked women. Susan Douglass writes, "...any power at all completely corrupted women and turned them into monsters. In their hands, power was lethal: it was used only to bolster their own overweening vanity and to destroy what was pure and good in the world" (29). They are much more active than the princesses, and they have much more agency. But they only do evil with their power, and as such are undesirable role models. Better to be passive and good and loved than active, if activity implies being evil and being hated. More than that, of course, is that "they all suffer the same fate—destruction" (Davis 107). The more power the woman had, the more horrible her fate. Lady Tremaine, the least powerful of the villainesses, simply sees the ruin of all her plans, losing the prince, her desired son-in-law, to her stepdaughter. Snow White's stepmother-queen, who researches the magic required to disguise herself as a crone and to put Snow White into an enchanted sleep, dies quickly, suddenly, and with relatively little pain as the jagged outcropping on which she stands is hit by lightening. Maleficent, whose name implies that power she wields so evilly is part of herself, who has the power to lay a curse that transcends time and space, who has the power to transport herself magically and to transform herself into both a transfixing point of light and into a powerful dragon, dies most hideously. Her multi-step death is the climax of the film. After a thrilling pursuit, Maleficent, in the form of a fire-breathing, mouth-snapping dragon, backs Phillip to the very edge of a precipice. Bolstered by the good fairies' magic, he takes aim and throws his sword into the dragon's chest. The rocks under the dragon crumble, sending her down into a ravine. Her magical green fire turns into mundane black smoke. Phillip, creeping to the edge, looks down and sees his sword, glowing, upright in the shadow-stain of her cloak/dragon-skin. The sword goes black in shadow, and Maleficent is dead.

The distinctly unhappy endings of these powerful women are not necessarily linked to their evil, but to their agency. Interestingly,

> it is these evil women who are the active women in their films, and that their activity
> is forced upon them by their own jealousy and unhappiness....Real happiness seems
> to be linked to one trait alone — passivity. If you are willing to wait patiently for

your happiness, it will surely come to you. Try to make it happen for yourself, and you will only end up defeated and alone. (Davis 108)

The lesson here is in two layers: the princesses, passive, end up happy. The wicked women, trying to take control, are destroyed. Emulate one; eschew the other: your chances of a happy ending increase.

Another lesson of the wicked women is that they are the enemies of the young. Female-on-female violence is a factor in these princess stories, much if not all of it based on male attention. Seeing the prince fall in love with Snow White, having already been told that Snow White is the fairest in the land, causes the stepmother-queen to order her death. When using an intermediary does not work, she comes after the princess herself. Lady Tremaine encourages her daughters to destroy Cinderella's mouse-made dress. In a surprisingly violent scene, the stepsisters forcibly remove the trimmings, tearing the dress itself and leaving Cinderella in tatters. Maleficent, of course, spends sixteen years in pursuit of Aurora, seeking to revenge herself on Aurora's father by killing the girl. Girls are thus taught not to trust the generation just ahead of them, because they are still rivals, harmful and untrustworthy even when in positions, like that of stepmother, which should be nurturing. The girls have also learned that they cannot save themselves; they need to be rescued. Only one type of woman can be of help: the fairy godmother.

Most critics compare the princesses to the wicked antagonists, linking the two inexorably. While this is quite valid—good/evil, youth/maturity, victim/victimizer, the list could go on and on—another pairing, another comparison goes largely unnoted. Bell contrasts the bodies of the wicked women and the fairy godmothers, but she does not delve into the implications of these differences. The contrast between the wicked antagonist and the fairy godmother is crucial, not just to the plot but also vis à vis the choices presented to the princess within the story. The princess, as evidenced by her romantic dreams, is reaching maturity. As she does—and as the audience that identifies with her does—a choice will have to be made as to what sort of woman she (and they) will become. Bell writes, "On the Disney cultural timeline, the young heroines will become their stepmothers; the stepmothers, too, will become the good fairies and godmothers" (121). While the relative ages of the princess-wicked woman-godmother do suggest that progression, in reality none exists. One cannot go from being a (young) princess to a (mature) wicked woman to an (old) godmother. As we have seen, the path of the wicked woman leads inexorably to destruction. Even Lady Tremaine, the only antagonist to survive, is effectively erased from the story, her plans in ruin. In order to reach old age to become the good godmother type, a princess must choose her direction. The wicked woman/godmother choice is her fork in the road, and the fairy godmothers must be read as the counterparts of the wicked antagonists.

Physically, of course, the fairy godmother is quite unlike her adversary. The tall, powerful, intimidating wicked woman finds her opposite in the fairy godmother: short, soft, and plump. The wicked magical women, although described by critics as brunettes, are in reality completely hooded, revealing not a single strand; the godmothers' hair, while covered, is visible under their hats and hoods. Their bodies reveal their characters: "As endomorphs, they fulfill the physical somatype/stereotype as calm, relaxed, cooperative, affable, warm, forgiving, sympathetic, soft-hearted, generous, affectionate, and kind" (Bell 118). In creating the godmothers, the Disney animators drew on many of the techniques they used in creating Snow White's dwarfs. The godmothers move not in a rotoscoped "real" manner, but comedically; the godmothers, like the dwarfs, move from their rumps. Schickel hypothesizes an anal fixation in this "rump-butting," but different centers of gravity allow different personality types to be expressed through body language. According to Ebert, "Disney did it because it worked: it makes the comic characters rounder, lower, softer, bouncier and funnier" ("Snow White"). The godmothers' movements make them funny, not frail; although the animator Frank Thomas professed to having studied old women in grocery stores for his models of Flora, Fauna and Meriwether (Bell 119), it seems that he really relied on earlier comic characters, including Disney's dwarfs, for physical inspiration.

The temperaments of the godmothers, while slightly differentiated (Flora is a planner, Meriwether is quick to anger), have many commonalities. The primary personality trait shared by the fairy godmothers is that they are addled, slightly discombobulated. Cinderella's fairy godmother misplaces her wand. Having conjured up the splendid accoutrements Cinderella will use to get to the ball, she nearly sends Cinderella off in tatters. Her patterns of speech are repetitive, daffy; even her most powerful language, her magic spell, is circular. The three good fairies of *Sleeping Beauty* can be kindly described as "slightly befuddled" (Solomon 198). They are kindhearted, yet bumbling. They conceive of the plan to keep baby Aurora safe, delighted to think that they will "have to feed it and wash it and dress it and rock it to sleep." But while they do manage to keep the princess hidden for sixteen years, their foolishness reveals Aurora to Maleficent on the girl's birthday. They have not managed to learn non-magical housekeeping in all the time they've tended Aurora, and on her birthday they resort to magic to create her cake and dress. But a magic battle ensues, as two of the fairies fight about the color of Aurora's dress. This use of magic—so close to goal!—reveals their location to Maleficent's agent and leads to the curse's activation. It is clearly meant by the animators to be comedic, but it is an inexcusable slip.

The fairies' use of magic is also limited. If Cinderella had a fairy god-mother all along, why has she not come to the girl's aid previously? Surely a life of servitude is harder than missing one ball. No explanation is offered in the film (nor does the submissive and grateful Cinderella suggest that her godmother could have arrived sooner), but perhaps the godmother's magic must be saved for special circumstances or fork-in-the-road moments. In *Sleeping Beauty*, the good fairies' magic is much weaker than Maleficent's, rendering them largely impotent against the evil fairy. They tell King Stephan that "Maleficent's powers are far too great" for them to remove the curse. When Meriwether declares she'd like to turn Maleficent into a "fat old hop-toad," the others chastise her, telling her "that isn't a very nice thing to say. Besides, we can't. You know our magic doesn't work that way. It can only do good, dear, to bring joy and happiness." While the idea of magic bringing only joy and happiness is delightful, unfortunately that renders the good fairies rather ineffective against their powerful adversary. They comfort themselves that "Maleficent doesn't know anything of love, or kindness, or the joy of helping others." The good fairies, of course, know of these things and little else; their magic is apparently used only in the service of others.

Their limited use of magic leads the fairy godmothers to be of limited help. Cinderella's godmother appears in one scene and is never seen again[11]. The godmother provides Cinderella the necessary trappings to meet the prince, but she never reappears; the mice do the work of rescuing Cinderella from her attic and of rejoicing at her wedding. The good fairies do have one moment of almost direct conflict with Maleficent, instead of partially negating her work behind her back or spending magic-less years in hiding. When Phillip, whom they've freed (quietly, surreptitiously) from Malefi-cent's dungeon, fights Maleficent-as-dragon, the good fairies stand behind him and work their magic to improve his aim. Their magic must be worked through Phillip in order to work against Maleficent. In the service of others and working through others: that is where the good fairies' power lies.

According to Bell, the range of ages and body types depicted in the Disney princess films show the "worlds of women…that offer alternatives to institutional hierarchy, science and technology, and divine rights of kings" (121). Yet the princesses ultimately fit into the hierarchy, the power of the wicked women is vanquished, and the kings get their wishes. The female bodies do offer a range of possibilities, but not a liberating world of women; after all, these films were produced, directed, and written by men, and they represent the vision of one man in particular. The princesses must not become the stepmothers/queens/wicked fairies. They must find a way somehow to become helpful, sweet, post-sexual competition godmothers without passing through the stage of wicked feminine power represented by the antagonists. To wield that power is to die.

But to reach the grandmotherly age of the positive role models without passing through the powerful stage of the antagonists—unfortunately, this is impossible. The answer seems to be to ignore the sexuality, agency and power exerted by the antagonists. The young princesses are docile, sweet, in service to others; the godmothers are the same. By remaining as they are, by accepting their fates (which seem positive at the end of their films, but which needn't remain so), by making the men in their lives happy and not attempting to undermine the powerful patriarchy for the own ends, the princesses can survive to serve others in their old age, as godmothers.

Conclusion

"The uniformity of structure, style and themes established in 1937 was further developed in…*Cinderella* [and *Sleeping Beauty*], which reek of sexism, sentimentality, and sterility" (Zipes *Breaking* 129). Had these films faded into obscurity, as have most films from 1937, 1950 and 1959, there would be little purpose to examining them. But these princess films have never passed out of American consciousness; constantly before the American viewing public, they have become most Americans' definitive versions of the stories. Each has been re-released to theaters repeatedly since its initial run; *Snow White* and *Cinderella* were on a seven-year release rotation (*Newsweek* 83), and *Sleeping Beauty* was re-released in 1970, 1979, and 1986 (Solomon 200). These re-releases provide easy money for Disney studios; minimal advertising outlay renders re-releases almost pure profit. With the advent of home video, children can watch these movies to their hearts' content. Not only that, *Cinderella* had two direct-to-video sequels for home viewing:

Cinderella II: Dreams Come True (2002) and *Cinderella III: A Twist in Time* (2007). There is also a series of direct-to-video princess films, "Disney Princess Enchanted Tales," begun in 2007. More than 14 million units have been sold direct-to-video since 2002 ("Disney Princess"), even though the quality of animation in these films is distinctly lacking.

Merchandising beyond direct-to-video sales also keeps these early Disney princesses before the public eye. Television, toys, dress-up costumes, theme parks:

> All these activities are firmly linked in the Disney concept of 'total merchandising.' As Roy Disney...puts it, 'Everything we do helps something else.' A television show plugs a Disney movie; the movie characters can move into Disneyland or be used as the basis for more television, comics, songs, and toys. In a circle of mathematical perfection, the secondary promotions build up new interest in the movie, which can be released again. (*Newsweek* 84)

In fact, "Disney Princess" has become its own successful franchise, marketing the princesses (first-wave and second, and now twenty-first century as well) en masse. Recognizing the profitability of the line, "The Walt Disney Company supports the Disney Princess brand year-round through consumer products, merchandise, theatrical releases, home videos, television, theme parks, a website, radio air play and live entertainment" ("Disney Princess"). They have done so to the tune of $4 billion worldwide sales in 2007 and $2.6 billion worldwide in box-office revenue for princess films ("Disney Princess"). It is nearly impossible to conceive of such numbers, let alone to ascribe them to the passive princesses of the Disney stories.

This merchandizing creates an abiding immortality for the films, a viability and popularity long past their time of conception and long past their time of cultural appropriateness. As Rozario writes,

> One of the major difficulties of dealing with Disney feature animation is that it is caught in a perpetual time loop created by the Magic Kingdom, and thus the day-to-day histories of the princess tend to be under-recognized. The Magic Kingdom...riddled with anachronism, seems to perpetuate a timelessness detached from social progress, yet it is a timelessness continuously updated and re-invented by the studios and marketers. (2)

Rozario refers to the way the characters are in theme parks and "on ice" and in stage productions, but she has not examined the changes made to the princesses in marketing "product." In order to make the first-wave princesses a cohesive unit with their more modern second-wave and twenty-first century associates, changes have been made to their appearances and attitudes. For instance, a 2008 McDonald's Happy Meal tie-in includes Disney Princess toys and collectible trading cards. The early princesses are represented by Aurora's crown, Cinderella's gloves, and Snow White's "magical toy mirror" (which belonged to her stepmother and was an instrument of Snow White's doom, but no matter). The back of the Aurora trading card invites girls to "Put on your tiara and enjoy a royal audience with Princess Aurora at My Disney Girls' Perfectly Princess Tea Party at Disney's Grand Floridian resort." The front features a picture of Aurora, but she is not quite the princess she was. She is no longer the lithe, attenuated figure of 1959. Her body is rounder, her breasts fuller. This Aurora has a wider face, with a perkier nose, and eyes with the slightest, saucy upward slant. She stands at 45° to the viewer, her arms behind her back, thrusting her chest forward. More than anything, her body language conveys a different attitude; this Aurora, with her cheeky head tilt—inviting? sassy?—would not meekly acquiesce to a betrothal. Girls collecting the toy and the card are invited to become like Aurora.

The constant re-releases and updating, the perpetual money machine that these first-wave princesses are part of, keeps them a "relevant anachronism" (Rozario 1)—anachronistic not only because they are princesses but because their Disney films versions are so dated. The current revisions of the Disney Princesses are an attempt to bring them into the late twentieth century and beyond, an attempt to recognize the social changes wrought by feminism and other social movements. Whether this has been successful will be discussed in Chapter Four, which addresses the second group of Disney princesses. The early princesses — Snow White, Cinderella, and Aurora—live on as a mix of the dated films and the modern merchandizing. The early films themselves stand inviolate, consumed avidly by audiences around the globe, teaching modern audiences their dated, misogynistic lessons.

❖ CHAPTER THREE ❖

Second-Wave Feminists
and
Ideologically Intent Princess Stories

IN THE 1960S, second-wave feminism became a force for change in society. Women sought and gained economic power, moving out of the household and into the workforce. Feminists began to understand the psychological and material implications of sexism and sexist stereotypes, and the feminist movement helped women move beyond such thinking to expand their life options and improve their lots. In the 1970s, some feminists turned their attention to fairy tales, encouraging women readers to understand the implications and ramifications of sexism and sexist stereotypes in literature, especially literature consumed by young girls. Not only did feminists in academia examine extant fairy tales, their undercurrents and their (presumed) ramifications, but some feminist writers began creating their own versions of fairy tales, using them to "depict the struggles women undergo to define their lives in opposition to the daily lives they experience" (Zipes "Introduction" 2). The feminist authors of these fairy tales had a larger purpose:

> By reconstructing fairy-tale worlds along non-sexist lines, the writers of feminist fairy tales address society at large, question recurrent patterns of values and the stable expectations about roles and relations. They do not naively believe that one can change gender arrangements and social behavior by simply reformulating the traditional fairy tales. On the other hand, it has been demonstrated by psychologists and educators time and again that stories and fairy tales do influence the manner in which children conceive the world and their places in it even before they begin to read. (Zipes "Introduction" xii)

This was the project of second-wave feminist fairy tales: to change the stories which acculturate children in the hopes of contributing to cultural change.

Some second-wave feminists would argue that "feminists don't believe in princesses" (Brownstein). Yet fictional princesses undeniably exist; a better statement might be that feminists don't support the princess agenda (although I hope that this book is proving that there are many different princess agendas). Indeed, many feminists may not "believe in" or support princesses when the princesses in question are the early Disney productions these feminists were exposed to as children. But some feminists do believe in princesses, or at least they believe in their potential, for among these revised fairy tales are a number of princess stories. These authors recognized the allure of princess stories and their importance in the lives of female readers; they sought to redefine the notion of the princess to their own political ends. Yet the stories, with few exceptions, were neither widely read nor long remembered. They did not achieve the sort of cultural acceptance—let alone the cultural saturation—that other, more traditionally patriarchal princess stories achieved and continue to achieve. For some second wave princess stories, this narrow audience was intentional; they were purposefully written for feminists. For others, though, this lack of widespread acceptance was unintentional, not at all desired, and it was caused by a variety of factors. Some were alienating in their dogmatic feminism; others were such a product of their time that they quickly became too dated to be relevant. This chapter will examine the uses to which second-wave feminists put princess stories, beginning with those stories authored and used by the originators of the Ms. Foundation for Women. Other second-wave feminist princess stories will then be examined, including the few that found lasting mainstream success and several that did not.

This chapter will first give a brief overview of feminist readings of traditional fairy tales to elaborate on the themes and lessons feminists found problematic in the traditional tales and to provide intellectual context in which the new ones were created. These themes were addressed and redressed in the feminist princess stories created in the 1970s and 1980s, and examining them is the main focus of this chapter. In what ways did second-wave feminist authors seek to create or use princess stories that reflected their own values and life experiences? Finally, some thought will be given to why the vast majority of these second-wave feminist princess stories have not (yet?) achieved the sort of mainstream cultural saturation that their authors might have desired.

Feminists and Fairytales

The history of feminist fairy tale studies has been outlined before, notably by Jack Zipes in 1986 and Donald Haase in 2000 (updated in 2004). Each locates the catalyst for the discussion as Alison Lurie's *New York Review of Books* articles, "Fairy Tale Liberation" (1970) and "Witches and Fairies" (1971). In these articles, Lurie argues that traditional fairy tales are more feminist than women raised on Disney films might believe. She supports this argument both by providing examples of strong heroines both in the classic tales and by showing how strong female characters are even more numerous in the lesser-known tales. Lurie attempts to put a positive spin on traditional tales, but in discounting Disney's effect on American culture, she operates with blinders. Her essays serve as the basis for the feminist activity of collecting and disseminating lesser-known, more positive works, but in general, feminist scholars strongly disagree with her thesis.

Marcia K. Lieberman's response to Lurie's argument gave rise to feminist criticism of fairy tales. Rather than agreeing with Lurie's position that fairy tales could be liberating, Lieberman's seminal 1972 essay, "Some Day My Prince Will Come: Female Acculturation through the Fairy Tale" sharply decries the ways that fairy tales "serve to acculturate women to traditional social roles" (Lieberman 185). Lieberman discusses the wicked stepmother and the fact that powerful, bad women vastly outnumber powerful, good ones; the ways the beauty contest "serves as a constant and primary device" (189) in many tales; and the fact that "most of the heroines are passive, submissive, and helpless" (190). She also notes the prevalence of courtship and weddings in fairy tales and that so few of them focus on actual married life. Lieberman concludes by positing that a scholarly examination of fairy tales may demonstrate just how much they reflect female attributes and how much they "serve as training manuals for girls" (200). Later feminist authors will take that final notion and use it to support their own projects through princess stories of the 1970s and 1980s, and in fact there is still widespread agreement with many of Lieberman's arguments.

For much of the 1970s, Lieberman's ideas were repeated in American feminists' writings; according to Zipes, "Most feminist critics tend to agree with Lieberman that the traditional fairy tales spread false notions about sex roles" ("Introduction" 5). He identifies Andrea Dworkin and Robert Moore as critics who follow Lieberman's lead, but he finds their analyses of fairy tales unrelentingly negative and overly simplistic: Dworkin for reductionist readings with an implied uniformity of messages and receivers and Moore for stereotyping the tales themselves as uniformly dark. Haase classifies Susan Brownmiller and Mary Daly with Dworkin, criticizing each of them for using fairy tales "simply as evidence to demonstrate the sociocultural myths and mechanisms that oppress women" (Haase 3).

Zipes finds great importance in that feminist scholarship which parallels his own academic interests, that which traces "the Utopian allure and historical evolution" ("Introduction" 6) of fairy tales. He credits Kay Stone's "Things Walt Disney Never Told Us" (1975) as doing the important work of discovering "how and why certain changes were made in the tales during the course of centuries so that women can regain a sense of their own history and possibly alter current socio-political arrangements" (6). He considers "the historical re-examination and rediscovery of matriarchal features in folk and fairy tales...some of the most important work being conducted in the field" (7); Heather Lyons and Jane Yolen are identified as examples of scholars doing that work.

By the end of the 1970s, however, Haase finds that feminist scholarship was becoming more nuanced in the ways it read fairy tales. In 1979, Karen E. Rowe's "Feminism and Fairy Tales" argued that, in a society "where romance co-habits uncomfortably with women's liberation, barely disguised forms of fairy tales transmit romantic conventions through the medium of popular literature" (Rowe 209). By linking traditional fairy tales to modern romances, she argues for their continuing cultural importance not only to modern-day children but to modern women as well. Haase sums up Rowe's view thusly: "the fairy tale...had a role to play in cultivating equality among men and women, but it would have to be a rejuvenated fairy tale fully divested of its idealized romantic fantasies" (5). This belief serves as the starting point for many feminist revisions of fairy tales, and more specifically, of princess stories.

Both Zipes and Haase consider Madonna Kolbenschlag's *Kiss Sleeping Beauty Good-Bye: Breaking the Spell of Feminine Myths and Models* (1979) and Colette Dowling's *The Cinderella Complex: Women's Hidden Fear of Independence* (1981) important. Elizabeth Wanning Harries explains the sort of reading provided by Kolbenschlag and Dowling:

> The 'sleep' of Sleeping Beauty or of Snow White in her glass coffin, the uncomplaining self-abrogation of Cinderella, the patience and silence of the sisters who work to save their seven or twelve brothers, the princesses who must be rescued

from towers or briar hedges or towers or servitude—all these seem to provide the
patterns for feminine passivity and martyrdom. (13)

These works, and others, such as Linda Chervin and Mary Neil's *The
Woman's Tale: A Journal of Inner Exploration* (1980) and Marion Wood-
man's *Leaving My Mother's House: A Journey to Conscious Femininity*
(1992), "encouraged a self-conscious, critical engagement with the classical
tales as a means to liberate women to imagine and construct new identities"
(Haase 7). The works use the situations set forth in fairy tales to show
women where real-world changes would be beneficial.

Additional feminist studies of fairy tales have followed since then, of
course, but as this chapter's real project is to examine second wave princess
stories—those written during the time that second wave scholars were first
theorizing and debating the role and importance of fairy tales in the lives of
women—this review of the literature can end here, at the start of the 1990s
(the start of feminism's third wave). Believing "the traditional fairy tales are
unacceptable today because of their atavistic notions of sex roles and their
ideology of male domination" (Zipes "Introduction" 11), second-wave
feminists sought alternatives. Some feminists focused on compiling and
publishing lesser-known fairy tales. Among these are Alison Lurie's *Clever
Gretchen and Other Forgotten Folktales* (1980), which bolstered her
argument that many fairy tales were already feminist. Ethel Johnson Phelps'
Tatterhood (1979) and *The Maid of the North: Feminist Folktales from
Around the World* (1982) were two other early additions to the project. These
collections have been created continually since they were first envisioned:
Suzanne Barchers' *Wise Women: Folk and Fairy Tales from Around the
World* (1990), Kathleen Ragan's *Fearless Girls, Wise Women and Beloved
Sisters: Heroines in Folktales from Around the World* (1998), and Jane
Yolen's *Not One Damsel in Distress* (2000) continue the mission of uncover-
ing and collecting empowered-female folk and fairy tales.

Other feminists—and in the case of Jane Yolen, the same feminists—
decided to create their own, more socially conscious and appropriate versions
of the fairy tales. According to Vanessa Joosen, second-wave feminists,
"convinced of the didactic potential of fairy tales...soon started to use the
stories to their own advantage. They reacted to the gender bias of the
traditional fairy tales...not only in literary criticism, but also in primary
texts" (130). The list of these authors is long: Angela Carter, Tanith Lee, and
Jane Yolen are among the most prolific writers of "experimental feminist

fairy tales which seek to provoke the reader to re-examine his or her notion of sexual arrangements and the power politics of those arrangements" (Zipes "Introduction" 12). The Ms. Foundation for Women also reclaimed fairy tales in a number of venues: on the cover of *Ms. Magazine*, as part of *Free to Be...You and Me*, and in *Stories for Free Children*. Among these revised fairy tales are a number of feminist princess stories. These authors recognized the allure of princess stories and their importance in the lives of girls and women; they sought to redefine the notion of the princess to their own political ends. The ways they put princesses to use as educative characters both demonstrates the tenets of feminism and acknowledges the allure of the princess. Their failure to break onto the widest cultural stage raises interesting questions, both about their strategies and about how quickly the culture was changing.

Linked to the Ms. Foundation:
Wonder Woman and Gloria Steinem

The connection between Wonder Woman, the comic-book heroine, and Gloria Steinem, one of the founders of *Ms. Magazine* and the Ms. Foundation for Women, is fascinating, and the influences the two had on each other even more so. When creating *Ms. Magazine*, Steinem was looking for a recognizable feminist icon, a powerful woman with whom American women could identify. She chose comic-book heroine Wonder Woman, the Amazon princess. Interestingly, *Wonder Woman* had originally been created as a feminist princess story, intended to teach little girls to be strong women. When Steinem appropriated the character, then, she was merely copying and reinforcing the intent of Wonder Woman's creator.

Wonder Woman burst onto the American comic-book scene in 1941. Her creator was William Moulton Marston (writing under the name Charles Moulton), an early, eccentric feminist whose belief system "was marked by a belief in women's essential moral superiority, combined with a demand for the equality of opportunity that would permit physical strength and social power to become feminine attributes alongside that superiority" (Robinson 45). In published interviews, Marston declared women innately superior to men. He also discussed the need for both fantasy role models and real-world opportunities for girls. He affirmed that rejection of the inferior social role was natural and inevitable, claiming that "Not even girls want to be girls, as long as our feminine archetype lacks force, strength, and power....the obvious remedy is to create a feminine character with all the strength of Superman plus all the allure of a good and beautiful woman" (qtd. in Robinson 46). Wonder Woman was Marston's answer to the perceived needs of little girls: a female hero. The comic books' covers and introductory panels repeatedly declared her "beautiful as Aphrodite, wise as Athena, strong as Hercules, and swift as Mercury." But feminist Marston was not content merely to create a female hero; he was out to educate his readers and inculcate them into his kind of feminism, albeit within the limits of his medium. *Wonder Woman* "did pioneer a kind of feminist questioning, however commercially packaged and conceptually limited, at a time when few other voices in American society were raising such questions" (Robinson 23). Marston explained:

> Frankly, Wonder Woman is a psychological propaganda for the new type of woman who should, I believe, rule the world. There isn't love enough in the male organism to run this planet peacefully. Woman's body contains twice as many love generating organs and endocrine mechanisms as the male. What woman lacks is the dominance or self assertive power to put over and enforce her love desires. I have given Wonder Woman this dominant force but have kept her loving, tender, maternal and feminine in every other way. (qtd. in Daniels 22)

Wonder Woman was thus intentionally created to sway readers to a more feminist (if scientifically questionable) mindset. As *Wonder Woman*'s readership has always been predominantly male (Daniels 33), Marston was not simply trying to encourage self-confidence in girls, but to expose "millions of boys (who would become men in the 1960s) to the ideals of feminism" (Daniels 33). Small wonder, then, that thirty years later Gloria Steinem would choose Wonder Woman as a propagandist emblem of the burgeoning women's liberation movement.

Gloria Steinem, seven years old when *Wonder Woman* was first published, describes herself as an admirer of Wonder Woman when the stories were Marston's, the years that *Wonder Woman* was most strongly feminist. Reading these adventures, Steinem "could stop pretending to enjoy the ridicule, bossing-around, and constant endangering of female characters. In these Amazon adventures, only the villains bought the idea that 'masculine' meant aggression and 'feminine' meant submission" (1995, 8-9). As a little girl, Steinem enjoyed identifying with a strong female hero; as an adult, she realized "how hard Charles Marston had tried to get an egalitarian worldview into comic book form....this female super-hero was devoted to democracy, peace, justice, and 'liberty and freedom for all womankind'" (Steinem 1995,

9). As an adult feminist, and as editor of two *Wonder Woman* collections, Steinem traced Wonder Woman's progression from strong feminist in the 1940s through weaker and weaker iterations and eventually to the truly un-super version of the 1960s.

The earliest *Wonder Woman* stories, written by Marston from 1941 until his death in 1947, espouse the same feminism with which he conceived the character. As described by Steinem in her 1995 essay, Wonder Woman had, together with her Amazon sisters, "been trained in [her many and amazing powers] from infancy and perfected them in Greek-style contests of dexterity, strength, and speed. The lesson was that each of us might have unknown powers within us, if we only believed and practiced them" (1995, 7). Nor are Wonder Woman's adventures happening in a fantastic world unlike our own, where such women might more easily be allowed to exist; Wonder Woman lives and works in a recognizable, contemporary United States. Marston alludes to the condition of modern-day women when he describes Wonder Woman as "defending America from the enemies of democracy and fighting fearlessly for downtrodden women and children in a man-made world" (qtd. in Robinson 35). Men, in these early stories, are clearly in need of Wonder Woman's feminizing, civilizing, loving control. Marston was intentionally setting Wonder Woman as an example to his readers, male and female—the males to know what to expect from women and the female to know what to become. She was thus created as an intentionally exemplary model for little girls to emulate, just as any princess story heroine. She is a princess with superpowers, but Marston claimed that all women "possess as their birthright the same abilities that Wonder Woman deploys so effectively. They even had access to the same tools, for the ones we see in the comic book, material extensions of her power, are simply visual metaphors for what women are and what they can do" (Robinson 46). All girls, then, can grow up to become an Amazon princess, just as all girls could become their own Sara Crewe.

Many of *Wonder Woman*'s storylines involved teaching the women around her to emulate the character, not just in their personal lives but in the world at large; her feminism had a civic dimension.

> Wonder Woman's speeches, as well as her sterling example, are about how women can do anything men can do, whether that 'anything' was the work of brain or brawn. A female superhero may be 'stronger than Hercules,' as well as being as beautiful as Aphrodite and as wise as Athena, but those who are not, we were told, could still rely on their common sense, their ingenuity, and their solidarity. The point she reiterates ... is that she merely leads the way for all women, since all have

within them ...the requisite power to conquer the forces that would restrict female
life and possibility. (Robinson 47-48)

The early comic books further enforced this notion that even non-super
women can be powerful by including cartoon biographies of women identified as real-life heroes, such as Florence Nightingale, Susan B. Anthony, and
Elizabeth Blackwell.

After Marston's death, however, Wonder Woman—both the character
and the comic—changed. Robert Kanigher was the writer and editor assigned
to continue *Wonder Woman* for the twenty years following Marston's 1947
death, and the character's deterioration in the 1950s and 1960s must in large
part be attributed to him. She declined from an "unquestionably liberatory
icon into something quite different" (Robinson 65). Heterosexual romance
was foregrounded, and Wonder Woman's mission changed from global
rescue to more mundane law enforcement. Kanigher diluted or deleted the
feminist message that Marston had so strongly emphasized. Steinem describes the alterations: "She became sexier-looking and more submissive,
violent episodes increased, more of her adversaries were female, and Wonder
Woman herself required more help from men in order to triumph" (1995,
14). Steinem links these changes to the social changes real-life women were
experiencing, as they moved from the public roles they filled in the 1940s to
the homebound roles they were directed towards in the postwar 1950s.
Wonder Woman was joined in these years by Wonder Girl, who was largely
occupied by choosing a boyfriend (Mer-Boy or Bird-Boy?), and Wonder Tot,
called a "saucy Amazon babe" in the cover copy (Daniels 113). These
younger iterations of the character further weakened the feminist stances
Wonder Woman had previously espoused.

In 1968, Wonder Woman was completely re-envisioned. This massive
metamorphosis "transformed the Amazon into a political symbol of national
significance and exposed her to an ideological scrutiny that she has never
entirely escaped" (Daniels 123). In the September-October issue of 1968,
Wonder Woman was stripped of her superpowers and re-introduced as "a
mortal woman in the modern world" (Daniels 126). The scriptwriter, Dennis
O'Neil, described the character's revision as "taking a woman and making
her independent, and not dependent on super powers. I saw it as making her
thoroughly human and then an achiever on top of that, which, according to
my mind, was very much in keeping with the feminist agenda" (qtd. in
Daniels 126). Her body was slimmed down and clad in hip clothing; she

looks significantly less Amazonian and much more 1960s-American fashionable. Now dubbed "The New Wonder Woman," she fought many female villains; "In these encounters, which have a lot more in common with catfights than with epic struggles, sexual jealousy or simple envy of Wonder Woman's good looks rate high as motivating forces and the old notion that female enemies can and should be redeemed has disappeared" (Robinson 81). Marston's lessons of female solidarity and empowerment almost entirely disappeared.

Most distressingly, Wonder Woman gave up her superpowers in order to stay in the mortal realm with Steve Trevor, whom she had saved from death in the initial episode and repeatedly thereafter. Ironically, Steve Trevor was killed in the third issue of "The New Wonder Woman," so her sacrifice was for naught—a sort of feminist message, "don't sacrifice your identity for a romantic relationship," but clearly unintentional. As mortal Diana Prince, Wonder Woman

> ...walked about in boutique clothes and took the advice of a male mastermind named 'I Ching.' She still had adventures and she had learned something about karate, but any attractive man could disarm her. She was a female James Bond—but far more boring since she was denied his sexual freedom. She had become a simpleminded 'good girl.' (Steinem 1972)

Steinem is perhaps overstating Wonder Woman's "goodness," as these stories have been characterized elsewhere as involving multiple romantic involvements (Daniels 129). And while some stories from this era are of dubious feminist value, and absolutely a departure from the Wonder Woman Steinem knew as a child, Carol Strickland characterizes the super-powerless Diana Prince as having "power and style, dignity, strength and humor" ("Diana Prince Era"). Steinem makes a convincing argument that in becoming less than super-powered Diana Prince lost her heroic identity and became mundane, but Strickland believes that in her more human experiences Diana Prince becomes more empathetic, and that the writers "showed Diana Prince to be a symbol of Modern Womanhood without preaching" ("Diana Prince Era"). Yet it was the feminist preachiness that Steinem valued, and without it—and without Wonder Woman's powers and her traditional costume— Steinem found the character far less compelling.

In DC's defense, by the end of the 1960s, *Wonder Woman* was experiencing the "Superman problem": the character had gradually become so powerful that the writers could invent no meaningful earthly menace to oppose her. Samuel R. Delany, who had been asked to write a series of *Wonder Woman* scripts that would reflect problems of actual women, describes the editorial decision to strip away most of her powers as "the only sane thing…. Certainly it made it easier to come up with reasonable plots for her, and alone made it possible for the plots to have some relevance to the real world" ("Author Q & A"). Delany's six-issue story arc included plots about a corrupt department store owner; "a college advisor who really felt a woman's place was in the home and who assumed if you were a bright woman, then something was probably wrong with you psychologically…. [; and] a gang of male thugs trying to squash an abortion clinic staffed by women surgeons" ("Author Q & A"). Only two issues written by Delany were produced; according to him, Gloria Steinem's push to revert Wonder Woman to the old character concept was responsible for the decision to cut Delany's remaining issues.

As Delany recounts, Steinem was dismayed at Wonder Woman's new costume and diminished powers. Steinem allegedly "complained bitterly: 'Don't you realize how important the image of Wonder Woman was to young girls throughout the country?'" ("Author Q & A"). The next day, Delany recalls, his plans were set aside when

> an edict came down from management to put Wonder Woman back in her American-flag falsies and blue bikini briefs and give her back all her super powers. Well, that's what happened. . . . There was no way I could work those in with the relatively realistic plot lines I had devised. So my stories were abandoned, and I was dumped as a writer–and Wonder Woman never *did* get a chance to fight for the rights of a women's abortion clinic. ("Author Q & A")

Of course, the odds are slim that Wonder Woman would ever have saved an abortion clinic; even today, that storyline seems incendiary. Furthermore, Delany's timeline is suspect, as it is highly doubtful that such sweeping changes were made as quickly as he indicates. Nor were Delany's stories as feminist as his recollection might lead one to believe. Delany's Nov-Dec 1972 issue indicates that Wonder Woman knew nothing about the women's movement and had to be taught to champion women. In one panel, she claims, "I'm not a joiner. I wouldn't fit in with your [female anti-sweat-shop] group. In most cases, I don't even **like** women…?" (Strickland "Worst Panel"). Wonder Woman's claim not to be a joiner is factually inaccurate; she had previously joined the Amazon army, the US armed forces, and the Justice League (a federation of superheroes). Most egregious, of course, is the suggestion that Wonder Woman doesn't like women.

Steinem herself discusses visiting the DC offices once during "The New Wonder Woman" years. Distressed by what she saw in the *Wonder Woman* pages during this visit, Steinem took up the cause of rehabilitating and restoring Wonder Woman to her original feminist glory. As "the character's best friend and severest critic" (Daniels 131), Steinem wielded influence in two ways—both on a personal level as a friend of Steve Ross, owner of DC Comics, and as the journalist who would become editor of *Ms. Magazine*, a Warner publication (as was DC). In 1972, Steinem took up Wonder Woman's cause on the cover and in the pages of the first regular issue of *Ms Magazine*. She had been casting about for a cover image, and "Since Joanne Edgar and other of its founding editors had also been rescued by Wonder Woman in their childhoods, we decided to rescue Wonder Woman in return" (1995, 15). Steinem characterizes persuading the publishers to let *Ms. Magazine* put Wonder Woman's image on the cover as a struggle. Amy Farrell, however, highlights the economic felicity that placed Wonder Woman on the cover "both because she was a figure that would resonate with the women's movement and because featuring her would please their major investor" (55), Warner Communications. This cover was "the result of an intricate merging of commercial and political interests" (Farrell 157), as were the *Wonder Woman* collection I will discuss shortly and the *Free to Be...* project discussed in the next section.

With a banner proclaiming "Wonder Woman for President," the Amazon Princess strode across the inaugural cover of *Ms. Magazine*:

> Dressed in her red, white and blue sparkling outfit, emphasizing pointed breasts, powerful hips, and high-heeled boots, Wonder Woman stepped forcefully over a miniaturized city below her. Her momentum, her strength, and her size expressed the enthusiasm and energy of the early women's movement; she represented the figure of "womanpower,' the public relations slogan used by national women's organizations to communicate the potential of women, economic and otherwise. (Farrell 54)

Steinem was purposefully reviving Wonder Woman "as a mascot for the magazine, and indeed as the symbol for the movement then described as 'women's liberation'" (Daniels 131). The magazine included reproductions of some Marston-era *Wonder Woman* stories and a two-page article by Joanne Edgar decrying Wonder Woman's current submissive state and hailing her 1973 return under a new female editor, the first in her then 30-year history. Consensus was that the cover and the accompanying story were a success. The publishers, too, were impressed, and soon thereafter "she was returned to her original Amazon status—golden lasso, bracelets, and all" (Steinem 1995, 15). Steinem takes credit for Wonder Woman's rebirth.

Building on the success of the Wonder Woman cover, later that year Steinem edited *Wonder Woman* (1972), a collection of early, Marston-written comics, choosing the stories and writing the book's introduction and each chapter's prefatory material. This hardcover volume "undeniably brought Wonder Woman a new measure of fame and respectability" (Daniels 132). It was a Ms. Book, and the selection of comic book stories wholly supported Steinem's political agenda, "playing down the wilder aspects of Marston's imagination in favor of the instructive narratives Steinem endorsed" (Daniels 132). Steinem was using the Amazon Princess as the heroine of a princess story, as Marston had used her, this time reinforcing the narrative's educative value by adding her own in essay format[1]. She very clearly encourages the women reading the collection to emulate Wonder Woman in a number of ways.

Steinem is quite clear about what she values in *Wonder Woman*, and what she desires both from and for her readers. In her account, Wonder Woman's gender is, of course, the quality that most immediately struck her as a child. She had read other superhero comic books, but:

> The trouble is that the comic book performers of such superhuman feats—and even of only dimly competent ones—are almost always heroes. Literally. The female child is left to believe that, when her body is as grown-up as her spirit, she will still be in the childlike role of helping with minor tasks, appreciating men's accomplishments, and being so incompetent that she can only hope some man can come to her rescue. (Steinem 1972)

The thrill of gender identification was enough to enthrall Steinem as a child and to sustain her through her youthful period of reading the comic books. That a woman could be a hero, and that as a girl she could identify with this hero instead of straining to identify either with a male hero or with the insipid and helpless females populating comic books, is characterized as nothing short of miraculous to the young Steinem.

Looking back on the 1940s *Wonder Woman* stories in 1972, Steinem wrote that she was "amazed by the strength of their feminist message" (1972). Although the message is simplified to fit the medium,

> Wonder Woman symbolizes many of the values of the women's culture that feminists are now trying to introduce into the mainstream: strength and self-reliance for women; sisterhood and mutual support among women; peacefulness and esteem for

human life; a diminishment of 'masculine' aggression and of the belief that violence
is the only way of solving conflicts. (Steinem 1972)

Steinem did not accept Marston's feminism wholesale, disagreeing with him
on a few points: she does not accept Marston's claim that women are
biologically superior to men; she doesn't want men and women to switch
places in the hierarchy, preferring to eliminate it altogether; and she has
some qualms about Wonder Woman's infatuation with Steve Trevor. She
also finds the comic's 1940s patriotism "highly jingoistic and even racist"
(1972). Ultimately, however,

> ...all these doubts paled beside the relief, the sweet vengeance, the toe-wriggling
> pleasure of reading about a woman who was strong, beautiful, courageous, and a
> fighter for social justice. A woman who strode forth, stopping wars and killing with
> one hand, distributing largess and compassionate aid with the other. A Wonder
> Woman. (Steinem 1972)

She ends the essay hopeful that the planned 1973 revamp of *Wonder Woman*
will have "the feminism and strength of the original Wonder Woman—*my*
Wonder Woman" (1972). She also posits that "...if we all had read more
about Wonder Woman and less about Dick and Jane, the new wave of the
feminist revolution might have happened less painfully and sooner" (Steinem
1972). This belief—that reading *Wonder Woman* comics could be educational, serving as an instrument of (feminist) social change—is the underlying motivation behind Steinem's prefatory material in the collection. It also
highlights just how much of a princess story *Wonder Woman* could be.

In the material prefacing each of the collection's four chapters ("Origins," "Sisterhood," "Politics," and "Relationships"), Steinem underscores
the messages she wants her readers to find in the comics. In the "Origins"
preface, she highlights that Wonder Woman had been created as an alternative to "bloodcurdling masculinity" (1972). Prefacing "Sisterhood," she
writes:

> Wonder Woman's final message to her sisters almost always contained one simple
> and unmistakable moral: self-reliance. Be strong. Earn your own living. Don't de-
> pend on a man or any force outside yourself, not even a friendly Amazon. In Won-
> der Woman's own words, 'You saved yourselves—I only showed you that you
> could!'

Clearly, these are also the messages that Steinem wants *Wonder Woman*'s
readers to learn and live by. Steinem outlines three of the character's political
positions in the preface the "Politics": violence is not good and should be

avoided; strength is necessary, but only for purposes of self-defense; and enemies can and should be re-educated. Steinem also highlights the ways Wonder Woman fights for the rights of foreigners. Again, these political views are clearly meant to teach Steinem's readers.

Finally, in the preface to "Love," Steinem pontificates "Romantic love is the device men use to trick women into giving up their strength and independence" (1972). This is not exactly a lesson from *Wonder Woman*, but rather one from Steinem and other more militant second-wave feminists. According to Marston's ideology, love is the source of Amazon strength, the means through which Amazon society was peaceful and superior to male society. Moreover, Wonder Woman loves Steve Trevor, leaving Paradise Island to become his assistant and secret protector in America. She admires his strength while declaring she could not love a man who dominated her. "Her constant message to society was love, equality, and justice. When that lesson is learned by the patriarchal societies of the world, will Paradise Island no longer need to exist? Will love be possible at last?" (Steinem 1972). Steinem's final preface is both most sharply negative about society and most strongly touting *Wonder Woman* as educative, a tool through which men and women can learn to love each other and live together as equals.

Wonder Woman did undergo a renewal after appearing on *Ms. Magazine*'s inaugural issue and after the publication of the Ms. Book collection of her 1940s adventures. Steinem claims credit for Wonder Woman's rebirth by relating a phone call from "one of Wonder Woman's tougher male writers" (tantalizingly naming no names). This tough guy listed the changes that had been made—Wonder Woman's powers returned, her relationship with the Amazons re-established, a new Black sister—before plaintively asking Steinem, "Now will you leave me alone?" (1995). Steinem rather smugly reports, "I said we would" (1995). It appeared in 1973 that Steinem had achieved her goal, that DC had restored Wonder Woman to her original feminist glory, and that the Amazon princess would go on to be a feminist icon—all a result of Steinem's persistence.

But did Steinem and *Ms. Magazine* really have that much influence on Wonder Woman's portrayal in the comics, her "rebirth as a feminist"? The *Ms. Magazine* cover depicted Steinem's Wonder Woman, not D.C.'s Wonder Woman; "the cover story refigured the nationalist, freedom-fighting Wonder Woman to become a more pacifist figure, a strong heroine, but nevertheless a nonviolent one" (Farrell 55). Additionally, whereas Steinem credits this issue of *Ms. Magazine* with *Wonder Woman*'s restoration, Robinson instead connects it "to the phenomenon that made *Ms. Magazine* successful, the rise of feminism as a mass movement" (Robinson 83). In other words, Steinem read this causal relationship incorrectly. Feminism is the cause behind two effects: *Ms. Magazine*'s success and *Wonder Woman*'s turnaround. In fact, if we accept the feminism of Delany's planned-but-scrapped stories, Wonder Woman-as-feminist was in the works well before the publication of *Ms. Magazine*. Her all-American image had to be restored, and her superpowers, but her storylines were (allegedly) to have been more feminist under Delany than they ultimately were in her (seemingly) restored glory. And her post-Steinem adventures "emphasize female power and female solidarity, but they continue, for some time, to be illustrated so as to send the old, sexist message to anyone experiencing comic books chiefly on the level of the visual" (Robinson 84). Wonder Woman's Amazon companions are depicted in transparent togas, their buttocks fully exposed. Thus DC brought back the original character, but perhaps this was not the unconditional triumph that Steinem suggests. "Wonder Woman got back her powers, her costume, and her Amazon sisters, but the series lacked the complexity and feminist flare of Marston's original stories" (Crawford). There was a distinctly mixed message sent by the writers and the artists involved in *Wonder Woman*—and this mixed message, I believe, has prevented Wonder Woman from being fully accepted as Steinem's hoped-for symbol.

Wonder Woman reached its widest audience through the television series starring Lynda Carter, which aired from 1976-1979[2]. The pilot episode was an origins story true to Marston's version, and the feminist ideology espoused by the character was similarly faithful to his. She lives on the strictly female Paradise Island, with her mother (the queen) and her female compatriots. She proves herself superior in a physical contest and wins the right to take Steve Trevor back to the United States, where she becomes first an oddity and then a superhero. In the 1970s, however, Wonder Woman was not alone as a feminist character on the small screen, and that contributed to her downfall. According to Hank Stuever, "in a jumble of strong pop culture heroines—bionic women, police women, 'Charlie's Angels'—Wonder Woman had outlived her usefulness to the collective unconscious. She stopped being the exception to the rule" (5). While it was a feminist step forward that Wonder Woman was no longer the sole strong female character in American popular culture, this multiplicity of available feminist role models sapped her of her iconic status shortly after Steinem had allegedly won it for her.

Today, Wonder Woman does not really survive as the widespread feminist symbol Steinem would have had her be. Stuever bemoans her lost fame, explaining: "This is what happens to spent icons. They become easily recognizable Halloween costumes with no context, aging reference points to outdated ideas that may have been a metaphor for something—which was what, in her case? Feminism? Love? Sacrifice?" (2). The most widely disseminated image of Wonder Woman recently was the February 2008 cover of *Playboy*, which featured a woman wearing a Wonder Woman costume made only of body paint. This may be *Playboy* intentionally tweaking feminist sensibilities, but the fact remains that for many people, Wonder Woman is more sexual than strong. DC/Time Warner, "which is notoriously overprotective of their trademark, has refused to comment on this [*Playboy* cover]—in the process, awarding it their implicit approval" (Edidin). It is hard to accept *Playboy*'s contention that the cover was meant as homage to Lynda Carter, an outspoken feminist.

The artwork in the comic book caters to the males which comprise the majority ("estimates run as high as 90 percent" [Daniels 33]) of the comic's readers: Wonder Woman is scantily clad, often in bondage, and her body has the hypersexual lines of most comic-book females. Steinem would remind us that the importance of Wonder Woman is her message: "Remember Our Power" (1995, 19). While her message has periodically been feminist through the years, and certainly Steinem tried to use her as the protagonist of an Amazon princess story, she has not maintained this feminism consistently. According to Lillian Robinson, Wonder Woman "has failed to keep pace with the women's movement. Even today, Wonder Woman is no sister" (qtd. in Glenn). Although Steinem tried to promulgate the Wonder Woman princess story, this 1970s appropriation of the character did not last.

Linked to the Ms. Foundation:
Free To Be...You And Me

Another of the original members of the Ms. Foundation, Marlo Thomas was the leading force behind the *Free to Be ...You and Me* project. She had been seeking stories to share with her niece, but was "shocked to find that all the children's books...reinforced old gender stereotypes" ("The History of Free to Be..."). Thus began her quest to find books "to celebrate who she was and who she could be, all the possibilities" (Thomas 7); this quest lead to the concept of producing a record album of such stories. Thomas told

Gloria Steinem that she wanted the proceeds from the album to benefit women and children; Steinem invited her to become one of the Ms. Foundation's founding members. Thomas was put in touch with Letty Cottin Pogrebin, an author and another of the four founders. The Free to Be... Foundation became a subsidiary of the Ms. Foundation. Thomas "thought we'd collect some already published stories that were truly humanist in feeling as well as well-written, amusing, or touching, and totally free of stereotypes of sex, class, and race. After a lot of research, it became clear that if I wanted such stories, I'd have to write or commission them myself" ("The History of Free to Be ..."). She did. The recording was released in November of 1972; the book and an Emmy award winning television special were released simultaneously in March of 1974. A theatrical adaptation was commissioned in 1991 and was picked up for distribution in the Rogers and Hammerstein catalogue. The album and book are still in print; the television special is available for home viewing; and the play is still produced all over the country. This continuing interest in the project suggests a continued relevance.

The entire project was intentionally didactic, and the book contains three prefatory pieces in the unlikely event that readers might have missed the point. Thomas swipes at traditional children's stories and warns that "those of you seeking Wonderland or Prince Charming or a sleeping or even a sleepy princess will not find them here" ("This Is the Forward..." 9). Steinem extols the uses of the proceeds, which will go toward the "development of learning materials, child care centers, health care services, teaching techniques, information and referral centers and...all the practical changes that are necessary to get rid of old-fashioned systems based on sex and race" ("What Buying This Book Will Do" 11). Pogrebin describes *Free to Be...* as a "book of humor—but the laugh is on old constraints and worn-out conventions....There are important messages within the merriment" ("A Note to Parents" 12). Most selections work to dispel gender myths or stereotypes which apply to both males and females (boys don't cry, girls are valued for their looks), and "two or three selections redefine fairy tales so that Sleeping Beauty can stay awake and look at her life with her eyes wide open" (12). Only one of the stories actually features a princess, a retelling of the Greek myth of Atalanta, and it is dedicated to teaching girls what sort of princess to be and what to desire besides a prince.

Although there are different versions of her story, the mythical Atalanta (whose name means "balanced", as she is a character balanced between two genders) "is best known for participation in male activities while at the same time having an aura of sexuality surrounding her" (Gibson). Her father, a king, so wanted a boy that when Atalanta was born, he ordered her left on a hillside to die. Rescued and raised by hunters, one of the events for which she became known is the Calydonian Boar Hunt, in which she participated as the sole female. During the hunt, two hunters attempted to rape her; she killed them both. After her performance at the hunt (she drew first blood and was awarded the boar's pelt), her father proudly reclaimed her. They were reconciled, and her father wanted her married to one of her many new suitors. Atalanta, uninterested in marriage (either from loyalty to a killed lover or heeding a warning from the Oracle), made a deal with her father: she would race any suitor, marrying the one who bested her. The losers would be executed. Many raced for her hand and were put to death, until Melanion (or Hippomenes) and Atalanta became enamored of each other. Knowing he could not beat her, Melanion prayed to Aphrodite, who gave him three golden apples with which to distract Atalanta as she ran. Whenever Atalanta pulled ahead of him, he rolled an apple in front of her; she then stopped to collect it, giving Melanion time to catch her. He won her hand (some versions indicate that Atalanta allowed herself to be distracted, throwing the race for love of Melanion), and they were married.

The *Free to Be* ... version of *Atalanta*, written by Betty Miles, is as follows: Atalanta is a clever, handy princess and a very swift runner. Her father is having trouble deciding whom she should marry. Atalanta tells him not to worry; "I will choose. And I'm not sure that I will choose to marry anyone at all" (128). The king decides to hold a race, with Atalanta as the prize. Atalanta agrees to this, as long as she is also allowed to enter; if she is not the winner, she "will accept the wishes of the young man who is" (131). Atalanta prepares for the race, running the course in the early morning. Young John from the village, who admires Atalanta from afar, is motivated to train for the race in the evenings. He reasons, "It is not right for Atalanta's father to give her away to the winner of the race. Atalanta herself must choose the person she wants to marry, or whether she wishes to marry at all. Still, if I could only win the race, I would be free to speak to her, and to ask for her friendship" (131). The day of the race comes, and Atalanta and Young John tie for first place. Her father awards Young John the prize, the right to his daughter's hand in marriage, but Young John refuses, stating, "I could not possibly marry your daughter unless she wished to marry me" (135). They spend the day together, becoming friends, and the next day they went off on their separate adventures. "By this time, each of them has seen wonderful adventures, and seen marvelous sights. Perhaps some day they will be married, and perhaps they will not. In any case, they are friends. And it is certain that they are both living happily ever after" (135).

There is much to be admired in this retelling, a princess story that teaches girls to be smart, athletic, and confident. Atalanta's qualities are described in such a way that she is very attractive both within the story and to the audience. Most important are the things *Atalanta* does to the concept of princesses in marriage: this is a princess desired for her cleverness, who herself is in no rush to marry. Most radically, she might choose not to marry at all. The source material features a remarkably athletic woman who defends herself from and competes as an equal with men, so in some ways the *Free to Be* ... version is not actually much of a departure. This retelling has made some interesting second-wave feminist changes to the source material, but even more interesting are the ways in which it is not as female-empowered as it first appears.

The focus of the story in the beginning is Atalanta, and it does read (at first) like a princess story, extolling the new qualities a princess should have. Atalanta is "so bright, and so clever, and could build things and fix things so wonderfully, that many young men wished to marry [her]" (128). This is an obvious change to the traditional qualities sought in a princess, goodness and beauty, neither of which is mentioned at all in the story. Atalanta is also assertive, securing herself a place in the race as a way of determining her own future. She trains hard and is determined to win: two more strong character traits. Yet the story essentially leaves Atalanta in training and switches to focus on Young John, his beliefs and his training. This seems egalitarian, which of course is one of the projects of *Free to Be* ..., but in reality switching focus to Young John strips Atalanta of her agency. The race ends in a tie[3] yet the king awards the prize to Young John. Surely Atalanta should have protested this change in the rules, but she did not.

Moreover, Young John's beliefs determine whether Atalanta will marry him; she does not take a stand on her own. At the end of the race, looking at the two runners who have tied, the king addresses John, "You have not won the race, but you have come closer to winning than any man here. And so I give you the prize that was promised—the right to marry my daughter" (135). In fact, the king seems to suggest that he was not going to honor the agreement he had made with Atalanta; Young John came closer to winning than any man there, true, but the same could have been said if Atalanta had beaten him outright. Coming in significantly behind Atalanta, Young John still would have "come closer to winning than any man;" the king is ignoring the agreement he had made with his daughter. Young John declines the prize on the basis of his feminist beliefs, not because of the rules under which they had raced. Atalanta shares Young John's feminist beliefs, and tells him that she could not marry at all until she has seen the world. But this statement is in response to him, not in response to her father trying to give her away, about which she says nothing.

Two other factors in this basically strong princess story are also troubling. The only clothing mentioned in the piece is Atalanta's. We are told that she does her morning training "dressed in soft green trousers and a shirt of yellow silk;" on the day of the race, she wore "trousers of crimson and a shirt of silk as blue as the sky" (131). It could be that these allusions to her clothes were meant to be empowering to readers in the early 1970s—the princess wears trousers instead of skirts, after all. Today, however, these sartorial details seem out of place. The paragraph describing her training is very similar to the one describing John's, except the reader (or listener, or viewer) is left wondering why Young John's sartorial choices are not mentioned.

Also disturbing is the relationship between Young John and Atalanta prior to the race. He admires her from afar, watching her as she "bought nails and wood to make a pigeon house, or chose parts for her telescope, or laughed with her friends" (131). These activities are meant to imply that he values her for the things she can do rather than for her beauty. He does not approach her, though, leaving her up on a pedestal as much as if he'd simply admired her for her appearance. He earns the right to talk to her by "winning" the race, not by approaching her as a respectful equal. Especially disturbing is the fact that he essentially rescues her from her father, declining her when her father tries to give her away. She has not rescued herself by her cleverness or by her speed or her sense of self; John rescues her by his own feminist sensibilities. How lucky for her that John believed in the rights of women to choose their own husbands, or her story might have ended quite differently.

Linked to the Ms. Foundation:
Stories For Free Children

The third *Ms. Magazine* project featuring princess stories is *Stories for Free Children*, a regular feature of the magazine, edited and collected into a hardcover book in 1982. These stories are intentionally educative, teaching their readers to "be yourself and be true to yourself...without having to measure up to other people's ideas of what a girl or boy is 'supposed' to be" (Pogrebin *Editor's Introduction* 8). Meant for "readers who are fed up with conventional children's literature" (7), *Stories for Free Children* are described as "relief from passive princesses and ugly stepmothers" (7). Not all of them are derived from fairy tales, of course, but some of them are. Jeanne Desy's "The Princess Who Stood on Her Own Two Feet" (1972) is one of the earliest, a beautiful and admonitory princess story.

A princess, "as tall and as bright as a sunflower," is given an enchanted dog who becomes her constant companion. As much as she loved the dog, however, she longed to marry, and she was thrilled to learn a neighboring prince wanted to marry her. At the betrothal feast, however, the prince ran off when they stood up to dance. The princess's dog explained to the surprised princess that the problem was her height; she was taller than the prince. "The dog privately marveled at her naiveté, and explained that in the world outside her kingdom, men liked to be taller than their wives" (Desy 43). She remained seated when the prince returned, and they happily rode out together on horseback. The prince jumped a fence, expecting to impress her; instead, she jumped it as easily as he. He coldly directed her to ride sidesaddle, and when she tried to jump the next fence, she was unbalanced and fell. He declared "Girls shouldn't jump," as he helped her up—and then became irritated when he saw again how tall she was.

Seeing his displeasure, "she made a decision to sacrifice for love" (44); she crumpled to the ground, saying she was unable to stand. No medical treatment helped, of course, but the prince was quite happy to stay with the apparently crippled princess. As for the princess, "The loss of the use of her legs seemed a small price to pay for such a man" (45). Bedridden, the princess thought up many witty and amusing things to say to the prince, but he received these with a sharp "Haven't you ever heard that women should be seen and not heard?" (45). The princess was soon "unable" to speak, and the prince was once again content. Her dog, her constant companion, remained silently by her side.

Then one day, the prince was annoyed to find the dog on the princess's bed. "He went to strike the dog from the bed, but the princess stayed his hand. He looked at her in amazement" (45). That evening, the princess and the dog discussed the difference between the prince and the dog, and the likelihood that the prince would force the princess to abandon her companion. She cannot believe her betrothed would abolish her beloved pet, but as the dog wisely reminds her,

> "He took everything else away," he said.
> "No," she said. "I did that. I made myself...someone he could love."
> "I love you, too," the dog said.
> "Of course you do." She scratched his ears.
> "And," said the dog, "I loved you *then*." (45)

A wizard, called in for consultation, sadly recognizes that everything comes in threes, and he points out that the princess has so far (only) given up walking and talking.

From that day on, the princess hides the dog whenever the prince comes to see her, putting off their inevitable separation. On the eve of the wedding, seeing the princess's pain and despair as she is torn between her betrothed and her dog, the dog says, "Sometimes one must give up everything for love" (46). He lies down, dead, and the princess realizes what she has lost. She wraps the dog in her wedding dress and carries him out of the castle, telling the astonished onlookers she is going to bury the one who truly loved her. The princess looks down into the astonished prince's face to tell him good-bye.

Later, watering the white rose she planted on the dog's grave, the princess is approached by a man on horseback; his standard is a white rose. He dismounts and kisses the princess's hand. He stands several inches shorter than she does and says, "It is a pleasure to look up to a proud and beautiful lady" (46). It becomes apparent to the reader that this man was the dog, freed from enchantment and miraculously reborn. Seeing them, the wizard observes, "I gather from all this—I shall make a note—that sometimes one must sacrifice for love." His cat replies, "On the other hand...sometimes one must *refuse* to sacrifice" (46).

The lessons in this princess story work on different levels. Some are quite obvious, such as the primary one: girls should not maim themselves to gain male approval. Others are also obvious, such as the ones the princess declares after the death of the dog, when she realizes that she has been unfair to herself and to her loving friend:

> It is not necessarily my duty to sacrifice everything... And I have other duties: a Princess says what she thinks. A Princess stands on her own two feet. A Princess stands tall. And she does not betray those who love her. (46)

The coda between the wizard and the cat demonstrates the complexity of the issue. It can sometimes be proper to sacrifice for love, if the love is worth having—if, like the dog, the person truly loves the one who will benefit from the action and if the sacrifice was not petulantly demanded. The prince was clearly not worth the princess's self-sacrifice, but the love between the princess and the dog was.

And certainly many girls would identify with elements within the story. Countless young girls (and women) try to change themselves to attract and keep male approval, although usually not as dramatically as the princess in the story. Certainly tall girls often wish they were shorter, especially in those years after the girls' pubescent growth spurt and before the boys'. And many, many people recognize the truth of the princess's reaction to her dog's death, either in the actual death of a beloved pet or in the event of not having recognized the value of someone until s/he was gone. "The Princess Who Stood on Her Own Two Feet" is a beautiful, complex princess story that deserves to have reached a greater audience than it has.

Successful Feminist Princess Stories

The founders of *Ms. Magazine* were among the first second-wave feminists to appropriate princess stories, but they were far from alone. Many other second-wave feminist princess stories were written, with varying degrees of success. The princess stories discussed in this part of the chapter were all published in America, but their authors are not necessarily American. Zipes writes:

> Since the late 1960s there has been a growing tendency on the part of women in England and America—and not only women—to express a non-sexist view of the world through fairy tales or through criticism about fairy tales. The political purpose and design of most of the tales is clear: the narratives are symbolic representations of the authors' critique of the patriarchal status quo and of their desire to change the current socialization process. ("Introduction" xii)

Because this project was transatlantic, and because the stories discussed were published and disseminated in America, I have not restricted myself to purely American princess stories in this section; rather I will examine feminist princess stories written in English and readily available to an American audience.

According to Diana Scrimshaw, not all of the stories accepted as second-wave feminist tales should actually be considered feminist, although "many who are interested in exposing children to princesses who are not passive have taken these books at face value" (17). In fact, of the stories in Scrimshaw's survey, only one satisfies her requirements for being truly feminist: Jeanne Desy's "The Princess Who Stood on Her Own Two Feet," discussed above. While some of the stories Scrimshaw examines explore gender issues, and the princesses do ultimately change their roles, they do so in ways that she does not consider feminist: through benevolent patriarchy, through maternal neglect, or through intentionally submitting to expectations as a means of obtaining their ends. Marriage of teenaged princesses, intended to benefit the monarch, is another plot element in allegedly feminist princess stories to which Scrimshaw objects. Although the princesses often "win the traditional male role in the spouse hunting business" (19), this is only a cosmetic change; the fathers still maintain control over their daughters' sexuality (represented by marriage). Scrimshaw concludes, "Generally, the princesses win their battles, but lose the war against the patriarchal world view they have internalized" (23). This section will examine those that are feminist according to Scrimshaw's notions, considering the factors that have and have not contributed to their cultural saturation.

Tanith Lee's "Princess Sansu," first published in *Princess Hynchatti and Some Other Surprises* (1973) and later anthologized in *The Mammoth Book of Fairy Tales* (1997), is an exemplary feminist princess story. Lee is often named as one of the most important fairy-tale revisionist writers, and this early collection demonstrates her facility, humor and nontraditional beliefs. "Princess Sansu" is the story of a princess literally trapped by society's expectations of female beauty; her hair, beautiful in every other way (golden, silky, curly), is considered too short. Her father the king is dismayed by this failure, but Sansu's attitude about her perceived shortcoming is incredibly healthy: she "privately thought it was all a bit silly" (34). Her father finds a witch willing to "fix" Sansu's hair, but the witch is vying for the "Wickedest Witch of the Year" award, and sees in Sansu's hair a chance to win.

The witch enchants Sansu's hair, making it grow incredibly long. But there is a catch: if the hair should touch the ground, a tidal wave will sweep away the kingdom (presumably winning the witch her prize). Only the witch's own magical scissors can cut Sansu's hair, and once it is cut it will return to normal. Sansu is taken to a tower, where her hair remains safely above ground. Every day another level is added to the tower, and Sansu is farther and farther removed from her family and friends. Finally, Sansu conceives a plan to save herself. With the entire kingdom carrying her hair to keep it from touching the ground, Sansu goes to the witch's cave disguised as a witch. She ties a package with braided strands of her enchanted hair. The witch, fooled into thinking she has won the Wickedest Witch award, cannot open the prize. Frustrated, she uses her magic scissors to cut the strands around the package, breaking her own spell. Sansu is free, and the kingdom is out of danger. The witch retreats to her cave, and the king declares he "shan't mind [Sansu's] hair being too short any more. I won't ever measure it again" (47). Sansu rides off to witch school to become a good witch.

Sansu is a resourceful and inventive character who successfully solves her own problem, freeing herself and her kingdom. She bests the witch fair and square, removes her disguise and looks her foe in the eye. Most interestingly, Sansu's story does not end in marriage. She chooses to educate herself, with plans for a career. The story is neither overtly didactic nor dogmatic, but it is clearly feminist in its stance and its resolution. It is not widely known, however, and *Princess Hynchatti* is long out of print. This is unfortunate, as the entire collection offers a variety of interesting and charming princess and prince stories with unexpected solutions to common fairy tale plot devices.

One very successful princess story is Robert Munsch's picture book, *The Paper Bag Princess* (1980). As a picture book, it is far simpler than many in this chapter, but it has been hugely, widely successful, with 52 printings and more than 3,000,000 copies sold (as of its 25th anniversary; more have certainly been sold in the three years since then) [Munsch 51]. It has been published in a dozen languages and turned into various theatrical productions. Other products have been spun off from the book as well, including an audio version of Munsch recounting the story, a Princess Elizabeth doll, and a storytelling kit. It is a simple story, but it has become a staple of feminist literature classes (Munsch 14). It has also found a fan base in feminists outside of academe. "One *New York Times* writer confessed, 'I pass along paperback copies to my sisters and friends as if it were a subversive leaflet'" (Munsch 51). Clearly, this feminist princess story has struck a chord.

The lessons are simple, but they work against traditional expectations and demonstrate what a princess should be, giving readers (or listeners, as much of the book's audience is too young to read) a princess to emulate.

Princess Elizabeth is first described as a traditional princess, beautiful, with "expensive princess clothes" (26) and engaged to a prince named Ronald. When a dragon smashes her castle and carries Ronald away, Elizabeth is left with nothing to wear but a paper bag. She is determined to chase the dragon and retrieve Ronald. She outwits the dragon, defeating him, and Elizabeth finds the captive Ronald. Rather than thanking her, Ronald sneers at Elizabeth, telling her to "come back when you are dressed like a real princess" (46). Elizabeth replies, "Ronald…your clothes are really pretty and your hair is very neat. You look like a real prince, but you are a bum" (48). She leaves him; the final picture shows her kicking up her heels into the sunset.

Princesses, according to this story, should be brave; Elizabeth wastes no time in going after the dragon. They should also be clever, as it is through brains and not brawn that Elizabeth defeats the dragon. Most importantly and radically in a princess story, marriage need not be the final disposition of a princess. When Ronald chastises her for her appearance, Elizabeth confidently and accurately locates the problem in Ronald himself and seeks to correct it, not by changing herself or her clothes, but by dumping Ronald.

Interestingly, children hearing or reading the story may not understand the same feminist messages that the adults reading it to them understand. In fact, all children hear the story in a subtly different manner, "this difference relating in part to the subject position s/he takes up in the story (positioning her/himself as Elizabeth or Ronald or the dragon), and in part on her/his understanding of gender roles" (Davies 63). Children find the story funny, which is much of its appeal, but the humor for them comes from Elizabeth unexpectedly and rudely calling Ronald "a bum", not from "the clash between the romantic frame and the feminist frame" (Davies 71), which is where adults locate the humor. In fact, according to Davies, most children hearing this story "are simply puzzled and want a different, 'proper' ending" (71). This is not to say the book is not popular with children; it is, and they will happily listen to it repeatedly.

> The conflict between woman as active agent and woman as romantic love object is one that engages them, and though they prefer at this stage the romantic version which fits their fantasies about male-female relations, Elizabeth is clearly a salient character who chooses, at least for the moment, to break that connection. For those who bring a feminist perspective to the story and who support Elizabeth's line of action, this is clearly an important narrative in which the female hero makes her own choices and does not depend on a man for her happiness. For these children it is a narrative in which the female copes with her contradictory positioning and in which

> the usual power relations are undermined and with it the binary that hangs on and
> supports those relations. (71)

The power of the pre-existing, traditional romantic narrative is great, present even in those stories in which it is not presented. For many girls hearing the story, Elizabeth is too improper, too dirty, too active, to be a princess. They do not understand why Elizabeth does not submit to Ronald's dictates in order to be reunited with him, and they do not understand her anger and agency.

Perhaps the ongoing success of the story results from the humor and the feminist message that adults, the ones with the purchasing power, find in it as adults—not necessarily because children fully understand and adopt it as an empowering narrative. And it has been on the market long enough that women who heard the story as children may remember loving it; when they buy it for their children, they appreciate the story's feminist message in ways they did not understand as children.

M.M. Kaye's *The Ordinary Princess* (1980) is another successful second-wave feminist princess story, first published in America in 1984. Although it hasn't had the phenomenal sales and adaptations of *The Paper Bag Princess*, it has gone through ten printings and is still in print today—a success by any standard. Unlike Munsch's story, which happened upon its feminist stance almost by accident, Kaye's work was intentionally created with a feminist ideology. As Kaye explains in her introduction, she was reading the Andrew Lang fairy books (*The Blue Fairy Book*, *The Green Fairy Book*, etc.) when she had a revelation.

> I noticed something that had not struck me before—I suppose because I had always
> taken it for granted. All the princesses...were blond, blue-eyed, and beautiful, with
> lovely figures and complexions and extravagantly long hair. I began to wonder just
> how many handsome young princes would have asked a king for the hand of his
> daughter if that daughter happened to be gawky, snub-nosed and freckled, with
> shortish mouse-colored hair? None, I suspected. They would all have been off chas-
> ing after some lissome Royal Highness with large blue eyes and yards of golden hair
> and probably nothing between her ears! (Kaye xii)

While the suggestion that to be blond is to be empty-headed is unfair, certainly Kaye was on to something in her critique of the desirable qualities in a traditional princess. *The Ordinary Princess* seeks to redress the notion that princesses should be valued for their physical attributes.

Her Serene and Royal Highness the Princess Amethyst Alexandra Augusta Araminta Adelaide Aurelia Anne of Phantasmorania, the seventh

daughter of the King and Queen of Phantasmorania, was born more beautiful, serene, and princess-like than any of her sisters. The fairies invited to her
christening bestowed upon her traditional gifts of wit, charm, courage,
health, wisdom, and grace—except for the oldest and most powerful fairy,
who bestowed her gift last. "My child...I am going to give you something
that will probably bring you more happiness than all these fal-lals and
fripperies put together. You shall be Ordinary!" (16). This gift changes the
course of the princess's life; despite her mother's efforts to fight "her
distressing ordinariness" (22), she soon becomes known as simply Amy. Nor
does she lose the useful gifts given to her by the other fairies, although
"because she was not beautiful, not one ever seemed to notice these other
qualities" (23).

One after another her sisters, typically beautiful princesses, are married
off. Amy worries that it will be her turn soon, and "I shan't like it a bit. No
more fun. No more forest. Having to wear best dresses every day. Crowns
and court curtseys and state banquets and things like that. No climbing trees,
and a very handsome husband with no sense of humor!" (29). None of her
suitors stays more than a day, however, because she is so very ordinary. This
bothers her not at all, but the King soon grew "flustered and peppery and the
Queen became more and more anxious" (30). The King agrees to a plan: he
will lock Amy in a tower and hire a dragon to lay waste to the countryside. A
prince will surely come to rescue her, and the romance of the situation will
encourage the prince to propose to Amy.

When Amy learns of this plan, she runs away and soon takes a job as a
castle kitchen assistant in the neighboring country. Here she befriends
Peregrine, a man-of-all-work. Much to her dismay, Amy's true identity is
discovered. Peregrine, however, also has a secret identity: he is the king, who
has been posing as a servant to spend time with Amy and away from his
princess cousin, who has come to induce him to marriage. Both royal, Amy
and Peregrine can be married. They spend their honeymoon in the hut they
had built together on Amy's days off, and presumably they live happily ever
after.

There are a number of lessons embedded in *The Ordinary Princess*. The
primary message is that no one should aspire to be a traditional princess.
According to the book, being a princess is far less desirable than being an
ordinary girl. Young princesses spend their time playing boring games and
keeping their dresses and skin from getting mussed; once married, they are
stuck with boring, humorless husbands. They are beautiful, yes, but that

becomes the only characteristic for which they are valued. Peregrine, disgusted, describes princesses to Amy:

> They are almost as alike as peas in a pod!....first of all, they are very beautiful...then secondly and thirdly and fourthly, they all have long golden hair, blue eyes, and the most lovely complexions. Fifthly and sixthly, they are graceful and accomplished. Seventhly, they have names like Persephone, Sapphire, and Roxanne. And lastly...they are all excessively proper and extremely dull...except when they are make-believe princesses who are really kitchen maids! (82-82)

Amy agrees; she pities her sisters for their dull lives. Peregrine's marriage-seeking cousin also strikes Amy as somewhat pitiful: "She was as beautiful as the evening star, but she bowed and smiled in a rather bored sort of way—like a mechanical doll, thought the Ordinary Princess" (63). Stereotypical princes, too, Amy considers boring: "they may seem wonderful..., but ... you'd be surprised how stiff and stodgy and tiresome they are" (60). Although (Princess) Amy and (King) Peregrine do fall in love, the ways they are common people and uncommon royals are made quite clear.

The value of paid work is also highlighted in the story. Amy's fairy godmother tells her she will need to find a job to replace her worn clothing. Amy is not sure she'll like work (her godmother very practically assures her, "Neither do most ordinary people—but they have to" [54]) but she sees the necessity of it. Even as a very junior assistant kitchen maid, Amy takes pleasure in her work.

> On the whole, the Ordinary Princess—who was now an ordinary kitchen maid—enjoyed life as much as ever. For when you have spent most of your life surrounded by ladies-in-waiting and polite courtiers who all expect you to do nothing but play the harp nicely and do a little elegant embroidery, even peeling potatoes has its charms. And there is nothing that gives you a feeling of such proud satisfaction as drawing a weekly wage that you have earned all by yourself. (59)

This is an incredibly important lesson: to find satisfaction and pride in financial self-sufficiency. Amy could have bemoaned her fate or returned to a life of luxury. Instead she finds fulfillment even in the most ordinary, low-paying job.

The final lesson of *The Ordinary Princess* is rare even in second-wave feminist princess stories: the romantic couple spends months developing their relationship before becoming engaged. They see each other whenever possible, and on Amy's one-half day off every two weeks, they build a hut together. This implies a long period of moving from just being friends to being romantically involved. They make each other laugh so hard they lose track of time, so hard they have to sit down. They play together, exploring the forest and playing ninepins and tickling trout. And when their royal identities have been revealed, Peregrine proposes to Amy in a practical and realistic manner, rushing to meet her before getting on with the day's business of state. She considers their engagement and their future together: "He *is* a dear…and I suppose I'm glad he is a king and everything is going to end happily ever after. But I still think that sometimes I shall be just the littlest bit sorry that I wasn't a real kitchen maid and he wasn't a man-of-all-work. It has been such fun" (100). She does not consider whether her father will benefit from the marriage at all, and she agrees to marry Peregrine with no eye toward his wealth.

Amy has found a life partner who values her for qualities having nothing to do with her appearance, another important lesson. The portrait Amy's parents sent to Peregrine is "not what one would call a speaking likeness" (108), because her parents are afraid that Peregrine will be put off by her looks. Amy sends him a note with the portrait: "Don't get worried…I haven't really grown like that. My nose is still turned up and I have as many freckles as ever" (108). She gets an extremely gratifying letter in return, assuring her that he hardly ever looks at the portrait, and when he does "I only think how glad I am that you are not a bit like it and that your nose still turns up and has as many freckles as ever! Darling Amy, don't ever change" (108). This is true love, love that has developed over time and that accepts and values the woman for who she is. This sort of relationship is not seen in traditional fairy tales, and rarely in second-wave feminist princess stories, which generally value career or singlehood over rewarding romantic relationships.

Less Successful Second-Wave Princess Stories

While *The Paper Bag Princess* and *The Ordinary Princess* have retained their popularity since their first publication (and *Atalanta*, as part of *Free to Be…,* is still selling as well), many second-wave feminist princess stories have not maintained any real presence in popular American culture. Yet this is troubling; there remains a need for them in American society as a counter to more traditional tales, which contain lessons potentially damaging to their audience.

> Girls learn through these stories that their value lies in their looks and that the way people look naturally determines the way they behave. They are also conditioned through these tales to become passive and unadventurous—to wait for their charm-

ing prince to arrive and save them out of the limbo and insignificance of their lives. The only women who have any sort of power in these fairy tales are both evil and good fairies—with whom children struggle to identify and therefore do not see as role models—and wicked step-mothers and witches. These powerful, active, independent females teach girls that these qualities are not desirable for women and will be punished (often by death); they also instill in female children a distrust for those of the same gender whom they are taught to see as threatening competition in their quest for romantic fulfillment. (Regel)

But not just girls may be taught harmful life lessons through traditional fairy tales. Boys, too, may learn "that only certain qualities are important in a wife and that they have to treat women as subordinate and fragile. They are in no way taught to deal with women as equals or even as significant others" (Regel). With such a clear need, why have second-wave feminist princess stories not maintained a larger presence in popular culture? There are several reasons for their quick decline; the rest of this chapter will examine different stories as a means of positing reasons why these stories and other of their ilk have largely vanished, remaining at best a niche market.

One reason these princess stories are not widely disseminated is that many of them are not actually feminist fairy tales; they are, instead, fractured fairy tales—funny, but without the ring of truth that actual fairy tales have. A feminist fairy tale is best exemplified by authors who alter "generic conventions in three main areas...to rework the discursive foundations of the traditional material: narrative strategy, representation of male and female characters, and renegotiation of patriarchal ideologies and values" (Kuykendal and Sturm 40). Giving voice, agency and subjectivity to characters within the story is a feminist narrative strategy, as is subverting stereotypes of males as well as females and changing patriarchal ideals into those based on other value systems (valuing the artistry of the weaving in Rumpelstiltskin, for instance, instead of valuing the spinning because it will lead to a good marriage). In contrast, fractured fairy tales (and fractured princess stories, by extension) simply turn the patriarchal hierarchy on its head, "disrupting the binary gender construction...fractured fairy tales challenge gender stereotypes and patriarchal ideologies only at the story level of the text. These changes rely on a straightforward reversal of gender roles and the substitution of strong female characters for more passive female characters" (40). Some second-wave feminist princess stories suffered as a result of being fractured, rather than truly feminist, fairy tales.

The stories collected by the Irish collective Fairytales for Feminists are fractured fairy tales, less successful as stories and more successful as in-jokes. As such,

> They demonstrate…little detailed knowledge of the fairy tale genre they utilize, alongside an overtly self-referencing use of feminism….The texts show a dismissive lack of appreciation of the vehicle they employ, and this leads to narratives that are shallow in their attempt to be fairy tale, though their purpose often makes humorous and satisfying reading as feminist stories. (Makinen 78-79)

These princess stories limit their audience, both by being so self-referentially feminist and by not being true fairy tales.

Two examples are Linda Kavanagh's "The Princesses' Forum" (1985) and Gráinne Healy's "Snow-Fight Defeats Patri-Arky" (1989). They are clever and humorous, but clearly written for a narrow audience. "The Princesses' Forum" envisions a group of fairy tale princesses meeting to discuss their conditions and to set out new rules by which to live. Snow White declares, "I'm tired of having to behave like a princess…I'm not delicate, I'm not silly and I'm certainly not weak. Anyone who could keep house for seven little chauvinists and not lose their sanity, has to be a very strong person" (36). While there is some mention made of not just "reversing the roles of oppressor and oppressed" (37), the princes portrayed in the story are reduced to fearful yet egotistical ninnies. There is also a side plot involving the question of Rapunzel needing an abortion; everyone is relieved that she is on the pill. This is obviously not written for girls, but its didactic tone is meant to educate readers not just on the stereotypes inherent in traditional fairy tales but also in how women (princesses) should expect to be treated. Unfortunately, "Retellings which explicitly address issues from literary theory are often experienced as overtly didactic, programmatic literature" (Joosen 137) and can feel belabored after the initial chuckle.

"Snow-Fight Defeats Patri-Arky" is primarily an extended play on words and, like many stories from *Fairytales for Feminists*, it suffers from its "reproduction of 1970s radical feminist clichés…[which] reveals a level of complacency that can alienate even many feminist readers" (Makinen 81). Snow-Fight battles with her cousins, the Arkys, to free Matri Arky from the rule of her most bullying brother, Patri. Snow-Fight argues "the politics of housework" (133) with her male cousins, Olig, Hier, Mon, Noh, and Patri. The battle escalates; Patri enlists the help of Otto and Techno Crat, and Snow-Fight calls on the Fury sisters. Patri poisons Snow-Fight, causing her to fall into a coma. When Furies move in, to help Matri take care of Snow-Fight, Patri retreats, seeking a new home where Snow-Fight's ideas were unknown. Ann Arky returns to wake up Snow-Fight with a potion and a song: "Women are we, sisters are we,/ We have the power to heal ourselves,/ We kill no beasts, we poison no lands,/ the power is ours, it is in our hands" (140). The women agree "they would live together, with and for each other" (140), while the Arky men ("boys") agree to build their own house in the woods and "never expect any woman to clean and cook for them" (140). This princess story, and many like it, comes from an author "writing firmly within the ghetto, and to the already converted" (Makinen 80); it is intentionally educative, but it preaches (writes?) almost entirely to the choir.

The alienating, dogmatic aspects found in the feminist/fractured princess stories can readily be found in the way the princesses frequently abjure marriage for career. In echoing Steinem's statement about romantic love being the device men use to trick women into giving up their strength and independence (1972), they ignore the fact that most people wish to find mates. Cinderella, in Maeve Binchy's "Cinderella Re-examined" (1985), is one such example. She only goes to the ball under duress. She has no desire to marry the prince, advising him "to examine his assumption that every woman would want to win him just because he was a prince" (13) and to see a professional about his foot fetish. Her happy ending involves a career as the king's caterer and "Chief Executive of Palace Enterprises" (15). It is a funny story, and it recognizably follows the broad outlines of more traditional versions of Cinderella, but career and marriage are not mutually exclusive. The marriage/career dichotomy as presented in "Cinderella Re-examined" is a false one, and leaving home to find a job is no longer in opposition to the daily lives of millions of women. Indeed, with the majority of women (59.3% in 2007 [Women's Bureau]) in the workforce, even women with children (76% in 2007 [Labor Statistics]), getting a job is no longer the stuff of fantasy; it's a given. Women readers of princess stories are more likely to fantasize about not having to work than they are to fantasize about getting a job.

There have been many studies examining the discrepancy between the numbers of girls and women who support the tenets of feminism and the numbers who self-identify as feminists. Paula Kamen's *Feminist Fatale: Voices from the twentysomething generation explore the future of the "Women's movement"* (1991) identifies three reasons women might not want to call themselves feminists. The first will be discussed below: they feel that the feminism's time has passed. Two other reasons may also come into play in considering why second-wave feminist princess stories did not achieve cultural saturation: feminism implies work (often seen as a difficult commitment), and feminism will upset men (a frightening prospect).

The outspokenly feminist nature of the second-wave feminist princess stories may well have scared away potential readers influenced by negative media stereotypes of feminists and feminism.

> Women may resist the feminist label out of a fear of the evaluative connotations which it may carry in their own minds and those of others. Common perceptions of feminists as embittered radicals may deter many women from applying the feminist label to themselves. This may be especially true for young, single, heterosexual, college women (e.g., Hogeland, 1994). Such women are often pursuing a relatively mainstream heterosexual lifestyle and consequently prefer that this be reflected in others' perceptions of them. Adopting the label of "feminist" conflicts with this pursuit because of the perceptions it may connote. (Williams and Wittig 9)

Some women may feel that a dislike of men is a requirement of feminism, or that individual achievement is more effective than collective advocacy. Williams and Wittig propose that there may be private and public aspects contributing to resistance to self-labeling as a feminist. "At the private level, avoidance might be due in part to personal ('cognitive') dissonance, for example, between one's positive self-concept and a personal negative evaluation of feminists. At the public level, one potentially risks more—e.g., social ostracism" (10). This "resistance to the f-word" (Evans 208) has created its own field of study within feminism, and is too vast for the scope of this study[4]. However, fear of branding oneself a feminist, even through one's choice of reading material, may have negatively impacted the sales and dissemination of second-wave feminist princess stories. In rejecting the label, these potential readers of second-wave feminist princess stories may be motivated to avoid specifically feminist works; perhaps the label of "feminist" alone is enough to limit the readership of these feminist stories because the potential readers shy away from applying the label to themselves through their reading as in their public personae and social lives. Negative connotations of feminists may also have deterred movie studios from adapting these stories to film, thus denying them the widest cultural dissemination. Those few female movie executives may not have wanted to "out" themselves as feminists by publically endorsing a film made from one of these stories.

Furthermore—and ironically—these stories' lack of widespread, lasting popularity can be blamed on second-wave feminists' general success. While few would argue that second-wave feminists achieved all of their goals, they made such great strides that their stories' dichotomy between love and career, for instance, seems largely irrelevant. Princess stories are wish-fulfillment stories, and "wish-fulfillment stories are about teaching people what they should wish for" (Poniewozik 2). When second-wave feminists were writing these princesses stories, "the wish was to be able to do everything men could" (Poniewozik 2); very quickly, however, that wish was realized for many practical purposes. Modern American girls take for granted that they can control their reproductive systems, play sports, and achieve their career goals. The culture changed too quickly for many second-wave feminist princess stories to gain a real foothold and achieve cultural saturation.

On this topic, Sheila Greene discusses Sue Sharpe's mid-1990s study of adolescent school girls. Sharpe interviewed two groups of girls, one from 1972 and one from 1991, to examine their attitudes toward feminist concerns and the futures they anticipated. "Less than twenty years separated Sharpe's two samples, but clear changes were evident at a psychological level in terms of confidence, independence and life expectations" (Greene 119). The girls from the sample of 1972 planned to have careers in addition to marriages, but "most still endorsed traditional values and adopted traditional goals" (119). The girls in the 1990s sample, however,

> ...were 'more assertive and confident' and took it for granted that women would be independent and equal to men. *At the same time they rejected feminism as not relevant to them since equality had been achieved* (Sharpe, 2001) [emphasis mine]. As Sharpe comments, the girls endorse the goals of feminism but refuse to identify as feminists. (119)

Sharpe's study, among many others, indicating that girls in the 1990s considered the goals of feminism met suggests another reason why these second-wave feminist princess stories have largely fallen by the wayside: potential readers believe the stories' time has passed.

Indeed, the status quo delineated as many princess stories' starting point is not today's status quo; they seem overblown and unrealistic as a result. Harriet Herman's *The Forest Princess* (1974) is one such princess story. The princess is raised in a vacuum: she lives alone in a tower, magically supplied with everything she needs. On her tenth birthday, she is given a rope with which to climb out of the tower and into the forest; there she befriends the forest animals. At thirteen, she is given a telescope through which she can see a golden castle. She watches as a terrible storm washes a boy, a prince, onto the shore of a nearby lake. She brings him home and they live together happily for some months. When she asks him to teach her to read, he replies, "In my kingdom girls do not learn to read, but things are different here" (Herman). She, in turn, teaches him "to cook and to make things with his hands" (Herman). Eventually, homesickness gets the better of the prince, and the two of them return to his home.

Once there, the princess learns the difference between the happy vacuum of her tower and life in royal society. When the prince tells his family where he has been and what he and the princess have been doing, "the king looked suspiciously at the princess. 'We are grateful to you for saving our son's life, princess, but gathering berries and nuts and cooking, that is girls' work!'" (Herman). The princess is led inside by the ladies-in-waiting, who giggle and say "We must teach you to be a proper princess" (Herman). They bathe her and dress her, and when she complains that she can't breathe in her corset, and that her clothing is too heavy to walk in, they reassure her that "You'll get used to it. All girls do!" (Herman). Most distressingly, the girls in this country are not taught to read, because "That is the way it has always been" (Herman).

The prince upholds social expectations, becoming angry with the princess when she questions them ("Why can't you accept things the way they are?"). The princess secretly teaches the other girls to read. When she is told she cannot ride horses with the prince, she secretly teaches herself horseback riding tricks; she reveals her stunt riding at the prince's birthday pageant. The king wishes to reward her for her bravery, and asks her to name her prize. She replies, "Your majesty what I have done today could have been done by any of the boys and girls in your land. As my reward I would like the boys and girls to ride horses together, to read books together and to play together" (Herman). The king declares, "The boys and girls are perfectly happy the way things are" (Herman), but the girls protest: "We are tired of these hoops and petticoats. We want to wear simple clothes and learn to ride horses and to read books like the boys" (Herman). The prince speaks up in support of the girls, but he is silenced by the king, who banishes the forest princess. No one knows where she went, but "If you go to the land of the golden castle today, you will find the boys and girls playing together, reading books together, and riding horses together" (Herman). So while the princess was banished without a word of farewell from her friend the prince, the reader is to assume that he has learned from her and, when he is king, he institutes the changes that his father rejected.

The social problems in *The Forest Princess* lie far outside the realm of American girls, many of whom wear jeans to school and who are, in fact, more facile readers than boys[5]. *The Forest Princess* is a second-wave feminist princess story so much of its time that it could not transcend that time. As Kuykendal and Sturm note,

> Children use fairy tales to identify cultural norms about the world in which they live. Contained within these cultural norms are the shared beliefs about gender roles held by the child's society. As fairy tales are often a child's early exposure to gender identity and how it defines a character, these gender roles should be as realistic as possible. (40)

The gender norms decried in stories such as *The Forest Princess* are no longer realistic in America (although they are distressingly realistic elsewhere).

Ann Tompert's *The Clever Princess* (1977), published by Lollipop Power, Inc. (identified on the book cover as "a feminist collective that publishes books to counteract sex-stereotyped behavior and role models presented by society to young children") is another victim of feminism's success. Princess Lorna's father, the king, has no time for her, so she spends much of her time studying or wandering around and asking questions. The answer to her many questions ("Why are you wearing that silly thing on your head? ... Can't you make anything but chocolate cake for dinner? ... Do all flowers look alike?" [4-5]) is always "king's orders." The king requires the footman to wear a silly hat; the king demands only chocolate cake be served for dessert; the king wants no flowers but tulips planted in the country. It seems the king is so busy micromanaging and making arbitrary decisions that he cannot make time for his daughter, so Lorna spends much of her time with Old Krone, a magical woman who lives in the forest. Old Krone teaches Lorna magic, but cautions her not to use it unless all else fails.

Eventually, the king grows old and wants to retire, but when he says the time has come for Lorna to rule, his counselors are appalled. "Girls don't rule kingdoms...She must marry a man who will make a good king" (10-11). The king is soon persuaded that finding Lorna a husband is the correct thing to do, but she turns down each prospect, saying she has "no wish to be married at all" (12). She asks her father to teach her to rule, but the counselors opine that "Princesses should spend their time trying on gowns and jewels and going to balls" (13). She is forced to spend her days trying on an endless procession of "dressing gowns, dinner gowns and ball gowns...and all the other things that the king's counselors thought made a proper princess" (14). Lorna, frustrated, refrains from using her magic, but she also refuses to consider marriage.

The counselors consider forcing Lorna to marry by throwing her in a dungeon or turning her into a toad, but eventually they simply ask Old Krone to help change Lorna's mind. She refuses, but does suggest testing the princess's fitness to rule, as her father had been tested before her. The counselors agree, and after passing series of challenges (initially because of the reading she has done and finally by magic), Lorna is crowned ruler. Lorna never marries, and she hardly rules: "Over the years, Lorna ruled wisely and well by NOT ruling for the most part, leaving most of the decisions to the people of the kingdom. Thus she was never too busy to wander through the fields and woods with Old Krone or to go fishing with her father" (38).

Again, the situation in the story is far removed from the situation of today's American girls. Britain, the country with a monarch with which most Americans are most familiar, has had a woman on the throne for decades. Her husband is not the king; he is Prince Consort, clearly a lower rank than she. Beyond that, this story has several problems. Princesses should use their wits, as indeed the story teaches, but the suggestion that girls should use magic in dire straits is pointless, as girls don't have magic. Ann Trousdale and Sally McMillan's study, "'Cinderella Was a Wuss': A Young Girl's Responses to Feminist and Patriarchal Folktales" (2003), suggests that real-life girl readers interpret such a magical resolution with dismay and disbelief. "'Why do you need a wand if you're a princess? ... You don't need a wand! .... Where did those magical powers come from? That was the good thing about her, that she wasn't, like, you know, extraterrestrial'" (21). For Trousdale and McMillan's reader in particular, the fairy tale princess should be "enough of a force in the world on her own strength not to need such superfluous female trappings as a magic wand" (22). The lessons from Old Krone are the most didactic bits of the story. To be even more memorable and special, they are told in verse. The first, and most important one (since the readers are shown the original scene, not just told about it later) concerns magic: "Though affairs may move slower than snails, / Don't use magic unless all else fails" (15). Again, a pointless lesson.

Certainly it's good news that Lorna did not adopt the same nonsensical micromanaging, dictatorial style as her father. But as an opponent, he is so foolish and weak that triumphing over him is hollow. Besides the question of who should rule, the completely arbitrary decisions against which she rebels are meaningless, which lessens their real-world application. Only chocolate cake for dessert, only tulips in the gardens, only striped smocks on the peasants...there is no rational reason for a king to institute these laws. He allows his counselors to override him in the matter of his heir; his initial decision, that "The time has come for Princess Lorna to rule the kingdom" (10), is quickly and repeatedly overruled. If he can enforce his iron will on every single person in the kingdom, it makes no sense that his counselors wield such power over him.

Finally, of course, Lorna becomes queen—or does she? She is never given that title, being called only Lorna or Princess Lorna throughout the story. She also staunchly refuses to marry, and the text highlights the fact that she always has time, as laissez-faire ruler, to fish with her father or wander with Old Krone. Her only relationships are with her parent figures; she never advances to adulthood. She resolutely refuses to marry before her father appoints her his heir, a decision that makes sense within the story; the counselors want her married so that her husband can rule as king. Once she has been declared ruler, however, there is little reason for her refusal to marry. The Junior Chief Counselor, who has watched her with growing admiration, proposes to her, but she rejects the notion. "Although she was very fond of him, she refused. 'Maybe, someday,' she said. 'For now, I have no desire for a husband or a king'" (36). Trousdale and McMillan's subject found a "lack of interest in marriage... 'unrealistic' and assumed that, at the end of [the heroine's] independent adventures, [she] would marry the prince" (22). As discussed above in reference to "Cinderella Re-examined," the majority American women will marry at some point; in 2007, the census reported that 75% of women were or had been married. When a princess-named-heir finds someone who loves and respects her, and of whom she is very fond, there is no logical, real-world reason for refusing his hand, and to do so plays against current definitions and expectations of happy endings (both fictional and real-world). Her position as ruler is assured; Lorna is not protecting her power by declining the Junior Chief Counselor's offer. Refusing to marry causes her in some sense to remain a child. Spending all of her time with her parent figures without taking on the role of wife (or mother) leaves Princess Lorna in maturation limbo, neither fully adult nor naively child.

An even more problematic princess story is Michael Foreman's *All the King's Horses* (1976), whose title seems an allusion to the nursery rhyme "Humpty Dumpty" ("all the king's horses and all the king's men couldn't put Humpty together again"). Perhaps this allusion is meant to refer to changing social conditions; once changed, they resist return to a prior state. On the other hand, this is a very strange Atalanta-esque story which does not directly point to realistic social change. It begins promisingly, with an unconventional description of a Princess: "She wasn't the milk-white, golden-haired, pink little number the way princesses are supposed to be. She was a BIG girl. And *dark*" (Foreman). This breaking of conventional description bodes well for the princess story, both recognizing the traditional princess and providing an alternative. The princess finds palace life boring, preferring to ride horseback over the grasslands. Her father the king "is anxious to get her married," and this is the source of tension in the story. Her first suitor is the richest man in the land, but she laughs scornfully before literally, physically throwing him down the stairs. "I don't want a husband I can throw downstairs...And I don't care how rich he is! I want a man I can respect. I want a man who can wrestle with me!" It is good that she doesn't care about her suitor's wealth, and if she had meant "wrestle" in a meta-phorical sense that also would have been a positive lesson. Unfortunately, she simply means wrestle in the physical sense; harkening back to Scrim-shaw's work, this element of violence is problematic.

The king declares that any suitor will have to wrestle with the princess for her hand; losing will cost the suitor 100 horses, to be added to the king's stable. Thus the courtship of his daughter is profitable for the king. The princess handily defeats each comer; "they were twisted and turned, mangled and mauled, and thrown out of the ring" (Foreman). Finally, a young woodcutter comes to wrestle the princess. The king, in a fairy-tale self-referential moment, thinks to himself that "It's always the woodcutter's son who wins the Princess" (Foreman). The princess appraises the woodcutter when they meet the day of their match, noting how handsome he is. Yet he still meets the same fate as all the other suitors. Then the princess turns, leaps on the back of the nearest horse, and rides off, followed by the king's thousands of horses. "Some nights they are still heard, rushing through the nightmares of kings and the dreams of princesses" (Foreman).

This, then, is meant to be a story that inspires its readers—but to what? According to the final line, kings fear this sort of princess and other princesses dream of (emulating?) her, but why? Surely physical violence is not the solution to problems of female inequality. Nor is running away from home a viable answer. Because neither the princess nor the king develop in any way through this story, readers are left to wonder what the take-away message really is.

Conclusion

While a few second-wave feminist princess stories are still widely available and widely read today, the vast majority were never widely read and did not become influential forces in American popular culture. Some reasons for this lack of cultural saturation have already been discussed: some stories were intentionally written for a narrow audience. Some are so overtly didactic that they are more screed than story, diluting the power of the story and frightening away some potential readers wishing not to be labeled feminists. And some, such as *The Clever Princess* and *The Forest Princess,* were so much a product of their time that they were unable to transcend it, to retain their relevance as society changed. There are two other related reasons that these stories never captured the widespread American imagination: such a small group of stories cannot overcome the layers of acculturation that accrete in other aspects of girls' lives, and there is no large corporation ensuring that the stories become widespread. In other words, the Disney factor defeats most second-wave feminist princess stories.

Ann Trousdale's 1995 piece, "I'd Rather Be Normal: A Young Girl's Responses to 'Feminist' Fairy Tales," discusses the problem of acculturation in potential readers of feminist fairy tales. Although Trousdale focuses her study on feminist fairy tales from the Alison Lurie school (recovered stories featuring strong women) rather than new versions or altogether new stories, her conclusions can reasonably be applied to the princess stories under discussion. Although the young girl in the story likes the strong female princesses featured in the stories in the study, this appreciation does not extend to emulation; she would rather "be normal" (174).

> In each of the feminist stories, Cindy was drawn to the female protagonist and named her as her favorite character. But as strong as her attraction was to [these characters], the attraction— to the point of emulation at least —was checked by these females' unconventionality, indicating the importance Cindy gave to such

gender markers as clothing, hair length, personal appurtenances (or accessories), and body inscription. (178)

It seems that alternative models of femininity provided though feminist princess stories could indeed counter or broaden the more traditional, widespread, patriarchal models. The need to be considered acceptable to the world at large is very strong, however, and difficult to overcome.

None of the second-wave feminist princess stories discussed in this chapter have been adapted to film, which, in twentieth and early twenty-first century America, has been the quickest and easiest way to widespread cultural dissemination. The Disney corporation, of course, is one of the major forces perpetuating the older forms of femininity through princess stories, and it has yet to adapt any of the second-wave feminist princess stories. The first wave of Disney princess stories was discussed in Chapter Two; the second wave of Disney princess stories, created in response to the second-wave feminist movement, will be discussed next. The Disney films and their merchandizing and advertizing campaigns were ultimately too much for most second-wave feminist princess stories to compete with, and the Disney version of "post-feminist" princesses became the dominant one in the 1990s.

❖ CHAPTER FOUR ❖

Disney's "Feminist" Princess Stories

DISNEY STUDIOS revisited princess stories in the 1980s and 1990s, with a nod toward feminism and the new expectations of girls and women in American society. The princess stories produced at this time support feminist beliefs and issues—superficially. Disney Studios' new batch of princess stories [*The Little Mermaid* (1989), *Beauty and the Beast* (1991), *Pocahontas* (1995), and *Mulan* (1998)] touted their new heroines as spunkier, more independent and more feminist than the traditional Disney princesses (Snow White, Cinderella, and Sleeping Beauty). But these new Disney princess stories were burdened by the patriarchal traditions out of which they came. This chapter will examine the new Disney princess stories, focusing on the ways their adaptations change the source material and on the ways that the messages remain anti-feminist, no matter how "spunky" the heroines.

The Disney Response to Feminism

The mid-1980s found Disney Studios in a state of flux. Critics had for decades received feature-length animated productions tepidly at best, and since the years leading to Walt Disney's 1966 death the studio had become better known for live-action films than for animation. While older animated films were re-released with careful timing (a seven-year rotation, discussed in Chapter 2), new feature-length animated films were rare. In 1985, Michael Eisner was chosen as Walt Disney Productions' CEO (Kanfer 216); Jeffrey Katzenberg was installed as studio head, and Frank Wells became president. This younger generation of filmmakers would revisit and change the Disney formula for animated films, leading to what many have described as Disney's renaissance.

Society, too, had changed. By the 1980s, the effects of second-wave feminism had permeated much of society, and women were reaping the benefits: higher education, better jobs, and different social expectations. When the new cadre of Disney filmmakers, seeking to recapture the magic (and profitability) of the classic Disney animated films, turned to a classic source of inspiration—the princess story—they knew they had to take into account the social changes wrought by the women's movement. But while Disney Studios offered their new princesses as spunky young feminists, their princess stories did not live up to their advertising. The princesses' presentations and the surface levels of their stories paid lip service to feminism and to the new expectations of girls and women, but in reality, their stories are traditionally patriarchal—even more than the source material, which was greatly changed in the films. And upon examination, this second group of Disney princess stories is anti-feminist in some disturbing ways. The characterizations of the princesses are not as revolutionary as touted; men, not women, are the dominant force in the films; the stories follow the standard Disney formula, with romance as their true, underlying plot; and the retrogressive, anti-feminist messages in the films undercut their allegedly feminist heroines.

The Characterization of the Princess

These newer Disney princesses are meant to seem quite different, both from each other and from those that preceded them, although each is a paragon of her own type of beauty. Ariel (*The Little Mermaid*) is a redhead, with long flowing hair, a tilted nose and purplish-blue eyes to match her bikini top. Belle (*Beauty and the Beast*) has light brown hair which she generally wears in a practical ponytail, and light brown or hazel eyes (depending on the scene). Pocahontas is statuesque, with classic Native American cheekbones and strong nose. Mulan is Chinese, with a slighter body frame than the European princesses, shorter than Pocahontas. Breaking away from the stereotypical blond-hair-blue-eyes princess was supposed to mark a breaking away from other traditional aspects of Disney princess stories: the princesses' passivity, the importance of the male rescuer, the traditional "good" girl character. Yet the princesses and their stories, while superficially more adventurous and full of more possibilities than the princesses in older Disney films, are still ultimately reduced to dreamy, romance-obsessed girls who simply travel from father to beloved.

Nor are these princesses, superficial differences of coloring aside, much of a departure physically from the earlier batch. Sharon Lamb and Lyn Mikel Brown declare that "Disney girls are women with Barbie doll bodies. And, like Barbie, one small size fits all....Let's face it, changing skin and hair color and adding some exotic clothing does not a woman of color make" (67). Ariel (*The Little Mermaid*) and Belle (*Beauty and the Beast*) were both based on the same actress; their teenage physiques "moved [Disney princess bodies] from the realms of classic dance aesthetics to popular conventions of cheesecake" (Bell 114). Susan Douglas describes Ariel as having a waist "the diameter of a chive" (296); Roberta Trites decries Ariel as "a doe-eyed heroine with a figure less realistic than a Barbie doll's" (6) and "anorexic" (7). To Dave Kehr, she is simply "a kind of underwater valley girl." Dismissed as "Bambi with curves" by *The Washington Post*'s Desson Howe, Belle's looks are of utmost importance; as one woman in the opening song highlights, "Now it's no wonder that her name means 'beauty'/ Her looks have got no parallel." Owen Glieberman, in his review of *Pocahontas*, describes the princess as "an aerobicized Native American superbabe, with long, muscular brown legs, regal shoulder blades, and silky black hair flowing down to her waist" (Glieberman). Other critics have dubbed Pocahontas "Native American Barbie" (*Newsweek*) and noted her "hourglass figure and Playboy face" (Ebert, "Pocahontas"). Gary Edgerton and Kathy Merlock Jackson suggest that her safe and sexy exoticness (created wholly by Caucasian males) comes from the fact that "Indian features, such as Pocahontas's eyes, skin color, and wardrobe, only provide a kind of Native American styling to an old stereotype." Even critics who hailed the movie admit that "Pocohantas looks like a Native American cast member on 'Baywatch'" (Ringel). Mulan, too, is only slightly differentiated from the average Disney princess. "Apart from her almond eyes, Mulan is a typical Disney heroine when we meet her: winsome, sweetly deferential, and with a lovely singing voice" (Mondello). She has the two classic Disney princess physical features: "the requisite tiny waist" (Ringel) and "the requisite Disney hair—a thick, lustrous mane that, whether loose or pulled into a masculine topknot, makes Mulan an animated approximation of a Tressie doll" (Bernard). She is somewhat slighter than her European and Native American counterparts, and she spends most of the movie disguised as a man, but a nude swimming scene leaves no doubt that her breasts are full and her legs shapely. At 16-18 years old, each of these girls is older than her target audience, and each one wears a body her audience can only aspire to.

As is traditional, each of these heroines introduces herself and her desires via song. Ariel is, ironically, first introduced in her own absence. Her theme, "Part of Your World," is first heard as an instrumental piece while the undersea world is first shown. Later, in what is to be her concert debut, Ariel is introduced by her six older sisters—but when her clamshell is opened (ala Botticelli's Birth of Venus), it is empty. She ultimately sings her song as she sulks: "Betcha on land/they understand/bet they don't reprimand their daughters/Bright young women/sick of swimmin'/Ready to stand." Ariel has a collection of human artifacts, and she wants to live in the world that produces such items. Soon, though, she changes her song to encompass a newer desire: after rescuing Prince Eric from a shipwreck, she declares, "I don't know when, I don't know how/But I know something starting right now/watch and you'll see/Someday I'll be/Part of your world." She no longer simply wants to live on land; she specifically wants to be with Eric. The rest of her story concerns how she wins the prince.

Belle's introductory song is somewhat different, as it is a duet between Belle and the rest of her village. She describes the town as utterly mundane, declaring, "There must be more than this provincial life!" The town sings of her oddness ("Never part of any crowd/'Cause her head's up in some cloud/No denying she's a funny girl, that Belle"), but it seems her reputation for strangeness is based only on her interest in books. This introductory song is also cleverly interspersed with spoken dialogue which gives further insight into Belle's character and the characters of those around her. She tells the bookseller that her favorite book involves "far-off places, daring sword fights, magic spells, a prince in disguise." Her favorite part of the story is "where she meets Prince Charming but she won't discover that it's him till Chapter Three." The town concludes that although she's beautiful, "very different from the rest of us is Belle." It is also during this song that we are introduced to Gaston, the hyper-masculine hunter, a "tall, dark, strong and handsome brute" over whom the rest of the townsgirls swoon. He has long since fixated on Belle; as the most beautiful girl in town, she is "the best" and he's "making plans to woo and marry Belle." Belle and Gaston fall into a duet, with Belle reasserting "There must be more to this provincial life" and Gaston bragging "Just watch, I'm going to make Belle my wife!" Belle, primed for fairy-tale romance by her reading, will not want to settle for an average married life with Gaston, and he, who disapproves of women reading, only wants her for her looks. Her introductory song tells us she wants "more," although that more is not realistic, based as it is on fantasy.

Pocahontas is, like Ariel, introduced in her absence. Her father returns from battle, but she is not there to greet them. An aged wise man excuses her absence: "You know Pocahontas. She has her mother's spirit. She goes where the wind takes her." The camera eventually finds her on a cliff top, hair billowing in the wind. She returns to hear her father's news: he has arranged her marriage to the staid and humorless brave, Kocoum. "He is loyal and strong and will build you a good house with sturdy walls," says her father. When Pocahontas asks "Why can't I choose —?" he cuts her off by telling her that as the chief's daughter, it's time she took her place with her people; as the river does, she must choose the smoothest path. He gives her the necklace her mother wore at their wedding, literally tying conventionality around her neck. Playing on her father's metaphor, Pocahontas then sings her yearning song ("Just around the River Bend") about the price of security. She dreams of something coming for her and wonders, "Can I ignore that sound of distant drumming/ For a handsome sturdy husband/ Who builds handsome sturdy walls/ And never dreams that something might be coming?" She does not understand her dreams, but she is fairly certain she does not want to give them up to marry Kocoum.

Mulan struggles more than the other heroines; she wants to fit in, she wants to meet her family's expectations, but she just cannot. In her attempt and failure to conform, she is truly miserable. Her poignant yearning song discusses her problem and her desire to be able to present her true self to the rest of the world, especially to her family.

> Look at me
> I will never pass for a perfect bride or a perfect daughter
> Can it be I'm not meant to play this part?
> Now I see that if I were truly to be myself
> I would break my family's heart.
>
> Who is that girl I see staring straight back at me?
> Why is my reflection someone I don't know?
> Somehow I cannot hide who I am though I've tried
> When will my reflection show who I am inside?

This is an incredibly poignant song; Mulan wants to fulfill her family's hope of achieving honor through a good marital match, but she has just failed the matchmaker's tests. Unlike the other "feminist" Disney heroines, Mulan is not personally interested in finding a husband (Pocahontas would rather pick than have the husband her father has chosen for her; she does not ask why she can't stay single); for Mulan, getting married is simply the means to an end—maintaining family honor.

Each of these heroines is "not there" in her introductory song. Ariel and Pocahontas are physically missing, Ariel searching for artifacts and dreaming of life on land, and Pocahontas on a cliff, trying to see around the river bend. Belle and Mulan are physically present, but mentally absent; Belle has her nose in a romance while all around people discuss her, and Mulan is masked by a heavy layer of white pancake make up which literally obliterates her face. Mulan is aware that she is foiling her parents' (and society's) expectations, which is why she is sad in addition to yearning. But indeed, none of the girls are living up to social expectations: Ariel has forgotten and forsaken her concert debut; Belle is reading a book and shunning Gaston; Pocahontas is not at home to greet the returning warriors; and Mulan is unable to learn or live by the rules of femininity.

Sean Griffin finds in these wish songs more substance than is to be found in the desires of the first Disney princesses:

> What marks Ashman's songs as different from the "wish songs" that already existed in Disney's canon…is a desire to specifically escape from the dull, conservative parochial values of the everyday. Ariel wants to get away from her father's restrictions on her life; Belle wants to avoid the societal pressure to marry Gaston…unlike the earlier "wish songs" in Disney's catalogue that only desire to find happiness in everyday life, Ashman's "wish songs" specifically want to forsake the "normal" world and find happiness somewhere else. (Griffin 149)

While I disagree that the earlier princesses wanted to be happier in their everyday lives—they each, to my mind, sing of romance taking them away and elevating them, not of being happy scrubbing floors—Griffin has a point, one which is lost in the still-relentlessly heterosexual worlds presented in these newer Disney princess stories.

For Griffin, a queer theorist, these yearning songs are evidence of the gay dilemma, of needing to choose between different worlds: the straight, associated with marriage and family, versus the gay, associated with fantasy, escape, and forbidden romance. While he wrote about Howard Ashman's lyrics for Ariel and Belle, the other girls' songs can be read as even stronger statements, as both Pocahontas and Mulan express discontent and doubts about their future married (heterosexual) roles. Mulan, who sings of hiding her true self from her family, could be any closeted homosexual fearing his or her family's reaction.

Ariel and Belle want husbands; Ariel specifies that she wants Eric, and Belle, who vaguely says she wants "more," clearly wants the Prince Charming she reads about in books. Ariel's desired mate is unsuitable, being of a different species; overcoming that obstacle will become the point of her story. Belle wants more romance than she has been offered, a desire that will prime her to offer herself to the Beast in lieu of her father. Pocahontas and Mulan do not begin their stories dreaming of husbands. Pocahontas does not know exactly who or what she wants, but she is fairly certain she does not want the humorless Kocoum. And Mulan, poor Mulan, just wants to fit in; as that means getting a husband, she is willing to try. Each of these heroines will, of course, find love interests during their stories, but not all of them began with that as a goal.

These Disney princesses' personalities are meant to be as different from their predecessors' as their physical attributes and their desires; they are meant to be spunkier, more feminist, and more strongly individual. And they are, to some slight extent; none of them remains in servitude, passively awaiting a prince. None falls into a coma, magical or otherwise. Unfortunately, that is where the personality differences end; their newer traits are as superficially different as their new physiques. Ariel was hailed as "a fully realized female character who thinks and acts independently, even rebelliously, instead of hanging around passively while the fates decide her destiny" (Ebert "Mermaid"). But she does not think very well, not recognizing bad information when it is given to her (Scuttle the seagull's information about using a fork as a comb at the dinner table leaves Ariel feeling sheepish, yet she continues to accept his information as valid). Her action leads her to impetuously imperil her father and her beloved; she runs straight to the sea-witch, her father's enemy, becoming a pawn in the witch's plan to defeat King Triton. Ariel then spends most of the movie batting her eyes at the prince, unable to speak—literally having given up her voice for the three days she has in which to make Prince Eric kiss her. A voiceless heroine whose goal is a kiss, who ultimately becomes a pawn of evil is not a feminist role model, no matter how "spunky."

Belle, too, is more independent than the earlier Disney princesses. She offers herself to the Beast so her father can go free, and she does teach the Beast table manners. However, she also tolerates emotional abuse from the Beast, who falls into terrible rages and spies on her in his magic mirror; as his prisoner, he declares "If she doesn't eat with me, she doesn't eat at all!" Belle is twice saved by males: the Beast saves her from wolves when she tries to escape his castle, and Chip, the boy-teacup, frees her from her father's basement so she can go to the Beast's castle. She is also the object of the villain; Gaston wants to marry her, and he threateningly snarls "I'll have Belle for my wife, make no mistake about that" before hatching a plan to blackmail her into marriage. The climactic scene shows Gaston and the Beast fighting over Belle, Gaston taunting possessively, "Did you honestly think she'd want you when she had someone like me? ... Belle is mine!" Gaston threatening to "have" Belle is what turns the fight, as the Beast goes on the offensive to defend her.

Pocahontas, too, is not as liberated as she might be. She wants to pick a different husband from the one chosen for her, but she does not suggest remaining single. And she basically falls in love with the first white man she sees: as soon as John Smith is introduced, it is clear that Pocahontas' story is taking a romantic turn. Although the film hints about ecological responsibility and racial harmony, and Pocahontas's yearning song speaks of desire for adventure, none of those inspire any of Pocahontas' actions. She disobeys her father (how spunky!), who decrees no one should go near the whites, but she is clearly doing so for the sake of romance, not for any greater purpose. Her friend (Pocahontas is the only Disney princess to have a human female friend, which is a nice change) lies to Kocoum for her, allowing Pocahontas to sneak off with Smith. Pocahontas is only inspired to talk to her father about preventing war with the whites when Grandmother Willow points out that "Only when the fighting stops can you two be together." Only her love of Smith inspires her to defy her father and save Smith's life. Every action Pocahontas takes that can be described as feisty in any way is motivated by her romantic relationship.

Mulan is the most feminist of the princesses, but as will be discussed in the final section, the entire movie is so rife with anti-female sentiment, Mulan the character does not make the impact she might otherwise make. She wants to be herself, but she is not a traditional girl; she tries to fit society's mold, but she is unsuccessful. She does try, however, to be as submissive as possible, allowing herself to be dolled up for the matchmaker and going as far as cribbing cheat notes on her arm. Her pre-matchmaker prayer is "Help me not uproot my family tree/Keep my father standing tall;" she is hiding her true self for her father's sake (the importance of the father in these stories will be discussed later). When she boldly, even admirably, speaks out against her father being drafted, her father is dishonored and Mulan is shamed. Mulan is smart; her ideas save the day not once but twice. But everything she does is for the men in the film: her father, her beloved Shang, and the Emperor.

The Dominant Male

Although the title character, the main protagonist, of each film is female[1], these new films are all framed by men, as were the first wave of Disney films. Each film opens on a man or men, the love interest in three instances and the secondary father figure in the fourth. Final or penultimate scenes all focus on males as well: the love interest and, interestingly, the princesses' fathers and mentors. The romance is not only primary to the plot, as will be discussed later; it has clear patriarchal approval.

The Little Mermaid initially focuses on Prince Eric's ship, showing Ariel's love interest happily active in his element before the 'camera' heads underwater towards (but not all the way to) Ariel. Eric is shown as a whole person, with colleagues and friends, a dog, a hobby in addition to being a prince. The last scene in *The Little Mermaid* shows Ariel on her wedding ship, bidding her father farewell (the final spoken words of the film are "I love you, Daddy"). She then links arms with Prince Eric, and there is a distant shot of the two waving as their ship sails away; this image is framed by the much closer (and therefore larger) figures of King Triton and Sebastian the crab as they nod and smile at each other. Triton casts a rainbow over the proceedings, and the freeze-frame final shot is a close-up of Eric and Ariel in a deep kiss.

Beauty and the Beast begins with a striking stained-glass telling of the Beast's back-story, the only portion of the film given the storytelling weight of a narrator. It is the Beast whose story begins with "once upon a time," and thus it is the Beast's story which is given predominance over all of the action to come in Belle's village. *Beauty and the Beast* ends with a scene of the two lovers dancing in the ballroom while Belle's father and the Beast's staff look on sentimentally. To highlight the significance of the scene and the satisfactory conclusion of the romance, the comic sidekick teacup asks his teapot mother (both now restored to human form), "Are they going to live happily ever after, mama?" Her response is "Of course, my dear. Of course." The camera draws back to show the lovers dancing again, and then changes to a stained-glass style still shot, harkening to the Beast's back-story at the start of the film.

The first scene in *Pocahontas* introduces the male settlers (who sing a rousing song justifying leaving England "for glory, God and gold") generally and the dashing Captain John Smith (who is "not about to let you boys have all the fun [of fighting Indians]") specifically. The men talk about Smith before he even appears, building excitement for his appearance. Women embrace their men in farewell, and the Englishmen set sail. The next scene is also about men, and an echo of the first; the Algonquin braves return home, and their women run to embrace them in welcome. *Pocahontas'* ending is somewhat unusual, as Pocahontas and John Smith are not going to be together physically; Smith is returning to England so his bullet wound can be tended properly, and Pocahontas, for all her previous talk of adventure and love, has decided that her people need her too much to leave. Smith, caressing Pocahontas' face, asks her to come with him. She tearfully declines. He declares that he will stay with her, then. She tells him he has to go back (having learned as she approached him that his only chance of survival is to return to England). "But I can't leave you," he says. "You never will. No matter what happens, I'll always be with you. Forever." Her romantic words echo an earlier conversation, in which Smith, awaiting execution, tells Pocahontas "You never will [leave me]. I'll always be with you. Forever." Thus sentimentally pledged, they kiss; the music swells; and the audience would be forgiven for forgetting the very final scene, in which Pocahontas runs from her father to the cliff top from which she can see Smith's ship sail away. There is a reprise of the song she sang to him earlier in the film, and magic leaves swirl from her down to Smith, suggesting that in some more mystical way the two will always be together. The freeze-frame is shot from behind her as she watches his ship; we watch her watching him, an indication of his importance.

The story of *Mulan*, too, begins with men; the Huns attack China, and when the news reaches the Emperor he sends for conscripts, explaining that "one man may be the difference between victory and defeat." Two men are thus responsible for Mulan's story: the leader of the Huns and the Emperor of China. There is no final kiss between Mulan and Shang, unique among Disney princess stories, but the film's two father figures have a hand in the romance, one encouraging the match and one approving it. The Emperor, watching Mulan ride off, urges Shang to go after her, first with the movie's tagline: "the flower that blooms in adversity is the most rare and beautiful of them all." When Shang does not understand, the Emperor clarifies by telling him, pointedly, "You don't meet a girl like that every dynasty." The final scene shows Mulan joyfully reunited with her father as Shang approaches, stammering and awkward. After exchanging a knowing look with her father, Mulan eases Shang's discomfort by inviting him to dinner. Her comic sidekick Grandmother chimes in, asking "Would you like to stay forever?"

Shang accepts Mulan's invitation, and the scene cuts to a different viewpoint; First Ancestor is watching Mulan's father coming to stand next to Shang, with Mulan's mother and Grandmother coming to encircle him from behind. Shang, the love interest, is thus fully embraced by Mulan's family and is the focal point of the scene. As stated above, there is no kiss between the lovers; Mulan instead thanks and kisses Mushu, her comic miniature dragon sidekick (whose story this was as much as hers; he helps her as a means of raising his status among her ancestors). Romantic kiss aside, males have thus framed Mulan's story as much as the others, soldiers and Emperor in the beginning and Fa Zhou (Mulan's father), Shang and Mushu in the end.

As the framing indicates, the men are extremely important in these princess stories. As in the first wave of Disney princess films (and most other animated Disney films), biological mothers and positive mother figures are almost entirely absent. While fairy tales often have orphaned or runaway protagonists to facilitate the plot and the protagonist's development, these films seem to go out of their way to obliterate any adult female role models and to venerate the father and/or his surrogates.

King Triton, Ariel's father, is first mentioned by the sailors on Eric's ship in the opening scene. A wordless version of Ariel's theme accompanies the camera as it heads underwater, but the first words spoken in mer society are of King Triton. His arrival is announced with great fanfare, and he arrives in his royal chariot, muscles rippling, hair billowing, trident blazing. The next focus of attention is "Horatio Felonious Ignacious Crustaceous Sebastian," the court composer crab who will become Ariel's protector and sidekick, deputized by Triton to look after her during her adventures on land. During the course of the film, Sebastian will get the most rousing, memorable songs ("Under the Sea" and "Kiss the Girl") and the funniest subplot (in which he foils Chef Louie). He counsels Ariel and encourages Eric to bring their bourgeoning romance to fruition with a kiss. King Triton is ultimately responsible for Ariel and Eric's marriage, as he transforms her into a human so the two can marry.

Belle, in *Beauty and the Beast*, lives with her befuddled father Maurice, a wacky, comic-relief inventor of zany machines. Her mother is neither present nor mentioned; very few females are present at all. Belle's father is thrice the hapless source of action in the film. He first needs to be rescued when the Beast imprisons him. Belle offers herself as prisoner in his stead. In a later scene, Belle uses a magic mirror and sees her father sick and helpless in the woods; she leaves the Beast, with whom she has been very happy, to save him. Finally, Gaston and the asylum-keeper haul Maurice away; Belle is forced to use the magic mirror to prove the existence of the Beast, thus precipitating the final battle. Gaston also knew the hold Belle's father held on her; he planned to use her love of him and her desire to save him as a means of forcing Belle into marriage.

Pocahontas' father, Powhatan, is somewhat less central to her story. It is through his question ("Where is my daughter?") that we learn of Pocahontas, and our knowledge of her is expressed through their relationship. He does not mention her name; we learn that from the wise man. Powhatan addresses her in the possessive as well: "My daughter." He is her only link to her mother; he gives Pocahontas her mother's wedding necklace as a tangible sign not of her mother, but of the marriage he has agreed to on her behalf. Interestingly, at the end of the movie, Pocahontas does not go away with Smith—she stays with her people, as signified by her father's grasp on her shoulders. Because her fiancé has been killed, and because she has pledged her heart to Smith, it seems Pocahontas is free to remain with her father; she will not need to accommodate the restrictions and expectations of a wife, so she can remain a daughter.

The importance of the father in *Mulan* cannot be overstated. Mulan, as mentioned earlier, is concerned with impressing the matchmaker for her father's sake, willing to consign herself to unhappy conformity to make him proud. She runs off to join the army in his place, wearing his armor, risking her life to save his. After Mulan is revealed to be female, her desire to save her father becomes briefly a commonality between her and Shang (whose father has just been killed) and he commutes her death sentence in part because of this. As she turns to go home in disgrace, Mulan sighs, "I'll have to face my father sooner or later." After the final grand battle, Mulan returns home to her father. In a truly touching scene, Mulan presents Fa Zhou with the Emperor's crest and the enemy's sword. Fa Zhou throws these tokens to the side and embraces Mulan, saying, "The greatest gift and honor is having you for a daughter. I've missed you so." Mulan's mother and grandmother watch from a distance; the mother sighs and the grandmother makes a quip. The only familial relationship of any importance is between Mulan and her father.

The fathers are not the only important males, of course; the love interests are also important, perhaps more so as the objects of the girls' desires. Although the girls are the title characters—and although they are much more active than the earlier wave of Disney princess stories—the girls do not ultimately get to save themselves. It is always the love interest who wins the final battle. Prince Eric steers a shipmast into the belly of the giant, trident-wielding Ursula, killing her and saving the seas from her wrath and evil power (power she would not have won had Ariel not stupidly become a pawn in her struggle against Triton). The Beast saves Belle from Gaston, who has been presented as the only alternative mate in the film. The two are clearly fighting for the right to "have" Belle, and the Beast ultimately wins this fight—a fight which would never have begun had Belle not shown the villagers the Beast in the magic mirror (she was trying to save her father, true, but this demonstration of Maurice's veracity ended up with Belle and Maurice locked in the basement and the Beast battling for his life and Belle's love). Governor Ratcliffe, *Pocahontas'* tepid villain, attempts to shoot Powhatan. Smith saves the chief by jumping in front of Powhatan and taking the bullet for him. Since the story is historically inaccurate anyway, why not show Pocahontas saving her father? In the first phase of the final battle, Mulan conceives of the plan to save the Emperor, but it is Shang who most successfully implements it. In the final phase, Mulan has the Huns' leader on a rooftop, but it is Mushu, her male protector-dragon, who kills him with a rocket. Males have the final heroic word in these films, no matter that the stories are supposed to belong to the heroines.

Men are so dominant that women, beyond the titular princesses, are hard to find in these films; those rare women who are included undermine the notion of feminism. Ariel's sisters are introduced in the beginning of *The Little Mermaid*, but their parts are so minimal that Ariel essentially functions as an only child. Her friends are all male: Sebastian, Flounder, and Scuttle. There are servants at Prince Eric's castle, one plump, motherly one who cries at the wedding and two ugly, gossiping laundresses, neither of whom interacts with Ariel. And of course there's Ursula, the evil, plotting half-witch, half-octopus with her lust for power and her overripe sexuality. This linking of female sexuality and evil has been discussed in Chapter 2; with the exception of her fleshy corpulence, Ursula is very much in the campy/scary mold of Maleficent.

Although there was a sea-witch in Hans Christian Anderson's original version of the fairy tale, she remains nameless and essentially blameless. She explains the natural laws of magic; she does not make the rules for her own advancement. She is not the caricature of overblown voluptuousness that is Ursula, and she does not seek to rule the sea. Ursula is all that is to be feared of female sexuality and power; she is ravenous, rapacious, and undulatingly repulsive. Disguised as Vanessa, she is a sultry siren who captivates Eric, trapping him with her voice (Ariel's stolen voice) and her magically seductive self. This characterization of the sea-witch accomplishes three things: she illustrates how foolishly unthinking and selfish Ariel is in eschewing her father's wishes and approaching her for help; she sets up a sexual competition between voiceless good-girl Ariel and commanding "Vanessa" for Eric; and she gives Eric a way to heroically earn Triton's acceptance and his daughter.

Beauty and the Beast also has few other women. There is the beautiful yet vindictive sorceress of the Beast's back-story, depicted solely in static, stained-glass shots; she has no action in the main body of the film. There is the trio of buxom blond barmaids in Belle's village, foolishly swooning after the hyper-masculine Gaston. And there are the Beast's female servants, transformed into a motherly teapot (essentially a talking head), a wacky wardrobe, and a sexy French feather duster. The teapot and the wardrobe assure Belle that the beast is not "so bad," and are thus complicit in her emotional abuse and in forcing her into the role of teacher/civilizer. Disney's Belle has no sisters, unlike in the original story, in which she is the stand out sister who asks for a rose, a nonmaterialistic souvenir from her travelling father (in Disney's characterization of Belle, she wants "more" and considers the villagers her inferiors).

Pocahontas is unusual; she has a girlfriend who is willing to lie (once) about Pocahontas' whereabouts when she's with Smith. Of course, this suggests that men cannot trust a woman (because she will lie to them) and that women also cannot trust another woman (because sometimes she'll tattle). She also has Grandmother Willow, a magic tree who encourages Pocahontas to be with Smith, literally pushing them together with her branches. She is one of the older women characters whose sexuality is used as comic relief. When Pocahontas brings Smith to meet Grandmother Willow, she mystically, sagaciously determines, "He has a good soul." Then she salaciously adds, "And he's handsome, too." In the absence of an evil woman such as Ursula, mildly lascivious sexual comments such as these are left to "inappropriately" old women. Their sexuality is used as comic relief (unlike the evil women, whose sexuality is used threateningly).

Most of the females in *Mulan* simply serve to humiliate the heroine. When Mulan goes to the matchmaker, she is disgraced by her inability to keep in step with the other girls, "each a perfect porcelain doll." The matchmaker herself is judgmental and harsh, criticizing Mulan first for her appearance ("too skinny...not good for bearing sons") and then for her demeanor. Yet the depiction of the matchmaker is also humiliating. She is heavy-set, and visual jokes are made about her breasts (a cricket jumps into her cleavage) and her rear (she sits on a brazier). In her final shot, she appears to be a man in drag: she wears a mustache and goatee of smudged ink, her makeup has run down her face, and her angry voice is loud and deep.

Two of the women in the film are members of Mulan's family, although their parts are fairly small. Unlike most Disney princesses, Mulan has a living mother, but her mother remains practically silent in those few scenes in which she appears; even when she and Mulan's father speak, we are only shown this interaction from a distance and cannot hear what is said. Mulan's mother exists largely as a foil to Mulan's grandmother, a more exaggerated, more salacious version of *Pocahontas'* Grandmother Willow. She looks remarkably like the cartoon character Mr. Magoo; her image signifies her status as a comic-relief character, even if her sexual remarks are too mature for her target audience. Upon Mulan's triumphant return, Grandmother Fa snorts, "Great. She brings home a sword. If you ask me, she should've brought home a man." When Shang appears and asks for Mulan, Grandmother Fa cries, "Whoo! Sign me up for the next war!" As mentioned earlier, Grandmother Fa also, to Mulan's embarrassment, invites Shang "to stay forever." Her interest in sex and men is played purely for laughs, suggesting that only the young should be interested in such matters.

Most Disney protagonists are motherless, and these films continue that tradition as well. The dominant role of the men and the absence of good women seriously undercut the suggestion that these films are more feminist than previous Disney stories.

Adhering To the Formula

In her examination of women in Disney animation, Amy Davis writes that "the category of 'princess' is fairly easy to define: a princess is a woman who is the daughter of a ruler or the wife of a prince" (176). And yet, as pertains to Disney princesses, Davis' definition is lacking. I include in my discussion of this group of Disney princess stories the story of one girl who is, technically, not a princess: Mulan, who fits neither of Davis' requirements. The first reason I consider Mulan a princess lies in Disney Corporation marketing. Mulan is marketed as a Disney Princess, a member of the "giant sorority aimed at little girls....a superbrand, a meta-brand which would transform a collection of rather antiquated fairy stories into a juggernaut of commerce" (Millard). As such, Mulan and her products are supposed to embody "the wonderfulness of being a princess" (Millard). Disney certainly does not let Mulan's technical lack of royal lineage remove her from the realm of princesses.

It can also be argued that the Emperor elevates Mulan's status to that of a princess. He admires and honors her, bowing to her and causing the entire Imperial city to bow in kind. He is also the mentor of Mulan's love interest, Shang; he stands in lieu of Shang's deceased father in encouraging Shang to pursue a romantic relationship with Mulan. By acting as surrogate father figure to Mulan's future husband, the Emperor becomes a sort of spiritual father-in-law to Mulan.

Most important in considering *Mulan* as a princess story, however, is the fact that the film follows the Disney formula for such stories. This formula, no matter how superficially updated for a modern, more-feminist audience, promotes archaic gender roles and allows no real power to the female. According to Jack Zipes,

> From *Snow White and the Seven Dwarfs* up through *Beauty and the Beast*, the writers and directors in Disney's studio have operated with a formula: there is an opening song that announces the yearning of a heroine; the young woman, always virginal and sweet, is victimized and is captured or imprisoned by evil forces; at the same time comical animals…provide comic relief and try to assist the persecuted heroine; at one point a male hero is introduced along with a romantic song or two; and because the girl cannot save herself, the hero is called on to overcome sinister forces represented by a witch, scheming minister, or dumb brute. ("Art of Subversion" 209)

I would argue that not only is this absolutely the formula used in *The Little Mermaid* and *Beauty and the Beast*; the two later films, *Pocahontas* and *Mulan*, are also princess stories in that they adhere to the formula. As has already been discussed, Ariel and Belle are introduced through their yearning songs. Ariel is victimized by Ursula, and Belle is imprisoned and abused by both the Beast and Gaston. Each girl has comic-relief assistants: Ariel has Sebastian and Flounder, and Belle has the household objects (and her horse, although their conversations are one-sided). The male hero/love interest is introduced with song; Ariel sings to Eric, vowing to be with him, while Belle and the Beast have a duet of their internal monologues (they think-sing to themselves about the other, and their thoughts turn into a mental duet). Eventually, of course, the male hero rescues each girl: Eric kills Ursula, and the Beast metaphorically kills his internal Beast before literally leading Gaston to his death.

The filmmakers strayed from a strict interpretation of the formula as the decade progressed, however. Pocahontas has a yearning song, of course, and she has little animal friends who disrupt the tone of the piece. But her enemy is no stock-character villain. Pocahontas is imprisoned by tradition and by the racial strife around her; her father expects her to marry Kocoum and to shun the white men. The sinister forces in Pocahontas are represented on both sides of the racial divide by Kocoum, Pocahontas' fiancé, and by Governor Ratcliffe, both of whom are opposed to the races mingling. Smith defeats both villains. He physically overpowers Kocoum, leading to the latter's death, and he morally defeats Ratcliffe by taking the bullet Ratcliffe intended for Powhatan. Pocahontas is ineffectual in the first case, helplessly trying to separate the wrestling men. In the second case, Smith's embrace has so overwhelmed her that she is blissfully unaware of Ratcliffe and his gun. Smith, of course, can cuddle and be alert to danger simultaneously; as he blocks the bullet meant for Powhatan, the other Englishmen turn against Ratcliffe, giving Smith the final victory.

Mulan similarly follows the Disney princess story formula; her yearning song is intact, and her comic-relief animals threaten to hijack the entire film (*Mulan* is the story of Mushu's redemption as much as Mulan's adventure). Mulan's adversary is similar to Pocahontas' in that she faces the largely amorphous enemy of social expectations, those of rigid gender roles, personified by bit-part villains. Her first enemy is the matchmaker, and it appears at first that the matchmaker has won. "You are a disgrace!" she screams. "You may look like a bride, but you will never bring your family honor!" Mulan slinks away, ashamed, and had she not escaped the matchmaker's sphere, she would not have brought her family honor. Mulan's other foe is Chi Fu, the Emperor's counsel, who reports on the status of Shang's training camp. When Mulan's true identity is revealed, Chi Fu, appalled, urges Shang to kill her: "A woman! Treacherous snake! High treason! Ultimate dishonor!" At the end of the film, Chi Fu descends upon Mulan; Shang shields her. "Stand aside! That creature's not worth protecting!" declares Chi Fu. "She's a hero," responds Shang. "'Tis a woman. She'll never be worth anything," Chi Fu states. Mulan is not even on screen as Shang grabs Chi Fu by the collar, preparing to physically defend Mulan's honor. Chi Fu is defeated when the Emperor offers Mulan Chi Fu's seat on his counsel; Mulan declines, so presumably Chi Fu keeps his job, but the blow has been dealt—by the Emperor, not by Mulan herself. Similarly, it is Shang who defeats the matchmaker for Mulan, when he follows her home. Their presumed eventual marriage will make Mulan the bride that the matchmaker declared she would never be, and it will bring the proper, feminine sort of honor to the family. Again, this is achieved through a male; had Shang not come to Mulan's house, they would have had no such honor-bearing relationship. The ways these males defeated the gender expectations trapping Mulan are less showy than Eric plowing a mast into Ursula, but they have rescued Mulan just the same.

The Precedence of Romance

Although the press for these newer Disney princess stories would have the audience believe otherwise, these films are almost as much about romance as were their predecessors. This is part of their appeal, of course. As Dave Kehr wrote:

> The hidden subject of 'The Little Mermaid' is a young woman's discovery of her sexuality, and the feelings of guilt and regret (she must now leave her beloved Daddy) that it produces. All of the great Disney films have a similar subtext, and it is their way of drawing on universal growing pains (and helping to imaginatively resolve them) that gives them their enduring, worldwide appeal.

Each of these princess stories has the same plot: the girls move from their fathers to their beloveds. But because the audience has been promised something new in and for these feistier heroines, this plot of universal romance feels like a betrayal, a not-so-hidden message of what girls should really find relevant. Sharon Lamb and Lyn Mikel Brown highlight the problem:

> The problem is so much of the courage and feistiness is either in pursuit of romance or later put aside for it. Beauty endures horrific abuse to change her man; Ariel gives up her voice for her man; Pocahontas's goal is saving her man as much as preserving her homeland; Mulan's amazing feats dissolve in the presence of romance. This feels like a bait and switch. Draw a girl in with promises of something different and then bring in the same old thing through the back door. (69)

Although the new princess stories feature allegedly liberated girls who act independently and know their own minds, their stories boil down to romances. While these princesses each have adventures, at some point the girls' focuses change from independence to romance. *The Little Mermaid* and *Beauty and the Beast* are both based on traditional fairy-tales, so no matter how liberated their heroines are purported to be, the romantic elements are expected. *Pocahontas* and *Mulan*, however, contained no romance prior to their Disneyfication.

While Ariel's story begins with a yearning to live on land, to break free from the mandates of her father, she very quickly turns her desire toward one man. She saves Eric's life and becomes a stereotypically besotted teenaged girl, spending hours grooming and humming and drifting through life. Ariel's obsession with Eric allows Ursula to manipulate her (and briefly allows Ursula to take Triton's place as ruler). Ariel spends her time on land smiling eagerly and batting her eyes at Eric, awaiting his kiss. Sebastian, the crab, preps her: "Now we got to make a plan to get that boy to kiss you. Tomorrow when he takes you for that ride, you gotta look your best. You gotta bat your eyes …. You gotta pucker up your lips..." While the two are out in a boat, Sebastian leads the lakeshore denizens in a song, "Kiss the Girl." The penultimate showdown of the story is between Ariel and Ursula, disguised as the sultry Vanessa—an apparent love triangle. Ultimately, Ariel loses her bet with Ursula; Eric kisses her, but the deadline has passed. Ursula agrees to take Triton instead (her plan all along) and for a frightening few minutes Ursula reigns supreme; she separates and prepares to kill the lovers, cackling, "So much for true love!" After Ursula's demise, Ariel sits on a rock near the shore, gazing longingly at Eric's weary body. Triton sees that Ariel really loves Eric, and he remarks with a sigh, "Then I guess there's just one problem left....How much I'm going to miss her." Triton transforms Ariel into a human, giving her to Eric, and blesses their wedding and their final, on-screen kiss with a rainbow. Ariel has literally transformed from a girl in her father's world to a girl in her husband's world, and the romance was the cause of all the action.

That Ariel is chosen as Eric's bride, that she wins her man, is a major change from the original story, and not necessarily a positive one. Her happy ending undercuts one of the messages feminists read in the original, which is that self-mutilation should not be attempted for the purposes of getting a man. By taking away Ariel's voice yet allowing her to win the prince, the film encourages girls not to speak. In fact, Ursula, the sea-witch, specifically tells Ariel that men don't like talkative women; the fact that Ariel cannot speak yet wins Eric anyway supports this notion and undercuts Ariel's strength. She is left yearning for a kiss, unable even to tell her prince her name. Moreover, in the real world, this is not much of a happy ending. As Diane Steinle writes:

> I don't think the Disney folks have any business making a modern-day feature that concludes with the 16-year-old heroine getting married. That's a happy ending? It is too bad that Disney today either doesn't understand that impact or doesn't care enough to make movies devoid of potentially damaging messages, such as the romanticizing of teen-age marriage. (2)

A spunky, rebellious girl's goal and ultimate reward should not be marriage at 16.

Romance is Belle's great interest. Portrayed as an intellectual, the only reading material the audience sees her with is fairy-tale romances; she is thus primed to fall into a fairy-tale romance herself. As told in the Beast's backstory, he and his domestics will only be returned to human form if the Beast can love someone and have her love him in return. The raison d'etre of his entire household, therefore, is to promote romance, for by doing so they save themselves; this is a change from the original. The terms of the Beast's redemption have also been changed for the Disney version. In the source material, by the time Beauty meets the Beast he has long since become kind and gentle; he has lived as a Beast long enough to have learned his lesson. Beauty must get beyond her own prejudices to appreciate him for who he is underneath his hideous exterior. In the Disney version, Belle spends a great deal of time civilizing and gentling the Beast. The scenes in which Belle and the Beast become "friends" involve Belle nurturing the Beast as she might have nurtured a child: tending his wounds, teaching him table manners, showing him how to be kind to animals. She even reads to him (and teaches him to read); the reading material is *Romeo and Juliet*, reinforcing her habit of reading romances. She also puts up with his emotional abuse during this process. Jane Yolen and Heidi E.Y.Stemple believe that this story "teaches our daughters exactly how to become battered wives. Its message…states clearly that no matter how beastly and cruel the monster you live with is, somewhere there is a prince hidden, and that if you just love him enough during his 'nice' periods, that prince will appear" (247). The film's emphasis on teaching the Beast, according to Susan Jeffords, makes it clear that "such ugly and repulsive men are not really to be shunned; they're to be nurtured until their 'true' goodness arises" (171). If men are beastly after the age 21, the age by which the Beast had to learn his lesson or remain unchanged forever, Jeffords says they must be excused because they simply were not taught in time.

The addition of the character of Gaston reduces Belle to a romantic commodity to be had, to be fought over, and highlights the romantic tension of the story. Had Gaston not been motivated by his desire to marry Belle, none of his boorishness would have mattered; he would have had no excuse to threaten Maurice, and he would not have gone after the Beast (no matter the rationale he uses to whip the villagers into a killing frenzy, it's the thought of the Beast having Belle that drives him in the final scene; he jealously observes to Belle, "It sounds like you have feelings for this monster."). Gaston functions as a contrast to the raging, uncivilized Beast:

> Only the purely and self-consciously self-centered Gaston could possibly make the petulant and childish Beast appear to be an appealing choice. Once the character of the dignified and worldly Beast was abandoned in favor of Disney's spoiled brat, Belle's choice to love the Beast could only have been made reasonable and effective by visualizing a worse man she could have chosen. (Jeffords 170)

Furthermore, by giving Belle no reasonable man to love, the film suggests that women have to settle: Gaston or the Beast? Or perhaps the ineffectual Maurice, Belle's father? Belle literally travels from her father's home to the Beast's twice in the film—once to save her father and once to save the Beast. She remains in the Beast's home, of course, because that is how she becomes a princess and how their romance is fulfilled.

The romance in *Pocahontas* was wholly invented by Disney; Pocahontas was a child of 11 and Smith a man of 28 when they first met in real life, but obviously those ages would not support the required romance of a Disney princess story. (One might think, however, that an 11-year-old heroine who lived a life similar to the historical Pocahontas' life would make a fascinating movie for girls in the Disney princess story target age range.) Although Amy Davis writes that Pocahontas "is motivated in her actions not so much by romantic love as she is by the greater wisdom which she possesses" (183), I disagree. Romance is so central to this story as presented that without it, there would be no story. Burgeoning romance is the magic that allows Pocahontas and Smith to communicate with each other; Grandmother Willow tells Pocahontas to "listen with your heart, and you will understand." Unlike *The Little Mermaid* and *Beauty and the Beast*, which save the romantic kiss for the climactic moment, Pocahontas and Smith almost-kiss and then actually kiss multiple times through the film. There are the pre-kiss preliminaries of holding hands and gazing into the other's eyes and leaning into each other after their soaring/ dancing/ running/ swimming montage (to "Paint with All the Colors of the Wind"), but they are interrupted by drums (which "mean trouble"). Pocahontas tears herself away, but it becomes clear that the racial war between the Europeans and the Native Americans is the true enemy of romance.

The two later kiss under Grandmother Willow's auspices; this kiss, seen by the sexually jealous Kocoum, causes him to attack Smith and subsequently be shot dead by another Englishman. Pocahontas disobeys her father when she sneaks off to see Smith, and Powhatan rightly lays the blame of Kocoum's death on Pocahontas. Pocahontas was aware of her responsibility, but she was not concerned with the death of her fiancé, only with the ramifications for her burgeoning romance: "All this happened because of me. And now I'll never see John Smith again." She calls on all the spirits around her for help in getting to her village in time to stop Smith's execution; she sings, "Is the death of all I love carried in the drumming of war?" but it is clear that "all I love" means Smith, as she races to stop his execution. "This is the path I choose, father; what will yours be?" is an unclear question, 'this' has a vague antecedent. Her path could be the path of peace between the races, or it could simply mean she chooses to love Smith. Within her story, the two are intertwined, but it is clear that peace is simply the means to the end of the lovers being together. Pocahontas caresses Smith's face while he is bound; she leaps into his arms as soon as he is freed. Even though the two of them are physically parting at the end, it is clear that they will love each other forever; although Pocahontas stays with her father, her heart is with Smith. Amy Aidman writes the lovers' separation "can be viewed on the one hand as a subtext that a strong woman cannot have it all, and on the other hand as Disney's inability to imagine sanctioning an interracial relationship in one of its animated films" (138). While both of these subtexts are present, also present is the distinct sense that Smith was Pocahontas' one true love, and that she will remain faithful to him.

At the start of Mulan's story, she is concerned about being an acceptable bride, but romance is far from her mind. Her marriage is to be arranged to bring honor to her family, not with an eye to love. Her failure at the matchmaker's has been discussed previously, but that does not mean that there is no romance in her story. Disguised as a man to join the army, Mulan becomes romantically interested in her commanding officer from her first morning at camp. In peril of her life and of her family's honor, struggling to pass as a man in a male culture that is totally alien to her, Mulan still takes time to notice Shang's bare chest. It becomes even more evident that Mulan is interested in Shang when she tries to comfort him after Chi Fu derides his leadership abilities and scoffs at his men. Mushu points out her interest, and though she denies it, the audience is shown her secret little smile as she walks away. Later, as Mulan loses consciousness from blood loss, her last sights are Shang's face and then his lips, a romantic marker. This romantic interest takes away from Mulan's triumph at the end; she has defeated the Huns, saved the Emperor, and been publically honored for her accomplishments. But when Shang can only stammer out, "Um. You—you fight good," Mulan walks away disappointed. He did not declare his love for her, and so she—and the audience—feels that the story is incomplete. Only when Shang follows Mulan to her home and accepts her invitation to dinner is the ending happy; the ancestors, who upon Mulan's victorious arrival have remained silent and glum, burst into a celebration as Shang and Mulan enter the house together. The fulfillment of their romance is the reason to celebrate.

Anti-Female Witticisms

Although it can be argued that these princesses are an improvement over the first group of Disney princesses, their films do not fully embrace female strength and independence. Many of the princess stories rely on witty remarks to undercut women. While these often come from the mouths of evil or comic characters, and thus are meant to appear to be jokes or evidence of wrongheadedness, one is reminded of the saying "many a truth is said in jest." One or two comments might be ignored, but taken as a whole, or on repeated viewing, they convey damaging, anti-female messages to their audience of little girls.

Ursula is the main source of anti-female remarks in *The Little Mermaid*. Not only is she a portrait of frightening femininity, she encourages Ariel to "get her man" in outdated, retrogressive ways. She sings a campy, wicked song to Ariel, assuring her that men prefer silent girls:

> The men up there don't like a lot of blather,
> They think a girl who gossips is a bore.
> Yes, on land it's much preferred for ladies not to say a word—
> And after all, dear, what is idle prattle for!
> Come on, they're not all that impressed with conversation—
> True gentlemen avoid it when they can.
> But they dote and swoon and fawn on a lady that's withdrawn—
> It's she who holds her tongue who gets her man.

Ursula assures Ariel that "your looks—your pretty face" will be enough to make Eric fall in love with her. "And don't forget the importance of...body language!" The fact that Ursula is apparently correct—Ariel does make Eric fall in love with her with no spoken communication—further validates Ursula's advice. Thus although Ursula is evil, and theoretically not to be trusted, her advice seems compelling and true. And if it works within the world of the princess story, is there a logical reason why holding one's tongue would not get a girl her man in the real world?

Belle's characterization as a misfit because she reads is a very negative message. Her eccentricity is pointed out with "cuckoo" finger swirls next to a villager's head, and Gaston opines that "It's not right for a girl to read. Pretty soon she starts getting ideas, and thinking..." These statements are meant to be funny, and they are, but that does not render them harmless. As the Beast looks for ways to impress Belle (forgetting the most important one, of controlling his temper), Lumiere, his oversexed French candlestick suggest, "There's the usual. Flowers, chocolates. Promises you don't intend to keep." Again, this is funny. But it makes unsavory elements in gender relations acceptable.

In no film more than *Mulan* are the witticisms and the heroine so much at odds. Mulan the heroine is "clever, generous, passionate and determined. But she's a good deal more than that; she's also vulnerable and funny, showing flashes of irony and slapstick humor. She's the best animated heroine in Disney's history not because she's the most politically proper but because she's the most fully imagined" (Durbin). Critics and academics agree: Roger Ebert writes "The message here is standard feminist empowerment: Defy the matchmaker, dress as a boy, and choose your own career" ("Mulan"), and Andrea Quong believes that "'Mulan' has a decent, clear message—100 percent unadulterated feminism." If the character of Mulan existed in a vacuum, these statements might be true. As it is, however, the feminism of the heroine is thoroughly undermined by the sexist world in which she lives. The entire film is about gender roles and fitting in, a huge change from the film's source material, *Ode to Mulan*; the poem ends with an image of gender-indistinguishable male and female hares.

Mulan's father undoubtedly loves Mulan, and in his reassuring conversation with her we are meant to understand that this love is unconditional, accepting of her limitations. But when left alone he clearly demonstrates what is important to him: he prays that Mulan will impress the matchmaker. Family honor is essential to him, and the way he sees Mulan bringing honor is through becoming a bride. He also chastises her for speaking out of turn, telling her she dishonors him and that it is time she learned her place.

As Mulan is prepared for the matchmaker, her mother, grandmother and dressers sing "Honor to Us All," [a catchy song about the only way a girl can bring honor to her family: by being attractive and catching a good husband] A girl must be "primped and polished" in order catch a man. Additionally, she needs "good fortune, a great hairdo…good breeding and a tiny waist." The women grooming Mulan also explain "men want girls with good taste. Calm. Obedient. Who work fast-paced." The sort of girl being described serves not just her husband, but her emperor; the men "serve by bearing arms, a girl by bearing sons." A rhetorical question in the final verse sums up the girl's position as a marriage commodity: "How could any fellow say 'no sale?'" As clever as this song is, it describes archaic gender roles and makes them upbeat and exciting.

"I'll Make a Man Out of You," the song sung by Shang during a rousing training sequence, suggests that to succeed one needs to be a man. One of the first lines is the scornful "Did they send me daughters when I asked for sons?" At the end of the song, Mulan will prove that a girl's brains can succeed where even the brawniest man fails, but the tone of the piece is derogatory; only after Shang tries to send her home in disgrace ("How could I make a man out of you?") does she triumph. There is ironic humor in this line, because of course he cannot make a man out of her; nothing could. But every insult in the movie has to do with being a girl; this song just provides the first instance.

Mushu mocks Mulan's "stupid girlie habits" when she wants to bathe. Yao, one of her soldier friends, plays king of the rock while swimming, boasting, insulting his friends by declaring "there's nothin' you girls can do about it." Another soldier-friend tells Mulan they have to fight, and exhorts her "Come on, don't be such a girl!" Again, the irony that Mulan herself is being addressed this way does not mitigate the fact that her gender, an integral part of her identity and that of much of her audience, is used as an insult. Chi Fu angrily denies squealing "like a girl." He later claims he knew "there was something wrong with [Mulan]. A woman!" [Mulan proves herself worthy, but she earns her accolades in spite of being a girl rather than because of being one. Her gender is an obstacle to overcome.]

The song "A Girl Worth Fighting For" recalls Mulan's preparation to meet the matchmaker, when the women grooming her promise, "Wait and see, when we're through/Boys will gladly go to war for you." In this case, the song is used as a character-development device for Mulan's soldier friends; their versions of ideal girls differentiate their personalities. Illustrat-

ing the sort of girl each man desires works as a means of character development, but its statements about gender relations are antiquated and frankly
sexist. Ping is interested in a very specific type of beauty; he wants a girl
"paler than the moon with eyes that shine like stars." Yao needs a worshipful
girl to "marvel at [his] strength, adore [his] battle scars." At first it sounds as
though Chien-Po might be more enlightened, since he "couldn't care less
what she'll wear or what she'll look like," but his interest is ultimately just as
traditional: "it all depends on what she cooks like." Each man has a very
specific need he wants his girl to fill; the girls' roles are simply to tend to the
men's physical or psychological desires.

Mulan (as her male alter ego, Ping) asks "how 'bout a girl who's got a
brain, who always speaks her mind?" The others drop out of song to scoff in
unison: "Nah!" Mulan is swept along, silent, uncomfortable, as the men sing,
envisioning idealized women or sculpting them from snow. Her unvoiced
discomfort is recognizable to women who have found themselves in similar
real-world situations, as the only woman in a group of men who are discussing women. The only other women shown during this song are workers in a
rice paddy; in a vision from the 1950s, they giggle appreciatively when
Mushu wolf-whistles at them. This is a clever, stick-in-your-head tune
glorifying stereotypes and archaic gender roles, and every man in the troop—
not just Mulan's comic friends—joins in.

Direct-To-Video Sequels

It is certainly possible to look at these princess stories and see feminist
evolution: Mulan is undoubtedly stronger, smarter and more independent
than Ariel, with Belle and Pocahontas ranged along the way. But the Disney
princess story is not all progress. Inspired by the record-breaking profits
from home-video sales of these princess stories, Disney created direct-to-
video sequels, all of which have sold in great numbers and all of which are
viewed repeatedly by their audience. While some may consider these home-
video productions outside the canon and therefore dismissible, their sales
suggest they are important enough to examine. With small exception, these
videos are retrogressive; the princesses and their stories demonstrate an
appalling lack of feminist awareness and a glorification of sexist stereotypes.

Beauty and the Beast has two direct-to-video sequels, *Beauty and the
Beast: The Enchanted Christmas* (1997) and *Belle's Magical World* (1998).
They are more properly called "midquels," as each takes place during the

time of the original film, after Belle came to live in the castle but before she and the Beast fell in love. They tell stories (one feature-length story in *Enchanted Christmas*, four short stories in *Belle's Magical World*) featuring a patiently, nurturingly didactic Belle and an angry, abusive Beast. *Enchanted Christmas* is the story of Belle bringing Christmas to the castle; the Beast does not celebrate the holiday, as he was initially transformed at Christmas. But Belle is determined to have her celebration, and she sets off toward the forest to find the perfect tree. Two new characters (Forte the organ and his pawn, Fife) are trying to thwart the burgeoning friendship between Belle and the Beast. First they manipulate her into leaving the castle grounds and going into the forbidding forest, and then they arrange an accident for her cart. Chip and Belle tumble into the river, and Belle becomes trapped beneath the ice. The Beast rescues her, carrying her to the castle. The next scene shows her in the dungeon, imprisoned for having the temerity to disobey the Beast's wishes regarding leaving the grounds and celebrating Christmas: "You broke your word, and for that you will rot in this dungeon forever." The Beast repents of this decision, however, when he finds a present Belle had left for him: a storybook about hope. He releases her from the dungeon, and Forte, enraged, tries to destroy the castle. The Beast then kills Forte, and the household celebrates Christmas.

The first story of *Belle's Magical World,* "The Perfect Word," best illustrates the gender/power relations in the Beast's castle, and it gives a clear picture of life in an abusive household. Lumière is coaching the Beast on how best to impress Belle, and Cogsworth comments on how unusually "tranquil" things have been lately. The connection is made clear: the Beast has been keeping his anger in check because of Belle. At dinner, the Beast, sweating nervously, demands the window be opened. Everyone else is cold, and Belle tells the Beast he is rude for ignoring the needs of others. The animate dictionary rattles off a list of synonyms for "rude," and the Beast angrily backhands him off the table. Belle leaves, and the Beast has a roaring, furniture-smashing tantrum. The servants urge the Beast to apologize; Belle refuses to leave her room until he does. When the Beast refuses to apologize, they urge Belle to do so. The Beast is clearly in the wrong, but she agrees to do it—"I suppose I do owe him an apology—for calling him rude, I mean." She is willing to apologize, but the Beast must do so first. He rages off-screen, "I will never apologize!" to the sounds of smashing furniture and Cogsworth and Lumière's terrified screams. Other household items—the pen, dictionary, and paper—conspire to forge an apologetic note to Belle, which she reads gratefully before running to apologize to the Beast. The deception is discovered, and, after chasing the forgers around the castle, teeth bared, the Beast banishes the offending items, throwing them into the snow. Despite Belle's pleas ("Let them go, I beg you...Please! I can't bear to see them harmed"), the Beast threatens harm to anyone who helps them.

As do many abused women, Belle then blames herself for what has clearly been the Beast's irrational, terrifying wrath: "If anyone committed a crime, it was me. None of this would've happened if I'd apologized." Mrs. Potts, the only other female with a speaking part, also tries to take some blame, because she knew about the forgery. Belle urges the banished items to return, but they demur, understandably afraid, saying, "No no no...that guy is a beast. He'll hurt us." Belle assures them, "Deep down, he has a good heart. We let things get so far out of hand. You're the ones who suffered the most. Please forgive me." The Beast then admits he has "been difficult" and apologizes. All is forgiven. Belle is the quintessential abused partner: she blames herself for the Beast's truly unforgivable behavior; she insists on excusing him and deludes herself into believing that "deep down" he is good; and the smaller, more helpless creatures around her suffer.

Pocahontas II: Journey to a New World (1998) is a true sequel, opening some months after the end of the previous film. News of John Smith's presumed death has reached Pocahontas, and she is in mourning. John Rolfe, a diplomat, has come to the colonies to attempt to prevent a war between King James and Powhatan; he and Pocahontas "meet cute" as he comes off the ship. They meet cute again when Rolfe brings a horse to present to the great chief, "Pocahontas." Powhatan refuses to travel to England, but Pocahontas volunteers to go in the interest of peace; she and a bodyguard and her comic-relief pets board ship with Rolfe the next day. When Rolfe stands up to the ship's captain for her, we see the beginning of a romance. This romance is the true story of the film, just as Pocahontas' romance with Smith was the true story of the original film.

Once in England, Pocahontas revels in her new surroundings while onlookers gape at her. Soon she is approached by Ratcliffe, who is evilly pleased to learn that the Algonquin ambassador is a lowly woman. King James has decided to send an armada against the Algonquin if he is not pleased by their ambassador, and Ratcliffe happily believes that Pocahontas will not be up to the task. Rolfe goes to court, where Ratcliffe convinces the king to have Pocahontas appear at a ball. Rolfe despairs, but his housekeeper takes on the task of grooming Pocahontas. Pocahontas first innocently prances out to Rolfe in her underwear, but the housekeeper soon has her under control. The housekeeper ties Pocahontas into a corset, makes up her face, and dresses her hair in a montage of styles. She sings a song, during which Pocahontas is dressed and passed off to Rolfe. The first verse of the song focuses on impressing the king, which is supposed to be Pocahontas' goal, but it very quickly becomes a song about impressing John Rolfe:

> Johnny's lucky they asked you to go....
> Wait till he sees you there in your curls,
> John's always had such a fondness for girls with curls....
> You two might come to see you were meant to be....
> Wait till he sees you, wait till tonight
> Fate has a way of arranging what's right
> After he sees you in your new clothes
> A lady of grace from your head to your toes
> Pretty and pink as the roses he grows
> Who knows, who knows, I can't wait!

At the end of the song, Rolfe gives Pocahontas a necklace. She resignedly removes her mother's necklace, saying "it doesn't belong here anymore." With the new clothes and the face powder to make her "pretty and pink", and especially with the change of necklace, Pocahontas has molded herself into a new person.

Pocahontas, initially a success at the ball, is imprisoned when she speaks out against a bear-baiting. A mysterious hooded figure hears of her plight and meets with Rolfe to plot her release. The hooded man is John Smith, and he and Pocahontas joyfully reunite as the men rescue her. Smith wants to reignite their romance, but Pocahontas is thinking of her people's needs. Rolfe supports Pocahontas' decision to return to court to plead her case, but Smith is dubious. Pocahontas returns to court and convinces the queen of the truth, but the king is skeptical until John Smith throws his support behind Pocahontas. The king has already sent the armada, however, so Pocahontas and the men must race to stop the ships. Smith boards the ship, wreaking havoc, and foiling Ratcliffe's plan. Smith has thus thrice saved the day: freeing Pocahontas from jail, convincing the king, and tossing Ratcliffe overboard.

The next day, as Smith is being fawned over by a number of women, Pocahontas tells Rolfe she will return home. The two are close to confessing their love, but Smith interrupts with the news that he wants to take Pocahontas around the world on the ship he has been awarded. Rolfe, thinking

Pocahontas still loves Smith, discretely leaves. Pocahontas, however, initiates a break in her relationship with Smith, but when she looks for Rolfe, he is gone. Pocahontas sadly sets sail for home, but Rolfe reveals himself to her on board, telling her he has given up his position in order to be with her. They kiss, Pocahontas' hair billows, and they sail into a glorious sunset. Pocahontas has given up Smith, an adventurer, for Rolfe, who only wants to "go home" to Jamestown with her.

The Little Mermaid 2: Return to the Sea (2000) is the most interesting of these direct-to-video sequels. It stars Melody, Ariel and Eric's 12-year-old daughter. Refreshingly, this protagonist's age necessitates the invention of nonromantic motivations. Because Ursula's sister, Morgana, is so threateningly angry at Triton and Ariel for Ursula's death, Ariel forswears going into the sea until the sea-witch is found. She decides (in a moment of terrible parenting) never to tell Melody that she is half-mermaid, and she has the castle walled off from the sea. Melody has a strange affinity for the ocean anyway, which she hides from her parents; just as Ariel did, Melody breaks the parental restrictions laid on her. The plot is simple: Melody finds a locket on the sea floor that her grandfather Triton had given her the day of her presentation to the mer-people. It has her name on it, and the tune it plays is captivating. When Ariel and Melody have an argument—Melody is sure her parents are hiding something from her, and Ariel is furious and frightened that Melody disobeyed her and went into the ocean—Morgana seduces Melody by promising to tell her about her locket and the undersea life her mother has kept from her. Morgana plans to use Melody to retrieve Triton's trident from his throne room; only a member of the royal family can remove it. To make this possible, she turns Melody into a mermaid.

Melody is delighted, and resents that she had never been told of her heritage. Triton sends search parties to look for Melody, and Ariel returns to mermaid form so she can search as well. Melody comes swimming up with the trident, and the two now-mermaids are surprised to see each other. Melody, furious, shouts, "All this time, and you never told me? ... The most important secret in your life and you never told me?" Ariel tries to explain, but Melody hands the trident to Morgana. Morgana sneers at Melody that what Ariel did, she did for love. The action quickens: Eric's ship is sunk, Ariel saves Eric, and Melody's tail turns back into legs. Melody's sea-creature sidekicks bring her to the sea surface; now that she's human again, Morgana does not control her. Morgana forces Triton to bow, and crows, "See that, Ma? Who's your favorite now?" Melody brings the trident back to

Triton, who freezes Morgana in a block of ice. Mother and daughter are reunited and reconciled, and Triton gives Melody the choice of remaining in the sea or living on land. Melody has a better idea, though, and the final scene shows the whole family—Eric, Melody, Ariel and Triton, frolicking together in the castle waters, the retaining wall removed.

In place of the romance, which was not included due to the young age of the princess-protagonist, there are lessons about the importance of mothering, shown specifically as the consequences of bad mothering and the struggle between maturing daughters and their mothers. The damage done in this film is not as horrifying as that done in *Snow White*—no mother figure attempts to kill her daughter—but it is more insidious. The implication is that Morgana is only evil because her mother favored her sister; through her evil actions, Morgana is trying to live up to her mother's expectations. Morgana's mother set her up in competition with Ursula: "all my mother ever did was criticize me. It was always Ursula this or Ursula that or 'Morgana, why can't you be more like your sister Ursula!'" When Melody finds the locket, Morgana gloats, "Finally, I'll succeed at the one thing Ursula never could!" Morgana bonds with Melody by commiseration, assuring her that "Oh, you're not the only one whose mother doesn't understand you." Morgana is emotionally damaged, deranged, because her mother did not love and support her enough. Melody's bad mothering at Ariel's well-meaning hands seems to be leading her to evil as well: she only gave the trident to Morgana to defy Ariel. I am not sure that the inclusion of a mother is a positive step, if this is the relationship that is shown.

In the original *Mulan*, Mulan was ultimately praised for following her heart: she defied social expectations to save her father and her country. *Mulan II* (2005) changes this message of self-sacrifice, of risking one's life for higher causes, into a message of self-indulgence. The film opens shortly after Mulan has returned home from war. She is a hero to the little girls in her neighborhood, and she trains them to fight. When Mulan herself was in training, the song was "I'll Make a Man Out of You," and the trainees were exhorted to be "swift as the coursing river, with all the force of a great typhoon, with all the strength of a raging fire." Mulan teaches her charges to "be gentle at the same time as we're being tough....[to] bring it all into balance." She sings:

Like a rock, you must be hard.
Like an oak, you must stand firm.
Cut quick like my blade.

Think fast, unafraid.
Like a cloud, you are soft.
Like bamboo, you bend in the wind.
Creeping slow, you're at peace
Because you know
It's okay to be afraid.

This is a much softer message than the one Shang gave his trainees. It seems odd to assure would-be warriors that they can be at peace because they know their fears are acceptable.

Shang comes to propose, and one of Mulan's little friends precociously suggests they go to her house (thus demonstrating that pre-pubescents, like grandmothers, find him sexy). Mulan accepts the proposal, and everyone is happy—until Mushu learns that when Mulan marries, he will no longer be her guardian. He then sets out to divide the pair, and this becomes the film's major sub-plot. Meanwhile, Mulan and Shang find that they disagree about some very basic things: wedding size, the number of children they want, favorite color, and acceptable levels of spice in food. Mulan's parents are concerned that they are not a harmonious couple, and Mushu will play on these differences as he tries to stop their wedding.

The couple is summoned by the emperor, who needs them to escort his three daughters to their arranged weddings, sealing an alliance and preventing war. Mulan is appalled at the idea of arranged marriages, but the emperor is confident that his daughters are prepared. Mulan and Shang bring Yao, Ling, and Chien-Po, Mulan's soldier friends, as their troops; the three reprise "A Girl Worth Fighting For." Each guard will find that one of the princesses will fulfill his romantic desires.

Mulan talks to the princesses about their upcoming nuptials. The girls assure her that these marriages are an honor and that they are happy to serve their country. Mulan is dissatisfied, explaining to Shang, "I realize our duty is to the mission. But I have another duty, to my heart." This phrase, "duty to my heart," will be repeated numerous times in the upcoming scenes, as the girls all justify scrapping the mission. Mulan in the first movie would never have worked against the safety of her country, but she does here. Seeing the princesses flirt with the three guards, she eventually convinces them that they, too, have a duty to their hearts. This sounds empowering, but in reality it's all coming down to romance. Mulan's original "duty to her heart" was never about romance, it was about doing the right thing even when society was against her. For the princesses, "duty to their hearts" means breaking their promises to their father, ruining their country's chance of peaceful alliance, and running off with their crushes. This is vastly more selfish and less noble than Mulan's original cause.

Mushu's plan to break up the engaged couple works. He sends their carriage over a cliff, and Mulan and Shang end up having a huge, sitcom-style argument about asking for directions. Meanwhile, the princesses are arguing about what they should do. The oldest daughter insists they follow through with their arranged marriages, reminding her sisters that "a princess must make every sacrifice for her country. It's our duty." They sing about the life of a princess, assuring their audience that they would much rather be regular girls. Of course, the sort of regular girl they wish to be is terribly anachronistic within the world of their movie; Mulan herself was headed for an arranged marriage and living a very confined life before her (unique) adventures began, and the penalty for a woman fighting in the army, which has conveniently been forgotten, was supposed to be death.

The guards and the princesses go to a nearby village on a date. Each girl admires her man for exactly those qualities the man values, and it is clear that the couples are perfectly suited. When they return to camp, the princesses excitedly tell Mulan, "It's love." She congratulates them, but when Shang approaches he scolds, "What would your father say to see you break your vows?" He and Mulan quarrel. Shang accuses Mulan, "The problem, Mulan, is you. You place your own feelings above everything. Duty, obligation, tradition. It all means nothing to you." She strikes back: "I have a duty. I listen to my heart. Do you even have one?" Mulan has morphed from an untraditional but honorable woman into a petulant, irresponsible romantic.

The group is ambushed, and Shang falls into a ravine. Everyone assumes he is dead. The princesses decide that they will go through with their weddings, but Mulan tells them she will see this mission through herself. She offers herself to the neighboring ruler as a daughter-in-law, bride to one of his sons. Surely she, the hero of China, is worth more as a marriage commodity than three regular princesses. Shang, who survived the fall, understands Mulan's plan and goes after her, followed by the three princess/soldier pairs. He stops the wedding. Mushu, who has reconciled himself to losing his guardian position, calls himself the "Golden Dragon of Unity" and declares Shang and Mulan married. He also proclaims that the three princesses may marry whomever they choose. There is no resolution of the marriage-for-alliance plot point, and romance has taken over the entire story.

Conclusion

These later Disney princess stories, which heralded Disney's re-ascendance to the critical and popular heap of animation studios, are not nearly as different from Disney's first princess stories as they are purported to be. The anti-female messages they send are all the more devious for being hidden beneath a veneer of feminist girl power. Modern parents may be aware enough to discuss Snow White or Sleeping Beauty's passivity and their archaic dependence on a prince, but when patriarchal attitudes come disguised in kick-butt training tunes such as "Be a Man," they are not as readily apparent. The princesses' superficial differences from each other are convincingly individualizing, at first glance, but their ultimate similarity to each other is almost as monolithic an image as that presented by the first group of Disney princesses. The films' formulaic stories, their dominant male characters, and their reliance on romance as central to the plot all serve to undercut the significance of their newer, more empowered princesses. Most subversive to the feminist message these films allegedly want to send are the anti-female "jokes"; the reputation of "feminazis" having no senses of humor might make some reluctant to protest the inclusion of such jokes. Fortunately, Disney's princess stories are not the only post-second-wave feminist princess stories available. The third-wave feminist princess stories of the 1990s and 2000s will provide their audience with princesses who have goals and desires of their own, and if they find romance, it never takes precedence over their other needs. They are the princess stories Disney Studios pretended to produce but which are available only in young adult novels.

❖ CHAPTER FIVE ❖

The Third-Wave Princess Story: A Redefinition

THE late 1990s through the late 2000s produced many princess stories for a young adult reading audience. These offered tweens and young teens new versions of older fairy tales or entirely new stories featuring princesses and, in many cases, specific princess lessons. These stories took into account feminism and the new expectations of girls and women in American society; this combination of new expectations and old role models produced some very interesting works, illuminating the tension between traditional romantic expectations and newer social expectations in a culture changed by the women's movement. The books chosen for this chapter represent a range of princess stories from this period, but they do not represent the entirety of princess stories produced during this time. The renewed interest in young adult princess stories can be seen in two publishers' new series centered on princesses and fairytales. Scholastic's *The Royal Diaries* series, begun in 1999, is a collection of historical novels, fictionalized young teen diaries and epistles of real-life princesses from many countries and times; as a sample, I have included four of their titles in this discussion. Simon Pulse, a teen imprimatur from Simon & Schuster, has the *Once Upon a Time* series, retellings of classic fairy tales which promise "fresh, quirky heroines" and "unique and original 'happily ever afters'" (according to the back matter from *Snow*); three novels from this line are also included. This chapter will survey some of the young adult princess stories published at the turn of the twenty-first century, highlighting the many ways they reflect the new culture in which they were produced and the new expectations for and of American girls and women. Finally, a comparison of contemporary novels with nearly-simultaneous Disney adaptations will investigate the subversive changes Disney Studios made in film productions of Meg Cabot's *The Princess Diaries* novels and Gail Carson Levine's *Ella Enchanted*.

The heroines of these stories were neither passively awaiting their princes nor scorning men altogether. These stories, conceived as they were in a society where the goals of second-wave feminism were largely realized, strive to combine adventures of smart, independent heroines with a hint of romance, both of which appeal to a young adult reading audience (whose members consider themselves smart and independent yet still often hope for romance). These stories are written by and for females who did (or will) mature with feminism as an established fact, and this informs the possibilities open to their princess-heroines. As Jennifer Baumgardner and Amy Richards write, "for anyone born after the early 1960s, the presence of feminism in our lives is taken for granted. For our generation, feminism is like fluoride. We scarcely notice that we have it—it's simply in the water" (*Manifesta* 17). Female writers creating new princess stories or revising old ones are informed by feminism; the characterizations and adventures of their princesses are likewise informed. Baumgardner and Richards would call these princess stories "girlie" and would recognize that these stories and interest in them come not from an anti-feminist tradition, but from third wave feminism.

> Girlie says we're not broken, and our desires aren't simply booby traps set by the patriarchy. Girlie encompasses the tabooed symbols of women's feminine enculturation—Barbie dolls, makeup, fashion magazines, high heels—and says using them isn't shorthand for 'we've been duped.'…Young women are emphasizing our real personal lives in contrast to what some feminist foremothers anticipated their lives would—or should—be: that the way to equality was to reject Barbie and all forms of pink-packaged femininity. (136-7)

Princess stories do often fall within the realm of "pink-packaged femininity," but that does not make them any less empowering for their readers. These novels, products of and for girlie culture, combine more traditional notions of femininity with more modern ideas of female power.

Roberta Trites' *Waking Sleeping Beauty: Feminist Voices in Children's Novels* (1997) delineates the qualities of feminist children's texts. Many, if not all, of these qualities are demonstrably present in the young adult novels discussed in this chapter. Trites writes that "feminist children's novels use techniques both simple and sophisticated to call the reader to awaken herself and to reject the role of Sleeping Beauty" (9). Feminist children's novels are those "in which a main character is empowered regardless of gender" (4); although most protagonists in these novels are female, triumphing over obstacles related to their gender, they need not be female nor must their obstacles all be gender-related. According to Trites, rather than employ simple gender switching, protagonists in feminist children's novels use their imaginations and trickery to transcend their gender roles. These novels also rise above gender roles by embracing and celebrating "certain characteristics traditionally linked to femininity. Instead of completely rejecting femininity…, feminist protagonists recognize and rely on traits that gave their literary foremothers strength: compassion, interconnectedness, and communication" (5). Finally, in a feminist children's novel, the protagonist's agency and voice are the most powerful tools in reversing traditional gender roles.

> Unlike her literary antecedents…, the feminist protagonist need not squelch her individuality in order to fit into society. Instead, her agency, her choice, and her nonconformity are affirmed and even celebrated….
>
> The feminist character's recognition of her agency and her voice invariably leads to some sort of transcendence, usually taking the form of a triumph over whatever system or stricture was repressing her. The character defeats some force of evil (sometimes magical, sometimes not), or she succeeds at a typically male task, or she comes to believe in herself despite the doubts of those around her. (6-7)

The techniques and ideals Trites finds in feminist children's novels are also to be found in feminist young adult princess stories.

Some second-wave feminists seemed to disdain princess stories even as they consciously used them to further their political agenda. By contrast, authors creating princess stories at the end of the twentieth century and start of the twenty-first seem to celebrate them. They have found ways of making the stock, passive princess real and relevant to their informed-by-feminism audience. The princess stories of the 1990s and 2000s are part of girlie culture, which

> …is different from the cultural feminism of the seventies….[F]or this generation, having or loving our own culture isn't the same as cultural feminism—a separate ghetto (or utopia) for women—it's just feminism for a culture-driven generation….Girlies say, through actions and attitudes, that you don't have to make the feminine powerful by making it masculine or 'natural'; it is a feminist statement to proudly claim things that are feminine, and the alternative can mean to deny what we are. (Baumgardner and Richards *Manifesta* 134-5)

In this way, the third wave princess stories are about female empowerment. Princesses, which are the most traditionally feminine of all female characters, can—if properly developed—still serve as role models for modern girls. According to these princess stories, girls do not have to disavow romance or beauty in order to lead independent, rewarding, adventurous lives.

The princess story novels and series that will be discussed in this chapter are feminist in the way they characterize their princesses, in their motivations and their adventures. They do not exclude men and romance, but neither do they center on them; the princesses have individual goals and dreams, and romance is just one of their many desires. These princess stories, whether historical fiction, retellings of classic fairy tales, or new tales altogether, all have elements in common. Their heroines are far from passive; as E.D. Baker writes, "I've never been able to stand wimpy fairy tale princesses who can't do anything on their own and need princes to solve their problems" (*EDBakerBooks*). They are educated, they have goals, and romance is not their sine qua non. They are models of independent, modern girls, princesses worth emulating. These are third-wave feminist princesses, independent and interesting, members of female communities yet not disinterested in men. As Shannon Hale, author of two books under examination, indicated in an interview,

> I'm very lucky to be writing after decades of writers have already fought for their genuine, interesting, and varied heroines. I don't have the burden of writing on the offense, trying to prove that girls can be main characters, strong and individual. It's a luxury to get to write what I think is true, not make a statement. ("A Conversation")

Third-wave feminists are reaping the benefits of their second-wave fore-mothers, and their princesses reflect those benefits.

The Princess's Body

One of the first elements in these books which differentiates them from traditional—and certainly, from Disney—depictions of princesses is their physical makeup. Many of the books consciously play against the blond-haired-blue-eyed "princess" type; Princess Cimorene (*Dealing with Dragons* [1990]) has six older sisters, "perfectly normal princesses, with long, beautiful, golden hair and sweet dispositions, each more beautiful than the last. Cimorene was lovely enough, but her hair was jet black, and she wore it in braids instead of curled and pinned like her sisters" (Wrede 2). She is also so tall that her parents are afraid no man will marry her, because she would need to "look him in the eye rather than gazing up at him becomingly through her lashes" (2). Princess Addie (*The Two Princesses of Bamarre* [2001]) was also dark complexioned and "was always tall for [her] age, and loose-limbed" (Levine 2). Other princesses are either atypically tall or dark-complexioned. Princess Rhis (*A Posse of Princesses* [2008]) considers herself "a tall, angle-faced beanpole with hair the color of a wooden plank" (Smith 37). Cleopatra (*Cleopatra VII: Daughter of the Nile* [1999]) writes that she plays outside during the day and that her Roman friend warns her of turning "dark like a commoner" (Gregory 107); Cleopatra's response, as recorded in her diary, is an insouciant "'And?' (It is so very boring to be royal all the time!)" (107). It is not necessary to be blond or petite in these stories, and staying indoors to protect one's complexion is too dull to consider viable.

Princess Ben (*Princess Ben* [2008]) is fat, with an "apple-shaped silhouette" (151). Her physique dismays the queen regent, Ben's aunt and guardian, who insists, "A princess...requires a graceful and willowy carriage, not the appetite of a swineherd" (Murdock 64). Ben is put on half-rations and forced to eat very slowly, yet she has a secret stash of food in her room and thus does not lose weight; her "waist did not shrink, and [her] cheeks retained a cherubic plumpness more common to well-fed babies than marriageable royalty" (142). In fact, she is an emotional eater, and in the unhappiness following her parents' deaths she eats to dull the pain. After Ben pops the seams and buttons on her clothes, her secret food supplies are discovered and removed. Her first act upon learning enough witchcraft to escape her room undetected is to steal food from the kitchens. Her body type would never be willowy, however; even after two months away from her sleeping body double (magically left behind as she escapes her room), during which she slaved for soldiers as a prisoner of war, she awoke slimmer but certainly not lissome. Her commentary on the transformation is "Not that I was slender, certainly, but where once I had bulged out, now I dipped in ever so slightly...I was simply no longer rotund" (252-3). Ben knows that the approbation she receives for her physical changes is ultimately unimportant, and she inwardly "vowed never to debase herself with such superficiality" (254); she goes further later,

> ...to clarify yet again that I was not willowy, slender, delicate, gauzy, diaphanous, fine-boned, or any of the other descriptive forever linked to the daughters of kings, and that my figure, however feminine, yet conveyed that I suffered little in cold draughts. The endless twaddle about my silhouette revolted me, and I grew ever more incensed over the general reliance on appearance alone for repute, rank, and virtue. I kept my ears pricked for any superficial judgment and would gently remind the speaker that the person of whom they spoke had many other qualities, good and poor, beyond complexion and waistline. (269)

Ben does "transform from dour chrysalis to eager butterfly" (264), but this change is one of attitude, not physique or wardrobe. There is a ball, and Ben is on display, but she is not looking for a husband; she needs to prove herself worthy of ruling her country to preserve its autonomy.

Other princesses confound physical expectations in other ways. Emma (*The Frog Princess* [2002]) has a boisterous, un-princess-like laugh. When the frog asks for a kiss, she tells us, "I guffawed, I chortled, I wheezed" (4). Small woodland creatures scuttle away at the sound, and the frog doubts that she is truly a princess because she does not sound like one. "I know…My mother tell me that all the time. According to her, a princess's laughter should sound like the tinkling of a bell, not the bray of a donkey. I've told her I can't help it. My laugh is not something I can control, not if it's sincere. I don't think about it" (5). Her distinctive laugh will be an asset after she has been turned into a frog; her aunt, skeptically appraising two talking frogs, will recognize Emma by her distinctive sound.

The Princess Test (1999) also addresses the issue of physical expectations, valorizing an average-looking princess-to-be while mocking standards of physical beauty. When Prince Nicholas first sees Lorelei from a distance, he thinks she looks pretty. Drawing closer, he sees she is

> Not a raving beauty, but definitely pretty. Light-brown hair. Ordinary color, but thick and wavy. Nose a little too big. But her eyes were big, too. Enormous. And she had roses in her cheeks. You didn't see roses in the cheeks of the noble and stuck-up ladies at court. (Levine "Princess Test" 71)

Lorelei is a regular, healthy girl. Later, the standards for the girls competing to marry Nicholas are laid out: "Every inch of the princess would be measured. Her waist had to be tiny. Her hands and feet had to be small, although her fingers had to be long. Her big toe had to be longer than her index toe. She had to be tall, but not a giant. And so on" (76). Lorelei passes the physical tests, although she did worry that her nose might be too big. Tumult created by a commoner bringing in a child for medical attention causes everyone to forget about the pea test, which Lorelei would have passed, having been forewarned. When the other princess remaining in the competition suggests that the commoners be killed for interrupting proceedings, Nicholas seizes the opportunity to highlight Lorelei's kindness in wanting to tend to the child. This kindness is ultimately what wins the two the right to marry; everything else is deemed irrelevant.

Kristina, the princess of Sweden whose goal is to be king, not queen (*Kristina: The Girl King* [2003]), has spent her life being told the ways she is "ill-favored" (Meyer 97). Her closest friend, Ebba, sternly tells her she is not homely, and must never think that about herself. To each of Kristina's complaints about her appearance, Ebba has a counter-description. When Kristina points out that her eyes are atypically dark for a Swede,

> Ebba shrugged and said they give me an air of *mystery*. And when I pointed out that my nose is much too big, she shrugged again and said that it has *nobility*. What about my complexion, which my mother complains is as dark as a gypsy's? She thought for a moment and decided that it is *vivid*. My stature, I reminded her, is short and ungraceful. She replied that my hands are my best feature, very lovely and expressive. (97)

When Kristina next sees herself in the mirror, she does not see what she has always seen. Instead, she considers herself "if not a truly beautiful girl, then one who is surely not displeasing" (97). Kristina has been judging herself by the harshest standards. When given other descriptive vocabulary, she can appreciate herself anew.

In *Snow* (2003), the importance of beauty is downplayed in favor of more significant characteristics. When the duchess, Snow's mother, is pregnant, she imagines her unborn child in the traditional "Snow White" manner. "I hope he will be handsome. I hope she will be beautiful…with skin as fair as snow, lips as red as blood and hair as black as ebony" (Lynn 7). She then thinks better of these dreams, and "shakes her head at her silliness. 'I hope he is *brave* like my husband. I hope she is *kind*, like—like I hope I am.' She willed the baby inside her to be strong…and be born healthy" (7). This passage indicates that bravery, kindness, strength and health are more significant than appearance, and that wishing for beauty is silly in light of the other, more important qualities. In this novel, the root of the stepmother's evil is clearly shown to be her perceptions of what is important in a woman: youth, beauty, and fertility. She bemoans the fact that "staying young and beautiful is a full-time job" (26) for a woman. The servant holding her mirror suggests that "Being kind and wise is a full-time job, for anyone, My Lady. You are clearly beautiful, but I am sure people notice more than that" (26). The stepmother cannot bear this contradiction, and she magically enslaves the servant, silencing him: her first act of evil. The stepmother clings to her beauty to the exclusion of any other positive quality, and the fears engendered in her by her gradual aging and by comparing herself to her maturing stepdaughter drive her to villainy. It is made very clear throughout the story that physical beauty, while delightful, should not be valued above actual traits of character.

The Princess's Interests

The princesses in these novels are not just atypical physically; they also find typical "princess" duties dull and uninspiring. Many of the princesses have neither the interest nor the aptitude for sedentary, ladylike activities. They find typical princess tasks confining, and they cultivate other life goals. Even a pretty princess, like Helen of Sparta (*Nobody's Princess* [2007]), wants more than admiration for her beauty—she will inherit Sparta, and she wants to be prepared. She hates spending her days working wool with the women. Her nurse and her mother tell her, "'This is what all women do, even queens,' but what [she] heard was: *This is all that women* can *do, and even queens have no choice about it*" (Friesner 33). She wants more than anything to train for combat with her older brothers, but they mock her, saying, "swords are for warriors, not little girls" (34). Helen deduces three points from one such conversation with one brother:

> Even if I was pretty, it wasn't going to be enough to bring me the life I wanted: one where I was free to make choices that mattered, one where people listened to what I had to say.
> Aphrodite had the beauty; Zeus had the thunderbolts. Everyone loved Aphrodite, but everyone *listened* to Zeus.
> I'd never get my hands on a thunderbolt, so if I wanted to be free, I'd better find a way to get my hands on the next best thing: a sword. (36)

Helen slips outside as often as she can, running to improve her physical fitness. When she is caught spying on her brothers' training sessions, she explains her rationale: "Even if I never have to use a sword, I want to know *how*. When I'm queen, I've got to be strong enough to protect myself. If I can't do that, how can I protect anyone else? And if someone thinks he can control my life and my decisions just because he's got a sword and I don't— I want him to get a *surprise*" (41). Her brothers' trainer allows her to work with them, agreeing that a strong leader makes a strong country, and silencing her brothers' protestations by telling them that unless they can think of an argument beyond her gender, they have no argument.

Aurore (*Beauty Sleep: A Retelling of "Sleeping Beauty"* [2002]) is confined to the castle for the first several years of her life; her mother is afraid that she will injure herself outside, thus activating the spells cast on her at her christening. Because of the threat posed by needles, she is not permitted "to engage in any of the more traditional princesslike activities, includ-ing...painstakingly boring embroidery. But there were other ladylike tasks [she] might pursue, such as painting bowls of fruit or braiding rugs" (Dokey 27). She does not excel at these tasks, however; she messily eats the fruit and her rugs contain "gigantic and mischievous bumps" (27). She finally wins her freedom to go outdoors, a freedom which her father wholeheartedly endorses. He believes this indicates "a desire to know *all* those [she] might rule one day, not just those who are noble-born" (50). Aurore's lessons in the world outside the castle walls include the menial, the dirty, and the difficult:

> I learned to plow and plant the fields, not letting the fact that I sunburned my face and blistered my hands stop me. I held on until I developed calluses and my skin settled down to the color of toasted almonds. I learned to cut peat for fires and the proper way to thatch a roof. I fell off. Twice. The second time I broke my arm....
>
> When my arm had mended, I learned to shear a sheep, to card and spin its wool. Lest I become too domestic, I also learned to shoot an arrow from my own bow and to throw a knife. Accurately in both cases....
>
> In short, I pretty much stopped behaving like a regular princess altogether and had the time of my life. (59)

These lessons bring her closer to her subjects, but they make her an oddity among the nobility. This peculiarity is most notable at the ball celebrating her sixteenth birthday. Although everyone has a veneer of politeness, Aurore feels their scorn and mocking laughter. Most painful, she suddenly under-stands others' view of her:

> My fingernails were clean, but my fingertips were stained a faint blue. I had been helping the village weavers dye wool for winter cloaks. There were calluses upon my palms....
>
> On the dance floor, I forgot the steps and trod upon my partners' feet, though, naturally, they were too polite to comment. My new shoes, which Maman had pro-claimed the height of fashion, were just a shade too tight and pinched my toes. The whole evening was like suffering through the clumsiest moments of my childhood all over again—this time with a whole court looking on. (67)

Aurore cries in a corner until duty and honor compel her to put on a brave facade to face the crowd. Although the disapproving nobles try to deny her position as heir to the throne, ultimately the lessons learned from her subjects make her a fair and beloved ruler.

Princess Emma (*The Frog Princess*), as a frog, defends her title by list-ing the common princess activities in which she participates: "I really am a princess! I can play the lute and embroider and sing and dance and do all the other things that princesses are supposed to do, though not as well as my mother would like. I can also do some other things that most princesses can't do. I can count and read and—" (84). This inventory of Emma's skill set highlights both the ladylike talents a princess is supposed to cultivate and the ones that are often neglected, the standard liberal education most American girls take for granted. This inventory also slips in a little commentary: Emma is not as good at the princess skills as her mother would like, perhaps because she has been cultivating her reading and her math. During the course of her adventures, reading will save Emma's life and the lives of her friends, and it will prepare her for her future education as a witch; her embroidery is not shown to improve her life at all.

The inanity and tedium of typical princess skills are discussed in book after book. Princess Cimorene (*Dealing with Dragons*) calls upon her fairy godmother for help when the lessons she has been surreptitiously taking are discovered and forbidden. Rather than lessons in fencing, magic, Latin, cooking, economics, and juggling, each of which has been banned upon discovery, Cimorene is frustrated to be limited to "embroidery lessons, and dancing, and—and being a princess!" (Wrede 5). Cimorene argues, "I want to do things, not sit around all day and listen to the court minstrel make up songs about how brave Daddy is and how lovely his wife and daughters are" (5). Abandoned to her fate by her godmother, Cimorene later disgustedly catalogues her skills: "I can curtsy…I know seventeen different country dances, nine ways to agree with an ambassador from Cathey without actually promising him anything, and one hundred and forty-three embroidery stitches. And I can make cherries jubilee" (10). This inventory, combined with the imminent threat of marriage to a dullard, convinces Cimorene to pursue a career, one that will play to her strengths: she will become a dragon's princess. It is "a perfectly respectable thing to do, so my parents couldn't complain. And it would be much more interesting than embroidery and dancing lessons" (18). Her new career will lead her to adventure and bring her new friendships and a better education; the happy ending of her story comes when "her" dragon becomes King of the Dragons. Cimorene has an "interesting and busy" life ahead of her "and in Cimorene's opinion that would go a long way toward making her happy" (212). She looks forward to sorting treasure, reading books, practicing magic and solving problems with the dragons, a far cry from the princess duties she had at home.

The lessons in *Princess Academy* (2007) begin with reading, as the mountain girls collected for princess training are illiterate. Once the girls mastered reading, their instructor focused in-depth on "princess-forming subjects such as Diplomacy, Conversation, and the one that made Miri want to roll her eyes—Poise" (Hale "Princess" 92). Poise encompasses all sorts of physical movement:

> During their lessons on Poise, the girls took off their boots and balanced them on their heads. They walked in circles. They learned how to walk quickly (on toes, toes kept behind the hem of the skirt, fluid, arms slightly bent) and slowly (toe to heel, toe to heel, hands resting on skirt). They learned a deep curtsy for a prince….they practiced a shallow curtsy for a peer and understood that they were never to curtsy to a servant. (92-93)

Conversation lessons seem equally nonsensical, focused as they are on "the importance of repeating the name and title, asking questions, and always bringing the conversation around to the other person" (95). The Academy girls ask for more valuable lessons: economics, geography, and politics. These more intellectual subjects will improve the lives of those living on the mountain; Miri's new understanding of economics and the value of the marble her village mines brings them enough money that they can afford enough leisure time for education.

Ella (*Just Ella* [2001]), having become Prince Charming's intended bride, needs to become a princess quickly. The transition from scullery maid to princess is not smooth, however, and she chafes at her lessons and new restrictions. Her table manners are scrutinized; her dinner companions, their spoons moving in unison, are shocked when she dips bread in her soup. Her instructors are seated with her at meals, "to correct any horrifying error…before it attracted too much attention" (Haddix 27). Ella has no time to herself, nor does she set her own schedule; she, "the supposed princess, never knew from one minute to the next what [she] was supposed to be doing or where [she] was supposed to be until someone hissed last-minutes instructions to [her]" (34). She has a variety of lessons, from pronunciation and posture and manners to royal genealogy and how to treat servants. She is also required to be well-versed in the official religion, to recite the long, incomprehensible catechism "that would make [her] a fit wife for the prince and a fit mother for a future king" (44). Ella is confined to the castle, doing needlework; the only lessons she did request, riding lessons, were withheld from her because "a princess would never be without her carriage" (42). Ella finds the lessons tedious, meaningless, and she finds the restriction of activity frustrating. She will ultimately decide that she does not love the prince enough to settle for the quality of life dictated by her position.

Ben (*Princess Ben*) goes on at length about her detested princess lessons, "comportment, dance, languages, history, penmanship, needlework, horsemanship, and music," designed "to produce a pearl of a princess from even a grain of sand such as [herself]" (55). Ben is to learn languages, but her instructor's "vocabulary consisted of fashion and dining terms and fawning, useless phrases" (56). Ben has no interest in penmanship, "for [she] had far less interest in the appearance of [her] words than in their substance" (56). Her instructors try in vain to motivate Ben with promises of princes; her needlework, they tell her, will be given as a token some day, and dance and music are ways of methods of attracting "well-born bachelors" (57). Most loathsome is comportment, which includes not only grace in walking and curtsying but also table manners:

> Unless the queen was occupied with state business, she demanded I accompany her to dinner, ostensibly to honor my position but in reality to watch my every gesture and mention its fault....
>
> I resented every moment of these meals. What was the point of dainty bites, feigning lack of hunger when actually famished, or delight in food that lacked all seasoning? And, worst of all, why was I never permitted to eat my fill? I spent the evenings in a misery of starvation, my stomach stating what my mouth could not. (59)

Their miserable dinners together come to a head when Ben is beaten for snatching food from another's plate. After Ben is beaten, the queen resumes conversation as though nothing had happened, and commands Ben to join them: "Insignificant as our conversation may seem, a queen's greatest responsibility is to learn the art of speaking well while saying nothing" (75). (Ben earns another, more vicious beating when she retorts to her barren aunt, "I was taught that a queen's greatest responsibility is to bear her husband a child" [76].) Ben does not become interested in these princess lessons until her country is threatened by another, at which point she finds herself more than competent. The promise of marrying a prince is no motivation, but she can and does become proficient when she perceives a real need.

A few of these unconventional princesses express disdain for their more traditional, limited peers. Some of this may be attributed to sour grapes; the princess-heroines are, to some extent, social failures for their inability to master or disinclination towards traditional princess skills. Many of the princesses are somewhat ambivalent about their misfit status; they do not know at the start of their stories that their peculiarities will become their strengths. Princess Ani (*The Goose Girl* [2003]) feels like a fraud when she compares herself to her maid-in-waiting, who "would be better at playing princess than I am" (Hale "Goose" 19). The thought hurts. "Ani wanted so badly to do it right, to be regal and clever and powerful" (19), but she "full of trips, stutters and stupidity" (25). She will develop the resources necessary to save her country, but not through the social niceties she finds so difficult.

Miri, of *Princess Academy*, is held hostage by bandits who sneeringly scoff at the notion that girls, especially those attending a princess academy, might present them with any real difficulty. Had the girls been typical princesses, they would have been easily subdued. But Miri and her friends are not typical princesses, and Miri rallies herself: "I'm no princess. I'm a Mount Eskel girl, and I know things you could never guess" (253). Her source of strength is her non-princess knowledge, and the bandits who hold her will find to their dismay that her actual skill set is more formidable than they had assumed.

Princess Cimorene (*Dealing with Dragons*) finds herself one of four princesses held by the same colony of dragons. When she meets the others, she finds "three beautiful, elegantly dressed princesses. They were all blonde and blue-eyed and slender, and several inches shorter than Cimorene" (62-63). The varieties of blond hair—sun-ripened wheat, crystallized honey, ripe apricots—are poetic, yet in the overblown description is a note of humor that indicates how ludicrous such descriptions actually are. The princesses are "taken aback by the sight of Cimorene in her dust-covered dress and ker-chief" (63); she had been organizing the library when they arrived. Upon hearing the first and haughtiest-looking princess declare that the three have come "to comfort her and together bemoan our sad and sorry fates" (63), Cimorene responds,

> "I don't need comforting, and I'm not particularly sad or sorry to be here, but if you'd like to come in and have some tea, you're welcome to."
> The first two princesses looked as if they would have liked to be startled and appalled by this announcement but were much too well bred to show what they were feeling. The princess with the pearl circlet looked surprised and rather intrigued, and she glanced hopefully at her companions. (63)

The first two princesses are shocked to learn that Cimorene volunteered to serve her dragon, and even more shocked that she would suggest they escape on their own, without waiting for rescue. These princesses are foolish snobs, and the princess with the pearls will later share with Cimorene how peer pressure from the other two made her feel inferior: one of them "goes on and on about correct behavior, and [the other] dissolves in tears as soon as it looks like she's losing an argument" (70). Cimorene's new friend was herself never a satisfactory princess at home; things kept turning out well (her christening, her spinning) instead of leading her into a traditional princess story. Cimorene and her new friend are practical and intelligent, unlike their traditional princess colleagues, and the text leaves its readers in no doubt as to which ones are ridiculous.

Kristina (*Kristina: The Girl King* [2003]) considers herself hopeless in her "lessons in feminine grace" (Meyer 50), but as she would prefer to be king rather than queen, she does not care. Her mother tutors her in her wardrobe and in her walk, and she is a failure—intentionally. She has no interest in wearing women's shoes or silk stockings, and she would rather ride astride than sidesaddle. She has no interest in bearing children, as she defiantly declares to her riding master when he warns her that riding astride will hinder her fertility. She tells her best friend that she has no desire ever to marry, and that she wants a life in which she can live freely. Kristina's life is "governed by customs and traditions that [she] has no authority to change" (98). She lists the things she is not allowed to do, just because she is a woman: "Ride my horse astride. Use bad language, if I feel like it. Dress in men's breeches when I go walking. Travel abroad" (99). She insists on being taught and treated as a prince, not a princess, and by the end of her story at least one of her advisors addresses her as "My King." Her intellect, honed by traditionally male studies, brings her the respect she craves; her walk, her clothes, her manner of riding are all ultimately irrelevant.

Princess Rhis (*A Posse of Princesses* [2008]) does not apply herself to her studies; as she is not in line for the throne, she has little motivation to do so. She spends her time playing and writing music instead, ballads particularly, although her very proper sister-in-law finds music inappropriate and Rhis's habits lazy. Rhis has been told that "only entertainers play. A princess might strum if a boy professes to like music, but only to look decorative, and that proper princesses summon entertainers when they want real music. But proper princesses don't ever want ballads" (Smith 32). Rhis secretly learns ballads from the cook's nephew when he is not traveling with his performance troupe. Her skill in playing and being able to pass as an entertainer will later help her "posse of princesses" sneak into the castle of the man who has abducted a princess, Iardith. Rhis and her friend Shera call Iardith the "perfect princess," and not with admiration. Shera describes her:

She really is a perfect princess—and if you don't happen to notice all her perfections, she will tell you about them. But only in private. In public, she's just as sweet and dignified and proper as [anyone] would wish.... Hair blacker than midnight with no moons, and glossy, and never messy, though it is quite long, and light brown eyes—the boys who like poetry call them *topaz*, how disgusting. She has long, dark lashes, and perfect features, and a perfect figure, and she dances perfectly, and uses her fan perfectly, she has perfect manners—when others are around. And she knows more than you do—as she will tell you, ever so nicely—about every fashionable subject, whether flowers or artists. (Smith 35-36)

Iardith puts on airs in order to attract men, whom she does not respect. She flirts with other girls' boyfriends. The other girls understandably resent her. Were she truly sweet and good at all times, they might want to befriend her, but since she puts off her good manners and becomes snide and superior when in single-sex company, they find her artificial and mean. The quotes and raised eyebrows around her title of "perfect princess" underscore the disdain they have for her falsity.

The Princess's Restrictions

The fictional princesses often relish the non-princess positions in which they find themselves. One reason they prefer non-princess life is that regular, required princess clothing is often quite restrictive. Jessica (*Snow*), under her stepmother's tutelage, recognizes that she is dressed like a "perfect little noblewoman" (Lynn 37), but she finds "the bows, underclothes, tight shoes, and hair ribbons" and getting dressed with the help of maids "a pain" (37). Emma (*The Frog Princess*) finds the freedom of movement as a frog a revelation after a life confined by her wardrobe: "As a princess, I had never been able to go outside unencumbered by heavy fabric and long skirts. The new feeling of freedom was exhilarating!" (Baker 32). While formal clothes may be fun on occasion, these princesses leave little doubt as to the impractical nature and physical discomfort of their corsets and long skirts.

Marie (*Marie Antoinette: Princess of Versailles* [2000]) has "fifteen pages of closely written rules and regulations concerning fashion and dressing" (Lasky *Marie* 62) by which to live when she arrives in France. As princess in France, she must be accompanied by at least four ladies-in-waiting at all times, and she will be carried in a chair from place to place. This is different and disturbing to her; in Austria, her home, such chairs do not exist. She goes wading in a fountain in her nightgown, which she is convinced would not be permitted in her future position in France. She wonders: "what is the point of being the Queen of France if one cannot wade barefoot in one's nightclothes?" (64). Marie's older sister, pock-marked and veiled and therefore without marital or royal expectations, is much more free to think her own thoughts and live her own life; Marie considers her "a woman completely free, free of Mama, free of Austria, free of empires and husbands and filled only with her own music and love of God. If people, especially women, knew the secret of Elizabeth, she would be the most envied woman in the Empire, in Europe, in the world!" (49). Later, when Marie pities Louis for his somber and lonely childhood, she "cannot help but think of the fun that Louis Auguste and I could have if we had been born just ordinary people. An ordinary boy and an ordinary girl" (198). Fulfilling royal expectations can be difficult.

Other princesses also wistfully imagine life as ordinary girls. Faced with her father's drunken inability to lead, Cleopatra (*Cleopatra VII: Daughter of the Nile*) "wanted to shrug or otherwise act like a girl of twelve" (71). However, she thinks of her hero, Nefertiti, and rises to the occasion. The following year, she realizes that she is the one who must take charge when her father is unable. She struggles with this responsibility:

> How I wanted to scream my fury at him, my frustration. I wanted to rage, to weep. Even so, there remained a part of me—a small part—that wanted to behave as a queen might. She must not lose herself to temper or else folly might capture her. The other part of me—the big part—wanted to be a thirteen-year-old girl who is taken care of by a wise father. (136)

A father who fulfilled his obligations to his country and his daughter would have gone far to alleviate Cleopatra's troubles, but as a princess she must rise to the occasion even when the king cannot.

Ani (*The Goose Girl*) also finds freedom as a goose girl that she had never had as a princess. She listens to her worker friends grumble, discussing the imposter who has taken her identity. She realizes, "*If I were where I was supposed to be, I never would have met the workers of the west settlement. I'd be the yellow girl from Kildenree, with the whiny accent and pompous manner.* Just then, that seemed a pitiable fate" (Hale *Goose* 136). She also has an episode in which she chastises a man from the palace for not approaching his horse properly: "she had ordered him and insulted him and mounted his horse to ride down the pasture like a crazed thief. The anonymity of her goose girl costume and name gave leash to a freedom that she had never dared exhibit when she had been the crown princess shivering in her mother's shadow" (Hale *Goose* 152). Ani had spent her princess childhood falling short of her mother's expectations and being cowed into insecure silence. As a commoner, she allows herself to speak freely and to act without fear.

Other princesses recognize that their lives would be easier if they were not burdened by their positions. Ella (*Just Ella*) tries to break her engagement with Prince Charming both because she no longer loves him and because the life she would have to lead as a princess is too restricted. The final straw for Ella is a tournament she and her ladies attend. Physically confined by her fashionable, breathtakingly tight corset, Ella is nonetheless excited to go to the tournament. She and her ladies, however, are not permitted to actually watch the competition. They are seated in a cloth tent, with all the walls closed, unable to see or be seen, both from fear they would distract the competitors and to protect them from the possible sight of blood. Ella is incredulous:

> 'You mean, you go to the tournament and don't watch it? Why? Why not just stay locked in the castle, doing needlepoint forever? .... Oh, I get it, it's a change of pace to do needlepoint in a cloth prison instead of a stone one—'
>
> ....I appealed to the others.
>
> 'Why do you put up with this?' I asked. 'Doesn't she make you want to scream?'
>
> Every single one of them gazed at me blankly.
>
> 'Don't you ever want to do something—something real? Don't you ever get sick of being ladies-in-waiting? Have any of you ever wondered what you're waiting for?'
>
> 'That is what women do. We wait,' Simprianna said primly. 'Men go out and have adventures, and we wait for their return. They like to know that we are safe at home, waiting. And in this case, we also wait on you, dear Princess.' (Haddix 102-3)

The life of servitude Ella endured prior to being chosen by the prince at the ball was paradoxically freer than the life of luxury she endures as a princess. Her past experiences have shown her that life has more to offer than needlepoint and "waiting," and she can no longer convince herself that marrying the prince is worth the limitations on her movement and conversation.

The Princess's Work

Beyond the restrictions of clothing and proper princess behavior, these new princess stories also acknowledge that ruling a country is in fact difficult work, and that in order to mature into a good ruler, a princess needs rigorous training. The instructor who allows Helen to learn swordplay (*Nobody's Princess*) does so because it will help her become a better ruler. La Cendrillon (*Before Midnight* [2007]) respects and aspires to her stepmother's strength, knowing she herself will also have to be strong. Elizabeth (*Elizabeth I: Red Rose of the House of Tudor* [2002]) must "learn the most challenging discipline of all—to become [her] own master in regard to [her] studies" (Lasky "Elizabeth" 150). To that end, she devises a schedule that includes Aristotle, statements of logic, reading and translating Cicero, and composing lines in Virgil's dactylic hexameter. Moreover, she trains herself against becoming easily upset, watching as her father's festering leg is lanced. Horrible though it is, she knows that Henry "must not see me feeling faint and squeamish...I must look strong" (153). Elizabeth's chances of ruling are slim, and she feels invisible much of the time, yet she prepares herself to reign regardless. Kristina (*Kristina: The Girl King*) spends hours memorizing the works of Livy and Cicero, a task she considers fairly simple. One of her teachers

> ...describes the problems that a ruler might face ... and has me consider both sides of the question, weigh everything in the balance, and then arrive at a conclusion. At times, I am overwhelmed by the responsibility I shall one day carry, although the chancellor reminds me that I am my father's daughter in every way and will make a brilliant ruler. (Meyer 64)

Swordplay, strength, Latin and logic: not the usual princess education as delineated in traditional princess stories.

Cleopatra (*Cleopatra VII: Daughter of the Nile*) has a gift of languages and of befriending people, both of which she cultivates with an eye toward the throne. She consciously models herself on the Queen of Sheba in her desire for knowledge and on Queens Esther and Nefertiti for their bravery. She calls on reserves of inner strength when Cicero speaks against her father; she writes in her diary, "I wanted to run and hide so I could weep privately, but I stayed, for a queen must bear bad news with dignity" (Gregory 146). Even harder for Cleopatra is knowing that she could lose her place as her father's favorite, so she keeps any uneasiness to herself. As she writes, "Another truth for a princess: It is folly to be an enemy of the king" (148). Unlike an average girl, she does not even have a father whose love she can trust. While much of her life is appealing, the ways she needs to brace herself emotionally and project an aura of strength and wisdom beyond her years is tiring, not the traditional way princesses have been portrayed.

Princess Addie (*The Two Princesses of Bamarre*) spends her time as a dragon's captive learning about her people through a magic spyglass. She watches the commoners' everyday lives, from the peaceful goatherds to the ever-vigilant archers. She sees the impact of an epidemic disease on her countrymen, and she comes to understand and share her sister's zeal to help them. Later, seeing herself garbed for her wedding, she knows she has learned what it takes to rule: "the maiden in the mirror was…assured. Not timid, not afraid of her own voice or of shadows lurking in corners. The maiden in the mirror looked resolute, strong-willed. The maiden in the mirror could lead a kingdom" (234). Addie has always been lovely, princess-like, but in the course of her story she becomes powerful.

As discussed above, Princess Ben (*Princess Ben*) resents the superficial lessons she is forced to endure when she first comes to the castle. But when her country comes under threat, she rises to the occasion and throws herself into the true work of a ruler: matters of state. She begs the queen's pardon and admits "for too long I have avoided the affairs of Montagne….I must commence to learn what I might" (Murdock 255). The queen regent is surprised, but allows Ben to join her conference. As the country heads toward war, the queen's attention is taken by military concerns. The domestic concerns, "the countless decisions of Chateau de Montagnee—the menus, the interminable cycle of cleaning, the food stores to be laid up for winter, the disciplining and acquisition of staff" (264), fall to Ben. The chores of the mistress of a castle are not glamorous, but they must be done, and Ben learned them on her way to learning to rule a country.

The Princess's Rescue

The princesses in these princess stories are not only depicted learning hard lessons and preparing for the difficult task of running a country, they are also shown to be quite capable of saving themselves when necessary. None of them waits for a prince to rescue her; each can devise and implement plans for herself and her friends. Addie (*The Two Princesses of Bamarre*) not only escapes from a dragon alone and unassisted, she develops the strategy by which she and her companions will attain the cure for the Grey Death. Ani (*The Goose Girl*) conceives of the plan by which she and her friends will confront the imposter who has usurped her. Princess Sonora

(*Princess Sonora and the Long Sleep*) is known for her erudition and cleverness; she figures out how the quick-witted prince who awakens her can ask her hand in marriage without offending and having to fight the dull yet strong prince who had been there when the spell was triggered. Rosella (*The Fairy's Mistake* [1999]) "wanted to solve the problem of Harold and his poor subjects all by herself" (49), and she did, by refusing to speak until she and Harold came to an agreement that half of the jewels that dropped from her mouth would go towards improving the lives of his subjects. Ben (*Princess Ben*) burns her way out of a dungeon, and then escapes the castle by hiding in a night-soil wagon. Emma (*The Frog Princess*) saves herself and her friends while her male companion sleeps off a spell.

Ella (*Just Ella*) saves herself twice. She managed to get herself to the ball not with a fairy godmother's intervention, but by her own ingenuity, altering her mother's wedding dress and winning glass slippers in a bet. Imprisoned in the castle dungeon after telling Prince Charming she did not want to go through with the marriage, Ella digs her way out through the latrine pit. Although she has a friend who obtains the shovel she uses, Ella is remarkably clever and self-sufficient.

The posse in *A Posse of Princesses* consists of a number of clever and talented young princesses. The one who conceives of the plan to rescue the allegedly abducted princess is Taniva, a warrior princess, who wants to rescue the abducted Iardith in order to prove her fitness to rule. Furthermore, she is not interested in creating an alliance through marriage; she believes that effecting the return of Iardith will save their host country enough trouble and be such a gesture of friendship that an alliance will be created without marriage. When the princesses finally get to Iardith's room, the truth of her abduction comes out: Iardith planned her own abduction in order to force her father to marry her to her "abductor." Once Rhis's identity is known, she is taken as hostage instead of Iardith; her country is richer and her bride price or ransom would be higher than Iardith's would bring. Rhis, imprisoned, uses a magical ring to call her sister the magician. But when offered an opportunity to escape on her own, she stays to help her friends escape as well. By stealing and holding hostage a magical diamond, Rhis effects her companions' and her own escape.

The Roles of Other Women

Not only are each of these princesses unlike their predecessors, the roles of the other women in their stories are different as well. The first difference in the characterizations of other women in these princess stories is that these other women have been included at all. Unlike Disney princess stories, which leave the princesses largely isolated, many of these princesses have female friends or even communities of women in their lives. Snow (*Snow*) develops a deep friendship with Cat, the only female Lonely One. Miri (*Princess Academy*), who is torn away from her loving sister when she is forcibly sent to school, develops friendships with many of the girls who accompany her. The posse in *A Posse of Princesses* is all female. These girls do not dislike men, but in addition to finding pleasure in male company they form solid female friendships.

Emma (*The Frog Princess*) has a beloved aunt who supports her unconditionally: "She's the best relative anybody could have. Grassina is the only one in my family who doesn't ridicule me for being clumsy. She doesn't expect me to be the perfect little lady every minute of the day, and she's taught me a lot of useful things that no one else would ever have thought of teaching me" (Baker 20). She makes another good female friend, too, a bat named L'il. It is immaterial to the story that the bat is female, but that is almost the point—not all boon companions must be male.

Addie (*The Two Princesses of Bamarre*) has a loving nurse and a sister who is her best friend. Meryl has spent her life protecting Addie, but now that Meryl has contracted the Grey Death, Addie can see that Meryl "was going to die without having the adventures she'd longed for, all because of her promise to me. She'd postponed her dreams just to set me at ease. How could I fail to help her, at least try to help her?" (77). Her sister's love, which has sustained Addie her entire life, and the desire to save her are the only motivations that can make Addie leave the castle and brave the dangers of the world.

La Cendrillon (*Before Midnight*) has a godmother who loves and supports her all her life, and a male friend who is brought up as her brother. When her stepmother and stepsisters join her on the estate, fulfilling La Cendrillon's birthday wish for a loving family, they eventually learn to love each other. It takes time because "to truly love takes truly seeing" (Dokey *Midnight* 118), and La Cendrillon had hidden her true identity. But in her stepmother she gets the mother she wished for, "a mother to love [her], a mother [she] might love" (117), and this mother, and the love they develop between them, sustains La Cendrillon.

Many of the princesses develop one dear female friend, a character who stands out from the others in the novel. Initially it appears that Selia, Ani's maid-in-waiting (*The Goose Girl*) is to be Ani's support through the story. But Selia ultimately betrays Ani, leaving her for dead and stealing her name and position. Ani, living as a goose girl with nothing but herself to offer, is befriended by Enna, who learns Ani's true identity. At first she keeps Ani's secret, but when Ani is attacked Enna builds support for her, telling the other workers the truth. Enna later follows Ani into battle, risking her life and rallying others to her aid.

Helen (*Nobody's Princess*) has a mother who loves her and a twin sister with whom she has a fairly realistic—loving, yet competitive—relationship. She makes two additional women friends during the course of her story. The first is Atalanta, whom she admires deeply. Atalanta recognizes in Helen another woman "as hungry for adventure as I am" (Friesner 256); each appreciates knowing that there is at least one other woman who wants more than a purely domestic life. Atalanta teaches Helen to ride a horse, outfitting her with comfortable men's clothing; Helen later serves as Atalanta's weapons-bearer. Helen's other girlfriend is Eunike, the Pythia, the voice of Apollo. Eunike prevents Theseus from abducting and raping Helen, and later helps Helen go to Iolkos disguised as a boy. Eunike appreciates that Helen can treat her as a regular person, that Helen can see past the office and befriend the girl. Helen could not have succeeded without the help of these young women.

Beyond having female friends, these princess stories also offer new possibilities in antagonists: not every antagonist is female, and when one is, the women are not at odds over a man. In *The Two Princesses of Bamarre*, there is no human antagonist; Addie's timidity and the Grey Death are the obstacles to overcome. Princess Cimorene (*Dealing with Dragons*) must work to defeat the league of Wizards, who have thrown their support behind a dragon who will permit them access to dragon lands if they help fix the results of the next dragon king-determining contest. In *Before Midnight*, the problem lies in the political machinations of La Cendrillon's father, inspired by his all-encompassing grief over losing her mother. Ella's antagonist (*Just Ella*) is Prince Charming and his minions, who conspire to have her imprisoned until the wedding upon learning that she no longer wants to marry him. The struggle ultimately comes down to Ella and Madame Bisset, her chief instructor, who is motivated by her desire for power.

Other female protagonists are also motivated by factors other than winning the love of the prince. The primary antagonist in *Princess Academy* is the hated teacher, who is strict and stern because she, like Madame Bisset, wants to maintain her life of privilege. The most antagonistic mountain girl is only motivated to surpass the others because if chosen by the prince, she can escape the life she loathes on the mountain; she is not interested in marrying the prince per se. Similarly, Selia, the antagonist from *The Goose Girl*, steals Ani's identity in order to marry the prince—for the power of eventually being queen, not for love of the man himself. Princess Sonora's antagonist is the evil fairy Belladonna, angry that she was overlooked at the princess's christening. Snow and her friends struggle against Snow's stepmother, who works her evil in order to maintain her power. Power, not princes, motivates most of the evil women in these princess stories; if a man is involved, he is often the antagonist's hapless tool.

Love and/or Marriage

Love and marriage, together the ultimate goal in many traditional princess stories, are often two distinct concepts for these third-wave feminist princesses. This is a more realistic depiction; for royalty, marriages are often arranged and the typical princess would be considered fortunate to love her intended. It is a princess's duty to marry well, to create alliances and to provide heirs to the throne. Real princesses were required to marry—or at least, it was intended that they marry—and fictionalized accounts of their lives reflect that. Elizabeth is well aware of this requirement, and on her twelfth birthday she celebrates "the fact that I am not betrothed or married. That is gift enough" (Lasky "Elizabeth" 148). Kristina is adamantly opposed to marriage; she has no desire to lose any control to the man who would be king, and she would rather appoint an heir than bear one. She admires Elizabeth of England "because she never married. If she could rule her country without a husband, then surely I can do so as well" (Meyer 66). Cleopatra knows she will have to marry the man chosen by her father. Marie Antoinette's life is consumed by her preparations to marry Louis Auguste as part of her mother's plans to recover Silesia: "We lay siege not through weapons of war but through marriages" (Gregory "Marie" 17). Marie explains that by marrying the Dauphin and eventually becoming Queen she will rule Lorraine, which once belonged to her father.

The (purely) fictional princesses are also concerned with their duties of marriage. Rhis (*A Posse of Princesses*) tries not to resent her duty, which is to marry to the benefit of her country. The prince she will ultimately marry explains the reasons royalty might wed: "There's the kingdom to think of, and sometimes a desperately empty treasury, and a wealthy spouse can bring about needed reforms. For others, a marriage might be necessitated by a treaty—the joining of two powerful families in order to prevent war" (Smith 108). Rhis and Lios will marry for love, but not until they have proven to Lios' mother that they are serious and adult enough to marry and to rule. Five years after the imposed separation, Lios proposes, pleased that his mother and country would approve. When Rhis asks what he wants, he tells her there is no pure Lios; he cannot forget his country's needs, even in a proposal. It is a less romantic, much more realistic portrayal of the requirements of royal marriage.

Ben (*Princess Ben*) is dismayed to find she must marry. Her aunt, the queen regent, tries to comfort her: "That is the fate of all princesses, my dear. Every storybook teaches it. If it is any consolation, I have heard that such unions may be more than pleasant, even tender" (Murdock 40). A ball is planned, and Ben has no part in its planning. She feels like a pawn. "All subterfuge surrounding the event had disappeared. My mate would be chosen whether I wished it or no; any small effort I might have on the decision would be determined solely by my abilities to charm the man I favored" (151). Ben takes control during the ball, becoming as charmless and loathsome as possible, trying in this way to avoid marriage altogether. But her plan backfires; the guests come away convinced that Ben would be completely incapable of ruling Montagne, and they plan a governmental coup to save their land from Ben. The neighboring prince, who has previously declared that every man and woman deserves true love, prepares to marry Ben's sleeping double (thought to be Ben herself), whom he believes to be "a sullen and graceless oaf" (219). The real, disguised Ben indignantly calls him deluded, scoffing, "you consign yourself and another to lives of pure misery that you might possess a well-proportioned ballroom" (Murdock 219).

Many of the princesses have no interest in marriage and resent the expectation that they will marry, even as they understand that it is for the good of the kingdom. The fictional depictions of Elizabeth and Kristina, historical princesses who continued unmarried as queens, show them actively wanting to remain single even as girls, even knowing that the people around them would prefer they married. Helen (*Nobody's Princess*) is not only concerned for her own freedom; she knows her sister will be married off and sent to live elsewhere. Helen wonders, "Would she get to choose him, or would she simply be told, *This is the man you're going to marry*, the same way that Ione told us, *This is the dress you're going to wear today*? Was that being free?" (33). As privileged a life as most of these princesses have, the thought that they will be married to someone whether they want him or not is galling.

For Cimorene (*Dealing with Dragons*) and Emma (*The Frog Princess*), their intended marriages serve as the catalysts for their adventures. Cimorene tries to convince the slow-witted Therandil to call off the wedding, but he is bound by convention and will not hear of it. She leaves him, discouraged, and becomes convinced she should run away. Emma is devastated to hear that her marriage to Prince Jorge has been arranged; she cannot think of anyone less suitable for her than Jorge, a "rude idiot who barely acknowledges [her] existence" (Baker 26). Emma's mother tells her, "Husbands and wives who love each other are the exception, not the rule....Many women have married fools and been perfectly happy. Negotiations have begun and despite what you may think, they do not require your approval" (23-4). News of this engagement and her mother's attitude about it prompt Emma to kiss the enchanted frog, hoping for a way to avoid the planned marriage.

Upon finding herself engaged to Prince Melvin, Princess Sonora contemplates pricking her finger with a spindle and initiating her hundred years' sleep. Her mother is pleased that the prince is handsome and a good dancer, but Sonora thinks the prince sounds like a fool, and despairs, "They had nothing in common. Nothing important. The fairies hadn't made him smart. They hadn't given him a loving heart" (Levine "Sonora" 145). When she is awakened from her enchanted sleep, she quickly devises a way to avoid marrying Melvin.

One reason the princesses would rather not marry is that they have other goals, most of which involve education and/or making a difference in the world; even those princesses who do find love do not marry immediately, preferring to meet their personal or civic goals first. Sixteen year old Rhis (*A Posse of Princesses*) plans to do her duty and marry well, but she would like to have some adventures first. Her mother forbids her to marry until she is twenty, assuring her time to discover who she really is. When she does find love with Prince Lios, his mother imposes a five-year separation; she encourages Rhis to "study magic, or statecraft, or whatever you like" (Smith

274). Rhis studies both, and comes to her marriage prepared to rule as Lios' equal and his mother's worthy successor. Similarly, after her adventures as a frog, Emma (*The Frog Princess*) does not agree to marry her adventuring companion immediately, as would a princess in a more traditional story; inspired by their adventures, she puts him off, saying she would rather not get married until she has gone to witch school.

The more time Ella (*Just Ella*) spends in royal captivity, the more fixated she becomes on finding a real life-goal. In her previous life of servitude to her stepmother, she had recognized her two avenues of escape, neither of which was appealing: hire herself out as a servant, or get married. She pins her hopes on one final possibility, becoming a tutor for rich children, and finagles her way to the prince's ball not to marry the prince but to find employment. After escaping from the prince's dungeon, she is faced with finding a way to become useful again. She becomes a medical and agricultural advisor in her former royal tutor's refugee camp and learns to appreciate the rewards that come even in such bleakness. Her happily ever after was not predicated on marrying the prince, or marrying at all (although to add romance to the story, she and her ex-tutor have fallen in love; they are separated and Ella has not yet agreed to marry him at the novel's end). Ella's happiness is predicated on finding useful, fulfilling employment.

Love is an important factor in many of these stories, however; unlike the second wave feminist princess stories, which largely eliminated or scoffed at romance, third wave feminist princess stories recognize its importance in many readers' lives. Even more interestingly, the stories value different sorts of love, not simply the romantic variety. "Let there be no more throwing away of love while I am mistress of this house," says La Cendrillon's stepmother (Dokey "Midnight" 118). The love that was evident in La Cendrillon's mother's portrait inspires all of the women to come together with affection and understanding; it breaks down barriers and creates a functional family. The stepsisters each find a happy romantic ending, and La Cendrillon, buoyed by their support, boldly declares her love to the prince even though "I know it's traditional for the man to speak first, especially when he's a prince" (191). Motherly love, sisterly love, come before romantic love.

Nor is La Cendrillon the only young woman to declare her love to her prince; many princesses articulate their feelings before their princes do. Ben (*Princess Ben*) realizes her love for Prince Florian and kisses his supposedly dead lips. He revives from near death, and the two are wed. Aurore (*Beauty*

Sleep) tells her aged cousin Oswald, who has waited for her for one hundred years, that she cannot marry the young man who rescued her because she loves him, Oswald, instead. She kisses him, and he becomes young again. Snow (*Snow*), under a spell of amnesia, experiences the vaguest stirrings of memory when she talks to Raven, one of the Lonely Ones. As he discusses the scientific/magical procedure he hopes will break the spell, "She reached up and kissed him…she put her hand around the back of his neck to keep him from pulling away" (Lynn 247). Her memories come flooding back, and when Raven is confused, she explains "they say true love can always break a spell" (248). The *Once Upon a Time* series, retellings of tales which generally end in marriage, seems particularly intent on demonstrating princesses being active in love, not passively awaiting a prince to declare or take action first.

The differences between love and infatuation are explicitly discussed in *A Posse of Princesses*, *Nobody's Princess* and *Just Ella*. Queen Briath, Rhis' future mother-in-law, discusses the perils of marrying for simple physical attraction, without really knowing one's intended. She and three of her royal friends, men and women, foolishly married pretty faces—marriages they all came to regret. One queen's consort, Briath explains, is "useless for matters of state. Iardith's father married a pretty face without a vestige of wit behind it" (Smith 269), and Briath herself married someone who "was spoiled rotten because he was so boyish, so charming, everyone always believed everything he said" (Smith 270). Briath intends that her son, Lios, will not be the sort of man his father was, and that he will not make the marital mistake that she herself had made. Her own unhappy marriage, which Briath ended by sending her husband back to his parents, leads Briath to impose five years' maturation time before permitting Lios and Rhis to wed.

Helen (*Nobody's Princess*) is initially stunned by Theseus' beauty, gaping at him thunderstruck. Her blood pounds in her ears and her breath is short just looking at him, and when he smiles at her she blushes. She fantasizes about marrying him, until he speaks. His egotism, overconfidence, and boastfulness instantly dispel Helen's physical attraction to him. The two have a run-in later, in an episode that further confirms Helen's dislike of him. He accosts Helen in the marketplace, refusing to leave her alone. He maintains a running monologue in which he discusses Helen's potential beauty, her foolishness in wielding a weapon, and how a good husband will make Helen settle down. When she tries to leave, he physically prevents her, twisting her wrist until she cries out in pain. Helen screams and thrashes, but to no avail—Theseus does not release her and no one tries to stop him from dragging her off. "Who'd dare interfere with a man who was so obviously rich and strong, especially when the victim was just a girl...?" (Friesner 234). No amount of physical beauty can compensate for being a boor, an abductor and would-be rapist.

Ella (*Just Ella*) is at first entranced by Prince Charming's physical presence, his "clear blue eyes, high cheekbones, rugged jaw, blond hair precisely the right length...muscular chest and trim waist" (Haddix 28-9). When he plays with her hair, she loses her train of thought. These physical qualities are unfortunately his only positive ones, and they will not be enough to sustain her interest through their engagement. She does eventually find a real relationship with her royal tutor, Jed, who proposes to her. She worries about marriage in general, with the bad example of her father and stepmother fresh in her mind, and she worries about her judgment, since she had thought she was in love with the prince. As she considers Jed's proposal, she realizes that her feelings for the prince "had been infatuation with an ideal, not love for a real human being. Jed was real. I knew his faults as well as his virtues" (202). She asks for six months in which to make her decision, during which time they spend long hours working together and conversing. The story ends before Ella makes her final decision, but Jed has said, "If we do get married, our marriage won't be like other people's. You may go off and study to become a full-fledged doctor. We may work as a team on everything" (214). Ella will be free to pursue her education and her interests, and she will have a friend as well as a husband.

Princesses in romantic relationships are shown to have standards and expectations for male behavior. Honesty, respect, and consideration are among the qualities princesses should expect in a spouse. Rosella (*The Fairy's Mistake*) resents the way her betrothed forces her to speak (to generate jewels) but disregards what she actually has to say. Emma (*The Frog Princess*) expresses her frustration when Prince Eadric, her enchanted frog companion, disregards her advice and foolishly eats a poison fly. She also berates him for sleeping while she is working towards their rescue. Rhis (*A Posse of Princesses*) is annoyed by one suitor's false flattery. "The pretense of, of, liking, or romance, is what I hate—it's too sickening when someone glops on about flowers and hearts and how beautiful I am and how smart, but not really meaning it. I guess that's because, well, if they lie to me when we are strangers, when does the lying stop?" (Smith 109-110). Although some princesses may initially be taken by a prince's appearance, more important qualities will ultimately determine the course of the relationship.

The primary quality these smart princesses value in a man is intelligence. Princess Sonora, mocked for her intelligence, is delighted to be awakened by a prince who is endlessly curious. Cimorene (*Dealing with Dragons*) finds Therandil, her intended, handsome but "he has no sense of humor, he isn't intelligent, he can't talk about anything except tourneys, and half of what he does say he gets wrong" (Wrede 6). Ella (*Just Ella*) falls out of love with Prince Charming because he is so stupid. One of the maids says "He wouldn't know how to get out of bed in the morning if he didn't have advisors telling him which foot to put on the floor first" (Haddix 115). Moreover, he does not value Ella's intelligence. When she tells him she has been thinking (gently leading up to breaking their engagement), Charming chuckles and says thinking is "Always a dangerous thing for a woman to do...especially one as beautiful as you" (121). In her fury, Ella reconsiders her determination to break the engagement gently. Ultimately she will fall in love with Jed, as discussed above; they are intellectual equals and as importantly, they respect each other.

These princess stories also warn against unrealistic expectations of happy endings. The whole point of *Just Ella* is that, as Ella puts it, "in real life, ever afters generally stink" (Haddix 189). Hers certainly did not turn out happily with the prince, and the happy ending she does ultimately find in a refugee camp is far from a fairy tale. Ella's non-fairy-tale ending comes from the plot; *Princess Ben*'s comes from the reality of marriage. Ben warns against delusions of marital bliss leading to "happy ever after" directly:

> Every fairy tale, it seems, concludes with the bland phrase 'happily ever after.' Yet every couple I have ever known would agree that nothing about marriage is forever happy. There are moments of bliss, to be sure, and lengthy spans of satisfied companionship. Yet these come at no small effort, and the girl who reads such fictions dreaming her troubles will end ere she departs the altar is well advised to seek at once a rational woman to set her straight. (Murdock 338)

Most of the princess stories do not address the issue this directly, but many have similar warnings embedded in the narrative.

Prince Lios proposes to Princess Rhis (*A Posse of Princesses*) by speaking of the needs of his country. "I wish I could give you the play's version of being a queen, with boxes of gems and a new gown every day, and an endless series of courtly plays and surprises" (Smith 298). But he cannot offer Rhis these things, because their world is unstable. War looms and traders are unhappy and "there is greed and ambition and danger aplenty out there in the world, and our job will be to ceaselessly guard against it. We will work hard" (299). Lios will find the work bearable if he has Rhis by his side, but he is quite explicit and practical in all the ways their lives will not be a fairy tale.

La Cendrillon's stepsister (*Before Midnight*) bitterly believes that she cannot marry the stable boy she loves, because "that sort of arrangement may work out well in stories and in dreams. But not in real life" (Dokey *Midnight* 129). The girls from the *Princess Academy*, the would-be princesses, contemplate reality versus fairy tales. One of the girls compares the reality of meeting the prince with the fairy-tale version. She concludes less than enthusiastically, with a shrug, "'Steffan was pretty nice, I guess, but...' She shrugged again" (Hale *Academy* 285). Some girls still envision a life more luxurious than theirs in the mountain quarry, but one girl argues,

> It won't be one long ball. It'll be boring work, long days talking to people you don't care about, and married to a dull boy with a fancy title. I can't believe after all our lessons in History, knowing about all the assassinations and political plots and wars and barren queens, that anyone would want to be a princess. (Hale "Academy" 285-6)

Some of the more foolish girls are not convinced, but every admirable character agrees: the life of a princess is not one long happy ending.

Snow, which twice references "fairy tale endings," does not end in a marriage (although there is the promise of romance). During a scene that develops into a near-rape, Snow receives her first kiss. She wonders if that means she will marry this man. She does not; in fact, she is punished for allegedly having encouraged the young man to cross the lines of propriety. Later, she does not marry the nobleman who has returned her to her home. They agree to part as friends, both relieved that although "proposing to [Snow] just seemed...what was expected" (Lynn 256), she declined. They were the only two pleased by their decision, though. "Everyone in the estate and town was disappointed with her, resentful that she had spoiled their fairy tale" (256). The stereotypical happy ending would have the princess marry her rescuer, but Snow holds out for love instead of friendship, pleasing herself instead of pleasing others.

The life of a princess in these stories is not a life of luxury. In some instances, it is not even portrayed as a life of safety—and dragons are not the real danger. The perils of a princess's life are highlighted in the historical fiction *The Royal Diaries* series. Elizabeth is often exiled, ignored and isolated, and the reasons often seem arbitrary; she lives a very insecure and dangerous life. Cleopatra's life as detailed in her journal was in danger from a variety of sources. She worries that her sister is trying to poison her. In another attempt on her life, a note pinned to her horse's stall warns her that an assassin will run her through with a spear if she is seen with her horse. Later, a message comes that confirms her earlier fears, warning her not to eat or drink because her sister's friends had been hired to poison her. King Ptolemy and Cleopatra sail for Rome, escaping the various other assassination attempts. At the end of the book, Cleopatra plans an educational tour of Egypt as preparation for her time as queen. She hides her intent from her father, because "if he knew my trip was planned for the purpose of making me a good queen, that I am seeking wisdom and knowledge, he might prefer to kill me" (Gregory 172). Cleopatra has been in mortal danger for the whole two years covered by this fictional diary, from the people who might, under common circumstances, be most expected to love and protect her.

Being a Princess, Being a Girl

Many of these new princess stories directly address the issues surrounding women and girls. Anne, the wicked stepmother in *Snow*, is driven to evil by her perceived position in life. She feels that being female puts her at a disadvantage, and she constantly, bitterly strives against the unfairness she observes. When she first comes to live with Snow, Anne is not evil at all; she is beautiful and smart, and she shows an affectionate interest in her stepdaughter. As Snow matures, however, Anne demonstrates a distinct ambivalence toward her and toward her developing womanhood. When Snow first begins menstruating, the duchess warns her that "things will have to change" in a conversation that clearly delineates the antiquated rules for women under which Anne operates:

> 'You are no longer a little girl. You are a *young lady*. A ... *pretty* young lady. Women will begin to hate you and men will want to—men are just terrible....Let me inform you right now that boys and men are not your friends. They will never be your friends again. They will want to do improper things with you if you're *un*lucky, and to own you if you are. Marriage....I suppose you will get married in a few years...I should start to work on that...A mother would....' She shook her head. 'That is what you will be someday.... A mother. Society has only two uses for women, remember that. Beautiful girls and mothers.'

.... 'Be one or the other, or both, but not neither. No one wants an old hag. Or a
trollop.'
And then the duchess started to cry. (Lynn 46-47)

The woman who will shortly become a truly wicked stepmother is here
shown as a figure to pity. She is unhappy with what she believes to be
women's lot in life. The story will show Snow having healthy friendships
with men and women while Anne becomes increasingly cruel, isolated, and
desperate.

This archaic belief system which pits women against women and positions men as women's victimizers or owners leads to Anne's downfall. The
duchess also demonstrates other archaic, anti-female beliefs. When Snow is
sexually set upon by a count, the duchess blames her for dressing "like a
slattern" (Lynn 59). Snow reflects on this later, when she is giving her friend
Cat an ornate mirror. She contemplates her past life as a "good" girl, "who
did what people told her, more or less, and was expected to stay pretty so
boys would like me, so men would like me—but it's still my fault when they
kiss me" (147). When Cat resists the gift, saying only sissy girls care about
their appearance, Snow corrects her hidebound thinking in a very strong,
third-wave feminist manner: "Don't be ridiculous, Cat. You can be beautiful
and strong and scary and still steal like a thief. You have that choice" (148).
When Anne the stepmother does not believe she has a choice, when she tries
to live by sexist rules, she becomes evil; the heroine, however, valorizes a
different belief system and confronts those who do not yet live by it, including, eventually, Anne. The duchess has brought Snow to her, in an attempt to
steal her fertility. She lulls Snow with tea and conversation, and she apologizes for her terrible treatment of Snow ("In my madness, I believed that
eating your heart would enable me to have a baby" [185]). She continues:

> 'But understand this. As mad as I was, there is some truth in what I am about to
> tell you....My desperation to have a child, my obsession with my looks—these are
> merely a mirror for society at large. Society has only two uses for women: as young
> and beautiful things, and as baby machines. You are only wanted or useful as long
> as you fill one of those two roles.'
> 'That's not true,' Snow blurted out. 'Women are wanted for the same thing as
> men—to be kind, to be wise, to work hard....What about your experiments? What
> about yourself, Anne? You have done great things—'
> 'All of which I had to keep secret or publish under a man's name!' the duchess
> hissed. 'Like Georges Sand, Margaret Murray Huggins, Nettie Stevens—all in the
> shadow of their husbands or of fake masculine names.' (Lynn 186)

Society has changed, but Anne cannot recognize the changes. Snow redirects the conversation in the face of Anne's obvious insanity. Anne's bitterness makes her evil, and she will shortly make another attempt on Snow's life in the name of her own fertility. Had Anne realized that women can be valued for more than their looks and their fecundity, Snow's story would have been quite different. Anne has the old motivation of the stepmother in the Grimm "Snow White," but in a modern retelling it must be acknowledged that the world, and women's place in it, has changed.

Nobody's Princess addresses sexism and gender role expectations head on. As discussed above, Helen is consumed by her desire to be free, to make her own decisions and live by them. When she asks for combat training, the trainer tells her brothers they cannot make any objection based on her gender. There are other feminist issues addressed in the novel as well. Helen's two female friends, Atalanta and Eunike, offer opportunities to reflect on women. Atalanta competes with men on their level, hunting and wrestling and running. Although Helen's brothers are impressed by Atalanta's skills, and Helen admires Atalanta and wants to emulate her, the other women in the court of Mykenae have nothing but disdain for the woman they call an "unnatural creature" and a "want-to-be man"(Friesner 151). They characterize the huntress as sick, scoffing that all she needs "is a good husband and a house full of babies...*That* will cure her quickly enough" (Friesner 151). Helen takes umbrage at these comments and meets Atalanta for another riding lesson. Helen's other friend, Eunike the Pythia, is arguably the most powerful character in the novel. As the Oracle of Delphi, she saves Helen from Theseus' attempted abduction by identifying him and predicting his unhappy future. Men and women from all over Greece pay homage to Apollo through her, and she can essentially do as she likes. She helps Helen on her way to her next adventure, knowing that she herself is untouchable if her role in Helen's travels is discovered.

Much of the commentary in *Just Ella* is about the importance of beauty and the privileges it affords those lucky enough to possess it[1]. Madame Bisset, Ella's primary instructor (and warden), opines that "our duty as women is to be protected from unpleasantness, so that our minds and our souls—and our brows—shall be unsullied by worry. Women were created to be like flowers, providing color and beauty to the world. We leave troubling matters to the men" (Haddix 22). Ella takes issue with this, noting that neither the female servants in the castle nor the village women were protected from unpleasantness. Her friend Mary, a serving girl, tells her how and why Ella was chosen to marry the prince, information Mary has because "Being ugly is like being invisible sometimes" (114), and the king's advisors never noticed her working in the room during their planning session. The Charmings are required to have beautiful children, which necessitates marrying a beautiful woman. Upon entering the prince's ball, the young women were immediately judged and either directed toward the prince or shunted into a different room. Ella remembered being announced as though she had been a beauty contestant, then she understands that she "had been a beauty contestant. And the prince had been the prize" (115). The prince, Ella realizes, had never been in love with her; he had done as required and picked the most beautiful woman at the ball. She believes that breaking the engagement will be acceptable, but instead she finds herself imprisoned.

Madame Bisset is thrilled at the prospect of how Ella will look emerging from the dungeon on her wedding day: "radiant...so thin, so pale" (140). The palace ideal of female beauty is such that a woman imprisoned, underfed and never seeing the sun (as Ella will be) or overworked and wan from exhaustion (as Ella was upon escaping her stepmother) is considered most beautiful. As Ella says, "If it didn't affect me, I could be plenty amused" (140). At the very end of the book, when the prince has married Ella's rotund stepsister instead of Ella (as a means of insuring silence on all parts), new standards of beauty are adopted; all the women in the palace strive to carry as much excess weight as possible, as Madame Bisset realized it would be easier to change the standards of beauty than to slim down the stepsister. Standards of beauty are shown to be both unhealthy and arbitrary, first in the pale and skinny imprisoned look (much like the 1990s 'heroin chic') and then in the fat-is-beautiful revision.

The princesses in these new princess stories are a different breed both from the ones presented either in the second-wave feminist tales of the 1970s and 1980s and from the pseudo-feminist Disney princess stories of the 1990s. These girls are fully developed characters who embody the feminism "in the water" of their culture. They are of different body types and coloring, and they want more for themselves than to sit around and look pretty. They train for and perform real work; they save themselves when needing rescue. They expect the same opportunities given their male counterparts and to be treated as men's equals as a matter of course. They demand respect from their male friends and romantic partners, and they do not expect their stories or themselves to end when they find romance. Two more of their number will be discussed in greater length: Mia Thermopolis, of Meg Cabot's *The*

Princess Diaries series, and Ella of Frell, from Gail Carson Levine's *Ella Enchanted*. The first is explicitly concerned with princess lessons, both for the protagonist and for the audience; Disney has made two Princess Diaries films, one "based on the novel" and one simply "based on the characters" created by Cabot. *Ella Enchanted*, a Newberry Honor book, was also made into a Disney movie; it strays almost unrecognizably far from the novel in its onscreen adaptation. These are the only two earnest[2] princess stories Disney produced for the theater in the 2000s, and they are live-action rather than animated, but they show a greater consanguinity with the animated princess stories of the 1990s than with the third-wave feminist princess novels on which they are based.

The Princess Diaries

One princess story worth examining on its own is Meg Cabot's *The Princess Diaries*, a sixteen-book series: ten full-length novels, four novellas, and two self-help books. These novels tell the story of Mia Thermopolis, who learns that her father is the crown prince of Genovia and that she will one day inherit the throne. The overarching project in the novels is Mia's transformation from average high school freshman, obsessed with her physical imperfections and crushing on the most popular boy in school, to princess. This transformation is effected by her Grandmère, the Dowager Princess of Genovia, and while some of it concerns Mia's appearance, much of it concerns the real responsibilities of being a princess: diplomacy and governance. The books are fun and chatty, and Mia is extremely realistic, but the series is also quite didactic, both in teaching Mia how to be a princess and in teaching the reader what it is to be a third-wave feminist along the lines described by Jennifer Baumgardner and Amy Richards.

The basic plot of *The Princess Diaries* (2000), the first in the series, is as follows: Mia begins writing in her diary as a means of relieving the stress of her mother's new relationship with Mia's algebra teacher. She very quickly learns of her newly-important status as her father's daughter; her parents had never married, and they thought it best to allow Mia to live a normal life, assuming that her father would eventually marry and sire children born in wedlock. His testicular cancer removes this possibility, and Mia, as his only child, will assume the throne. Her Grandmère comes to New York to teach Mia all she will need to know, and much of the story concerns Mia's struggle to master princess skills and her frustration with the ways her life changes as a result of her new status: fame, a bodyguard, her friends' responses. The most popular boy in school asks Mia to a dance, using her for his own publicity. She leaves him in the middle of their date and spends the evening talking and dancing with Michael, her best friend Lilly's older brother, in whom she has been interested for years. The story ends with Mia happy about her life and looking forward to a one-week reprieve from her princess lessons.

The second novel, *Princess in the Spotlight* (2001), centers on Mia's mother's pregnancy and planning her wedding to Mia's algebra teacher. Mia is caught between her grandmother, who plans an elaborate affair, and her mother, who prefers a small, intimate get-together. Mia is also preparing for her first national prime-time interview. To round out her concerns, she is also receiving anonymous love-notes and, while she hopes they are from Michael, they are instead from Kenny, Mia's lab partner. She finds herself dating Kenny but dreaming of Michael, and in the climactic moments of the story she races from her grandmother's black-tie celebration to a midnight movie, where she is delighted to hear that Michael thinks she looks beautiful.

Further novels in the series follow a similar pattern, with Mia torn between her Grandmère's expectations about a princess' duties and the activities and interests Mia prefers. *Princess in Love* (2002) involves preparations for Mia's official introduction to Genovia and the uses to which Mia puts her fame. *Princess in Waiting* (2003) highlights the struggle between Mia's duties and her desires, specifically how Mia will resolve the conflict between a required royal ball and a desired showing of *Star Wars*. Life as a princess is not what Disney would have Mia believe, and my examination of the first two novels will demonstrate the tensions inherent in trying to combine the princess fantasy and real life.

Mia is not thrilled to learn she is a princess. She feels betrayed by her parents hiding her identity; she feels stupid never to have figured it out herself; and she instantly worries about the ways people will perceive her. She bursts into tears, which demonstrates to herself how unsuited for the role she is. She also looks, to her mind, nothing like a princess; her hair is bushy, her breasts undeveloped, and her feet are size ten. She is alienated from her parents and she feels she cannot confide in her best friend, Lilly, because "she is vehemently opposed to any form of government that is not by the people, exercised either directly or through elected representatives" (*Diaries* 47). Mia has never aspired to princesshood. When her mother suggests that most girls would be delighted to learn they were royalty, Mia reflects, "No girls I know. Actually, that's not true. Lana Weinberger would probably *love* to be a princess. In fact, she already thinks she is one" (*Diaries* 56). Lana is Mia's classroom antagonist, and the fact that she acts like a princess is not a mark in her favor. As soon as Mia's secret identify becomes public, people start to treat her differently, just as she feared.

Princess Lessons

"You know as well as I do that I'm not princess material, okay?"
—*Diaries* 108.

Mia has not dreamed of being a princess. Mia can be self-obsessed, as are many teenaged girls, but she is also aware of the world around her and is a passionate activist, eventually even learning to use her princess status for the greater good. Her dreams involve saving the world; she is an anti-fur vegetarian who wants to work with Greenpeace. She tries to refuse princess lessons, but she acquiesces when her father offers to donate one hundred dollars to Greenpeace for every day she takes lessons. When her identity is publicized, she faces the press wearing all of her "Greenpeace and antifur buttons, so at least [her] celebrity status will be put to good use" (*Diaries* 209). The only time she almost stops to answer the questions from the press is when a question is posed about her feelings on the meat industry. Her vegetarianism is one of her defining characteristics; her friends recognize that the most popular boy in school does not really like or know Mia when he orders her a steak for dinner. She finds it hard to believe that anyone besides her grandmother cares about her deportment, asking "Shouldn't my future countrymen and women be more concerned with my views on the environment? And gun control? And overpopulation?" (*Spotlight* 27). In one late-night conversation, Mia outlines her plan to give homes to stray animals, training some as seeing-eye guides and taking others to hospital in-patients (*Spotlight* 186). While her princess lessons will change some aspects of her personality, Mia will remain an activist and will strive to find ways of making her life as a princess reflect her personal passions.

Much of Mia's time is spent with her grandmother, the dowager princess, a cigarette-smoking, Sidecar-drinking nightmare (in Mia's estimation), being schooled in everything a princess needs to know. Grandmère has no sympathy for Mia's lack of desire to be a princess: "You are the heir to the crown of Genovia...And you will take my son's place on the throne when he dies. This is how it is. There is no other way" (*Diaries* 108). Grandmère has high standards for a princess' appearance, behavior and character. When Mia joins her in the penthouse at the Plaza, Grandmère greets her with a litany of complaints:

> Why are you wearing tennis shoes with a skirt? Are those tights supposed to be clean? Why can't you stand up straight? What's wrong with your hair? Have you been biting your nails again, Amelia? I thought we agreed you were going to give up that nasty habit. My God, can't you stop growing? Is it your goal to be as tall as your father? (*Diaries* 106)

Mia is expected to converse in French, to wear stockings, nail polish, and lipstick, and she is expected to report for lessons every day immediately after school. She bemoans the fact that she does not have a sweet, cookie-baking grandma, but over the course of the series she will find many of her princess lessons useful.

Under pressure from her grandmother, Mia unhappily changes her appearance. She undergoes a makeover at a high-end spa, where her hair is cut and dyed, acrylic fingernails are applied, and every inch of her has been "pinched, cut, filed, painted, sloughed, blown dry, or moisturized" (*Diaries* 129). Grandmère has also purchased Mia an expensive new wardrobe. In many books and films, this would leave the protagonist feeling wonderful, exuberant about her transformation and ready to face all obstacles. Mia, however, wonders how she allowed this to happen. She recognizes her own fear of confrontation, but she was also caught up in the moment. She writes, "it is sort of hard when all these beautiful, fashionable people are telling you how good you'd look in this and how much that would bring out your cheekbones, to remember you're a feminist and an environmentalist, and don't believe in using makeup or chemicals that might be harmful to the earth" (*Diaries* 128). Mia here wants both to be feminist and to be feminine; in other words, she wants to be "girlie." Baumgardner and Richards declare that it is okay to be drawn to feminine things, that one can be a feminist and still wear makeup. "Using makeup isn't a sign of our sway to the marketplace and the male gaze; it can be sexy, campy, ironic or simply decorating ourselves without the loaded issues" (*Manifesta* 136). Lilly, much more the voice of second-wave feminism, will scornfully insult Mia for her makeover. Lilly here is the personification of what Baumgardner and Richards call "the feminist mystique... the attitude that made us feel guilty for embellishing ourselves with girlie things" (*Feminism* 66). Mia's makeover is no anti-feminist crime, but one could argue that she should have been allowed to dress as she liked.

But Mia's physical appearance, although easy to criticize and easily changed, does not make up the bulk of her princess lessons. Her grandmother requires her to prepare a list of admirable women as her first night's homework (her list includes Madonna, Princess Diana, Hillary Rodham Clinton, a lady cop she once saw, and her mother). Grandmère educates and tests her on a wide range of subjects, from how to behave in a restaurant to Marx's discussion of capitalism to how to respond when someone declares his love. She lists the lessons she has mastered: "how to sit; how to dress; how to use a fish fork; how to address senior members of the royal household staff; how to say thank you so much and no, I don't care for that, in seven languages; how to make a Sidecar; and some Marxist theory" (*Diaries* 203). She is also taught that a princess must always be ready to compromise and to be kind to strangers. Mia does become more assertive as a result of her lessons, standing up to Lilly, Lana Weinberger, and Josh Richter (who will be discussed below). Her personal growth and absorption of her lessons is brought home in the second novel, when she convinces Grandmère to rejoin the wedding celebration Mia's mother has refused to attend. "I thought you were always telling me a princess has to be strong. I thought you said that a princess, no matter what kind of adversity she is facing, has to put on a brave face and not hide behind her wealth and privilege" (*Spotlight* 236). Grandmère has been seeking to impart not just fashion sense but dignity and fortitude through Mia's lessons, all characteristics a reigning princess needs.

Romance and Sexuality

> *"I know it's misogynistic and sexist and all, but it's also really, really neat"*
> —*Spotlight* 202.

Mia calling herself a feminist yet being twitterpated about boys, specifically Josh Richter, the most popular boy in school and Michael, Lilly's older brother, is not a contradiction. Those who would suggest that real feminists would not be so interested are again voicing Baumgardner and Richards' "feminist mystique," which "leaves us to assume that the feminist label belongs only to those who have sorted out all their issues and are no longer conflicted about men, sex, their bodies, their incomes, or fashion" (*Feminism* 66-67). Mia is conflicted, and no wonder: she has grown up with outspoken feminists, as represented by her mother and Lilly, but in a culture saturated by traditional princess messages, as represented by her frequent allusions to Disney. Her and her friend's reading of romance novels also colors her expectations of romance.

Mia has two strong feminist influences in her life, her mother Helen and her best friend Lilly. Helen, Mia's primary caregiver, never married Mia's father, telling Mia she "was a feminist who didn't believe in the male hierarchy and was against the subjugation and obfuscation of the female identity that marriage necessarily entails" (*Spotlight* 38). Although her father has been involved in her life, Mia has grown up with her mother's last name because her "mom doesn't believe in what she calls the cult of the patriarchy" (*Diaries* 44). Lilly is also an outspoken feminist and activist, involved in all manner of causes. She is fearless, and "she totally doesn't care how she looks....Lilly isn't afraid of anything" (*Diaries* 24). The only princess Lilly admires is Xena, Warrior Princess; emulating her, Lilly "can kickbox like nobody's business" (24). She is environmentally and economically aware, alert to injustice, and skeptical of Mia being guided by romance novels in male/female relationships. Mia both admires Lilly and fears her, and Lilly has had a great influence on Mia's activism.

Yet for all the times Helen and Lilly have demonstrated feminist values, Mia is not untouched by more traditional forces in popular culture. Lilly of course has strong views about the Disneyfication of America, but Mia references Disney princess stories whenever she feels especially princesslike or when her romantic dreams seem close to being fulfilled. Her favorite musical is *Beauty and the Beast* ("I don't care what Lilly says about Walt Disney and his misogynistic undertones" [*Diaries* 36]), and one of her tests for whether she would be physically intimate with a boy is his ability to watch the Broadway production without mocking it. Mia is also very aware of the life of Princess Diana, and as a princess she wants to model her own good works on Diana's. She reads romances and watches *Baywatch*, defending the latter from accusations of lameness and sexism by pointing out that both women and men are scantily clad and that in the later episodes, a woman is chief lifeguard. Her likes and dislikes are influenced by the entirety of popular culture, not just by those more feminist ones.

Mia is well aware of misogyny, but she cannot help wishing for traditional romance. Although she has crushes on both Josh Richter and Michael Moscowitz, she confesses this only to her diary. When her royal identity is revealed, Josh Richter breaks up with his girlfriend, antagonistic Lana Weinberger, to ask Mia to the school dance. Even though "this tiny part of

[her] brain—the only part that wasn't completely stunned by his asking [her] out—went: He's only asking you out because you're the princess of Genovia" (*Diaries* 231), she ultimately does not care about his motivations, and she accepts his invitation. Josh, intent on being in the spotlight, tips off the paparazzi and, much to Mia's humiliation, kisses her for the cameras. Mia realizes that this, her first kiss, was simply a photo op for Josh. She compares this experience with the ones she and her friend have read about in teen romance novels; there was no "warm gushy feeling" (*Diaries* 264), no sense that "the guy is drawing her soul up from deep within her" (264). It feels strange, "having this guy stand there and smash his mouth against [hers]" (264), and she is extremely embarrassed.

Mia realizes the kiss was a set up, that Josh was only with her so he could brag about dating a princess. And she realizes that she has changed. "If I hadn't turned out to be a princess, maybe I might still be all that stuff. You know, unassertive, fearful of confrontation, an internalizer. I probably wouldn't have done what I did next" (267). She demands an explanation from Josh, telling him she appreciated neither the publicity nor the kiss. When he protests that he really likes her, she retorts that he does not even know her, and offers as evidence the steak he ordered her for dinner. She turns and walks away, realizing "I would rather not have a boyfriend at all than have one who is only using me for my money or the fact that my father is a prince or for any reason, really, except that he likes me for *me*, and nothing else" (270). Mia has come a long way. She is no longer blinded by her crush on a pretty but thoughtless boy, and she has the courage and self-possession to stand up to him in public.

Yet she still wants a boyfriend. She seems to have found one by the end of the first novel, when Michael and she dance and talk all night at the school dance. She receives anonymous email love-notes in the beginning of the second novel, and although she hopes they are from Michael, evidence suggests they are not. When Lilly becomes involved with Mia's model-handsome cousin, Mia is envious: "*I* want a boy I can tell all my deepest secrets to. *I* want a boy who will French-kiss me. *I* want a boy who will be jealous if I spend too much time with another guy" (*Spotlight* 191). She recognizes that her desire for a boyfriend is not as independent and feminist as it might be, yet she owns her feelings all the same: "No boy has ever referred to me as his girl! Oh, I know all about feminism and how women aren't property and it's sexist to go around claiming them as such. But, oh! If only somebody (okay, Michael) would say I was his girl!" (214). As

Baumgardner and Richards attest, one can be a feminist and conflicted about sex simultaneously. Of course Mia wants a boy to claim her; that is what her reading and viewing habits have taught her to want.

Mia is also concerned about what sort of boyfriend or husband she can hope to one day have. She initially worries whether her father has already arranged her marriage ("Good God, no," is her father's reassuring response [*Spotlight* 58]). She has further cause for concern when she learns of the deferential protocol for a royal consort, which is what her husband will be. The sort of person who would follow protocol seems like no one she would want to marry. She frets:

> What kind of dweeb am I going to end up with?
>
> Actually, I'll be lucky if I can get anybody to marry me at all. What schmuck would want to marry a girl he can't interrupt? Or can't walk out on during an argument? Or has to give up citizenship of his own country for?
>
> I shudder to think of the total loser I will one day be forced to marry. (*Spotlight* 122)

She understands now why her mother would not have wanted to marry her father, having to live under rules such as those. And she believes that Michael would not agree to live under them, either.

She does experience a moment of romance with Michael by the end of the second book. She runs to a movie theater, dressed in the gown her grandmother chose for the formal wedding she hosted. Michael complimented her on her appearance, and Mia "smiled up at him, feeling just like Cinderella all of a sudden... You know, at the end of the Disney movie, when Prince Charming finally finds her and puts the slipper on her foot and her rags change back into the ball gown and all the mice come out and start singing? That's how I felt, just for a second" (*Spotlight* 254). Mia is misremembering the details of the Disney movie, but she has the sentiment correct: a moment of transformation when the man of her dreams recognizes and honors her beauty. Again, this is the sort of romantic feeling modeled by the popular culture in which Mia lives, and it is only natural that even a girl with a feminist upbringing would have expectations of this sort of romance.

Princess Lessons for the Reader

"Do YOU have what it takes to be a princess?"
—*Princess Lessons* cover material

Meg Cabot has taken the idea of princess lessons and modeling princess-like behavior even further in two of the series' books. *Princess Lessons* (2003) and *Perfect Princess* (2004) consist not of fiction but of princess lessons for the reader, written in the voices of Mia and her friends and acquaintances. These funny, breezy books are consistent in tone with the novels, but they are also forthrightly didactic. Rather than glean princess lessons from those given to Mia, here the reader is addressed and taught directly.

Princess Lessons is Mia's passing along and commenting on the lessons she has been receiving. The chapters—Beauty, Etiquette, Fashion, Character, Education, and The Mysterious World of Guys—have subsections written by different members of Mia's circle, from Grandmère to Lana Weinberger to Mia's bodyguard. Mia first addresses her public, warning that, while intriguing to outsiders, "being a princess is actually pretty boring, and princess lessons with Grandmère pretty much—well—stink" (*Lessons* xi). She extols the virtues of normal girlhood, but has put together this book so those who are interested may practice being princesses (although she does warn a second time "I honestly don't know why you would want to. See above re: stinkage factor" [*Lessons* xi]). Mia's voice lends humor to this book, and her commentary balances out the traditional, nonfeminist messages of princess lessons.

The first sections (written by Grandmère) demonstrate just how archaic these lessons are. Under "lingerie" Grandmère lists girdles as basic necessities. Mia's commentary refutes not just the garment but the principle: "Why a princess should be forced to conform to the Western standard of idealized beauty... is beyond me" (*Lessons* 62). Grandmère specifically forbids combat boots, but Mia defends them, citing their comfort. Furthermore, she appreciates the statement combat boots make: "I refuse to conform to the petty rules laid out by society's fashionistas. I am just me, Mia Thermopolis, princess, Greenpeace-supporter and high school student" (66). She goes on to disagree with her grandmother's approved jewelry, writing that every pearl resulted in a dead oyster, and that "I learned in World Civ that it is really important to make sure that your diamonds were not mined in a foreign country that uses child slave labor or engages in guerrilla warfare with neighboring villages. This is something I have noticed they do not mention in those Diamonds are Forever ads" (67). Mia's running commentary, especially when juxtaposed with her grandmother's traditional views, demonstrates her social and environmental awareness.

But there is more to being a princess than simply dressing the part. Mia writes, "You are probably as surprised as I was to find out that being a princess isn't all about being graceful and having good manners and what you wear. There's a bunch of other stuff involved, too…like being kind to those who are less fortunate than you, and being socially aware" (75). The lessons in the chapter on character include making friends, being a good sport, and the (un)importance of popularity. Mia herself contributes a subsection on the environment, the cause for which she is consistently most outspoken.

The book ends with a final note from Mia: "As you can see, there is a lot more to being a princess than just how to wear a tiara and pluck your eyebrows" (*Lessons* 125). She gives a final few pointers: be kind; be assertive ("It is princesslike to be assertive. It is unprincesslike to be walked all over" [*Lessons* 125]); be gracious. The most important tip for would-be princesses, according to Mia, is to be yourself:

> Can a girl with green hair and a belly-button ring really be a princess? Absolutely, if she selected that green hair and belly-button ring because she wanted them, and not just because everyone else is wearing them.
>
> Remember, being a princess is about how you act, not who your parents are, what kind of SAT scores you got, what extracurricular activities you choose to take part in, or how you look. (*Lessons* 127)

Cabot has created a princess-heroine whom she hopes will be a good role model for her readers. But in case modeling princesshood does not suffice, her heroine has become a teacher.

Perfect Princess has a similar project, teaching princess behavior that is appropriate for a modern audience, but it goes about accomplishing that project differently. Rather than have Mia's friends teach lessons directly, *Perfect Princess* categorizes princesses who are worth emulating. This book is "about other princesses—past, present, and pretend—who have made major impacts on society, and what we, as princesses in training, can learn from their triumphs and mistakes" (*Perfect* xvi). Rather than offering herself as a role model, here Mia discusses her own role models and why they should be her readers', too.

The chapter about those who became princesses by dint of marriage begins with this preface, which once again addresses the role of romance and
marriage. Mia defends romance, declaring that it need not sound the death
knell for female empowerment; it is possible to marry and to remain one's
own woman.

> Since the dawn of time, millions and millions of women have dreamed of being
> swept up and carried off in the arms of a handsome prince.... While some people ...
> might say that this fantasy is the result of an impressionable young mind warped by
> too many viewings of *Ever After* or *The Slipper and the Rose*, and that in this day
> and age it shows a terrifying lack of feminist empowerment, I'm here to tell you that
> just because you've married someone who happens to be royal, rich, and famous
> doesn't mean you have given up in your quest for self-actualization! Look at the
> examples of the following women, all of whom became princesses after marrying
> the men they loved, and tell me if you think they've lost their grip on their own
> identity! (*Perfect* 49).

Unfortunately, two of the princesses in this chapter are Disney-fictional,
Cinderella and Beauty (of *Beauty and the Beast*), and a third is Mia's own
(fictional) grandmother. Of those remaining, Grace Kelly offers little in the
way of role modeling.

But Diana, Princess of Wales and Queen Noor of Jordan each offer
strong messages, in Mia's interpretation. She encourages her readers to "Be
like Diana: Adopt a cause about which you feel strongly. Educate your
friends about it, and enlist their support, as well. Remember: To think
globally, you have to act locally" (*Perfect* 54). Noor, too, is a royal to
emulate: "Noor has worked hard to address issues of education, women and
children's welfare, human rights, environmental and architectural conserva-
tion, and urban planning" (55). And she always looks perfectly polished,
according to Mia, which can be "even more subversive" (56) than wearing
combat boots, because looking polished can lull people into a false sense of
complacency about one's politics.

There are entries about "power princesses" ("women who ruled not only
wisely but well" [*Perfect* 67] such as Eleanor of Aquitaine and Cleopatra)
and "action princess" ("kick-ass princesses whose stories deserve to be told"
[87] such as Boadicea, Matilda, and Wonder Woman), "politically correct
princesses" (an entirely fictional list, including The Frog Princess and
Princess Mononoke) and "wannabe princesses" (including Gwyneth Paltrow,
Barbie, and Sara Crewe[3]). Each entry offers a summary of the princess' life
and a different lesson for the would-be princess reading the book. The entry

on Snow White, from the "politically correct" chapter, is particularly interesting:

> There's no point in even going into this one, since you all know it so well. I mean, some of us even had Snow White birthday cakes when we turned six, and dressed like her for Halloween four years in a row, and memorized all the songs from the movie and went around singing "Someday My Prince Will Come" until our mothers threatened to buy us *Free to Be You and Me*, so we'd learn that it is both inappropriate and unwise in today's day and age to wait for princes to come rescue us... (*Lessons* 114)

The only "politically correct" aspect of Snow White is the commentary supplied by Mia, telling us what her mother had to say about her fixation on the story. The lesson Mia finds in Snow White is "Don't take fruit from strangers. This includes people you meet on the Internet" (114). Once again, the cultural saturation of the Disney princesses is highlighted. One cannot but think that the girl fixated on Snow White and threatened with *Free to Be...* was Cabot herself; the vignette rings true, and Cabot was a child when *Free to Be...* was at its most popular.

The final chapter in *Perfect Princess* is "Should-Be Princesses," and the final entry in the category is "You." Mia writes,

> Because who deserves it more? I mean, you know now that all it takes to be a princess (besides a country to rule) is kindness, confidence, observation of proper hygiene, generosity with your time, and consciousness of the environment... everything, really, that makes a model human being. Because in the end, that's all princesses really are: human beings, just like you. Only they happen to come with a crown. (139)

When "princess" is defined in this manner, every girl can in fact become one. And in the conclusion, Mia seems to believe that "there is one thing we all have in common: We think princesses rule" (*Lessons* 143). Cabot (through Mia) acknowledges the attraction that princesses have always had for girls and uses that attraction for good, intentionally attempting to offer princesses as strong, positive role models for modern girls.

Disney's Mia

Disney brought *The Princess Diaries* to the screen in two films, *The Princess Diaries* (2001) and *The Princess Diaries 2: Royal Engagement* (2004). The first film was based on Cabot's first novel; the second film was based on her characters. Cabot's stories were changed in significant and telling ways as they were brought to the screen; in the decade since their last animated princess story, Disney Studios had not changed much. I will discuss Disney's continued undercutting of feminist messages in depth in the following section on *Ella Enchanted,* but it is worth noting some of the many changes made in the Disney versions of *The Princess Diaries.*

Disney's *The Princess Diaries* differed from the novel in many superficial, family-friendly ways, although the basic plot remained the same. Mia's parents were divorced in the films, not never-married as in the books. Grandmère, played by Julie Andrews, was far nicer than the one depicted in the novel, and she and Helen have an amiable relationship instead of the antagonistic one depicted in the books. The movie grandmother also has a romantic relationship with Joseph, her head of security, which makes her more vulnerable and less the battle-axe she is in the novels; this character and his relationship to the grandmother were invented for the film.

Mia's story in the film is far more like a sitcom, with her academic Achilles heel being public speaking, not algebra. This allows her to publically vomit from nerves, rather than receive tutoring for solving equations. Since much of her relationship with Michael develops during their tutoring sessions in the novel, we simply must accept it as a given in the film. The setting has been changed to from New York to San Francisco, which allows the school dance to be moved to a beach. This new setting permits a nearly-naked scene of Mia being caught changing out of her bathing suit, an embarrassment arranged by Lana and her henchgirls. San Francisco also provides hills, on which Mia is unable to successfully drive; mayhem ensues. Mia is sitcomishly uncoordinated; she falls off chairs, fails gym class, and accidentally lights things on fire. Another sitcom touch is the "leg-pop" Mia discusses in a cringe-worthy conversation with her mother. She hopes for her first kiss, and she tells her mother she hopes her leg will pop up, as women's legs do in the movies. There is also the sitcom-plot-crisis: will Mia accept the role of princess, or will Genovia cease to exist? This was a non-issue in the novels, as Grandmère very firmly tells her she is a princess.

Mia begins the movie ridiculously unnoticed at her private school; she tells her grandmother at their first meeting, "my expectation in life is to be invisible, and I'm good at it." The principal does not know her name, and boys literally do not see her (one boy actually sits on her, unaware of her presence). Although her grandmother promises "I can give you books. You will study languages, history, art, political science. I can teach you to walk, talk, sit, stand, eat, dress like a princess" (*Princess Diaries*), we see none of a princess's more intellectual work in Mia's transformation. We do see her grandmother evaluating her looks: "Well, carriage, obviously. Hairstyle. Complexion. Eyes—lovely. But hidden beneath bushman eyebrows. The neck is seemly. Ears...like her father" (*The Princess Diaries*). Mia's transformation to a princess is entirely about her appearance. There are no political lessons, no lessons in language; we see Mia tied to a chair to eliminate her slumping and "hilarious" scenes of her emulating her grandmother's walk.

This first Princess Diaries film is also very father-centric, as we have come to expect in a Disney princess story. Ironically, the film-Mia's father is dead, and he was distant while alive (unlike in the novels, in which Mia's father takes an active role in her life)—yet the film still manages to provide father-figures who eclipse Mia's living mother. Joseph, Grandmère's head of security, is dispatched as Mia's bodyguard and chauffeur. He offers solemnly smiling advice when Mia needs it, and he speaks on her behalf when her grandmother thinks Mia cannot become a princess successfully. When Joseph romances (and weds, in the sequel) Mia's grandmother, he literally becomes her grandfather.

Mia's father, about whom his mother and ex-wife lovingly reminisce, is a strong presence in the film. Mia has never met him, but she romanticizes him based on her birthday presents and on the fact that he paid her tuition. His death two months prior to the opening of the film triggers her becoming a princess, and her grandmother gives her a diary and a locket. In this diary is a letter from her father; the diary and locket were to be her birthday presents from him. Mia finds the letter as she is planning to run away from being a princess. Reading it, her father encourages her to stand up and be fearless. This pater-ex-machina exhorts and reassures her in an oddly disjointed and not entirely relevant voice-over:

> Courage is not the absence of fear, but rather the knowledge that something is more important than the fear. The brave do not live forever, but the cautious do not live at all. From now on, you'll be travelling the road between who you think you are and who you can be. The key is to allow yourself to make the journey. I also want you to know I loved your mother very much and still think of her often. Happy birthday, my Mia. All my love, Your father.

This letter gives Mia the courage she needs to go to the ball. She tells Joseph "I'm not so afraid anymore. My father helped me." It is a very strange letter, given that her father could have had no idea he was about to suffer an accidental death, but it does firmly cement the distant-now-deceased father's central role in Mia's life.

Princess Diaries 2: Royal Engagement veers even further from any plot conceived by Meg Cabot. Rather than focusing on Mia's makeover or on any semblance of princess lessons, the film focuses almost entirely on her romantic exploits. In it, Mia is required to be married to take the throne; the law, enforced by Viscount Mabrey (who schemes to have his nephew reign), states that "Genovia shall have no queen lest she be bound in matrimony. [Therefore,] Princess Mia is not qualified to rule because she is unmarried" (*Princess Diaries 2*). Michael, the love of her life, is touring with his band and the two have ended their romance.

Mia thus must find someone willing to marry her within the thirty-day timeframe granted by Genovia's parliament. She initially balks at the notion of an arranged marriage, although her grandmother assures her that she and the husband chosen for her grew very fond of each other. When Mia protests, saying "I dream of love, not fondness," the queen gives her a chance to decline the marriage and with it, the throne. Mia decides to marry rather than abdicate; a flashback to her father's final letter (and the voice-over from the first film), with its message about courage, helps her decide to marry, to "be up there next to my father. I'm sure I want my chance to make a difference as a ruler" (*Princess Diaries 2*). A husband-shopping scene follows, in which Mia and the other women review eligible bachelors and decide whom to tap as Mia's husband. She settles on Andrew Jacoby, Duke of Kenilworth. Mia is lukewarm at first ("He seems…decent"), but his resume wins her over. Andrew has always expected an arranged marriage, and he is amenable to the match.

But Viscount Mabrey has other plans. He wants his nephew Nicholas to rule, and tasks Nicholas with distracting Mia from her fiancé. Nicholas does so, and standard romantic comedy mishaps ensue: Mia flirts with Nicholas, unaware of his family ties. Mia's grandmother invites Nicholas to stay in the castle for the next thirty days, ensuring that Mia and Nicholas will have many opportunities to bicker, which demonstrates their mutual attraction through most of the rest of the film. Mia is determined to marry Andrew, however, and the wedding plans move forward. Nicholas convinces Mia to spend an evening picnicking on the grounds with him; they fall asleep together; and the Viscount tips off a gossip columnist to their whereabouts.

Mia, enraged and blaming Nicholas for the publicity, prepares for her wedding. She flees the ceremony, however, struggling with her choice of a pragmatic marriage rather than a romantic one. Her grandmother, who has refused Joseph's proposal of marriage, urges Mia to follow her heart:

> Darling, listen to me. I made my choice. Duty to my country over love. It's what I've always done, it seems. It was drummed into me my whole life. Now I've lost the only man I ever really loved. Mia, I want you to make your choices as a woman. Don't make the same mistakes I did....Now, you can go back into that church and get married, or you can walk away. Whatever choice you make, let it come from your heart. (*Princess Diaries 2*)

This outrageous advice comes from a woman who has spent her life dedicating herself to something larger than a marriage. Choosing "as a woman" seems to mean that duty, honor, and country are less important than the hope of someday marrying for romance.

Mia returns to the church, where she and Andrew decide not to marry. She then makes a passionate speech about deserving the throne:

> My grandmother has ruled without a man at her side for quite some time, and I think she rocks at it. So as the granddaughter of Queen Clarisse and King Rupert...I ask the members of parliament to think about your daughters, your nieces, and sisters, and granddaughters, and ask yourselves: would you force them to do what you're trying to make me do? I believe I will be a great queen. I understand Genovia to be a land that combines the beauty of the past with all the best hope of the future. I feel in my heart and soul that I can rule Genovia. I... I love Genovia.... I stand here, ready to take my place as your queen. Without a husband. (*Princess Diaries 2*)

She loves Genovia enough to rule, but not enough to marry to secure the crown. Her heart and her love of Genovia are apparently enough, however, to convince the wedding guests that she should be queen. Mia moves to abolish the law requiring marriage for female rulers of Genovia. The members of Parliament among the guests decide in favor of change, and the law is passed. Mia quickly consults with her grandmother ("Just because I didn't get my fairy-tale ending, doesn't mean you shouldn't" [*Princess Diaries 2]*), who proposes to Joseph. They are wed right then and there. One romance has thus had a happy ending.

That there is also hope for Mia and Nicholas' romance is indicated when Nicholas speaks on Mia's behalf and announces that he will not accept the crown even if it is offered to him. In one of the final scenes, as Mia prepares for her coronation, Nicholas comes to her and tells her, on bended knee, that he is in love with her. He asks if she is in love with him, and although she does not answer in words, she flings herself out of her throne and into his arms. When they kiss, Mia's leg "pops", and the audience is left in little doubt as to where this relationship is going.

The entire film valorizes romantic love over all, from Mia's first voice-over in which she talks about living in a "fairy-tale castle," to the ball thrown in honor of her twenty-first birthday, at which she has to dance with every eligible bachelor, to the clichéd, bickering interactions between Mia and Nicholas. The brief moments of declaring women's rights to rule are almost incidental to Mia and Nicholas' romantic plot and Grandmère and Joseph's sub-plot. Once Andrew and Mia agree to marry, in a mature and self-sacrificing move, there would have been no story—except that romance is more important and thus, while Mia triumphs by having the archaic law abolished, no thought or effort has gone into that (had any thought been given it, the law could have been repealed when the issue was raised in an actual parliamentary setting, not at a wedding). Upon lighting the ceremonial coronation flame, what would have been her moment of triumph had the story actually been about her quest for the throne, Mia is far from triumphant. She is sad, and she sits gloomily on the throne in the next scene as well. The real resolution, the real happy ending, comes when Nicholas declares his love. Then the audience can breathe a sigh of fulfilled relief; the all-important romance has concluded satisfactorily.

In *The Princess Diaries* films, especially the sequel, Disney has taken a fairly realistic twenty-first century teenage girl and turned her into a helpless, hopeless romantic, with no plans and desires greater than falling in love. Men and relationships with men are as important in these films as in any Disney princess story; they are the heroine's primary goal and desire, and the men offer guidance, rescue, and romance. The princess, who in modern young adult fiction has become a strong, independent character, who values education and has goals of her own, here is reduced to a nervous girl re-formed by a makeover and redeemed by love. The anti-feminist Disney revisions of strong female heroines are even more apparent in the Disney adaptation of *Ella Enchanted*, which will be discussed next.

Ella Enchanted

Gail Carson Levine's *Ella Enchanted* (1997), a 1998 Newberry Honor Book, features a strong, funny, independent heroine who struggles against a terrible curse and ultimately wins her freedom. This retelling of "Cinderella" exhibits many of the characteristics of the other third-wave feminist princesses: she is smart, she rescues herself, and she finds romance at the end of her story but not as the plot's climax. The movie version, released by Disney subsidiary Miramax in 2004, is markedly changed from the novel, with a heroine more droll than fiery (although she has been given a thin veneer of politically correct causes to chirp on about). Comparing the two versions will both demonstrate the third-wave feminist ideals of the novel and further highlight the ways the Disney corporation subverts that feminism into the 2000s, even given unabashedly feminist source material.

Both in the book and in the film, Ella's obedience stems from a spell placed upon her in infancy. The fairy Lucinda meant this obedience as a gift, but it quickly became a curse; Ella is compelled to obey all direct orders. In the book, if the command is something she can do, she must comply; if she cannot follow the order (as when her sewing instructor tells her to take small, even stitches), she is compelled to exert herself until she can comply. In the film, Ella's obedience is played for laughs: a comic "magical" sound is issued when the command reaches Ella, her back instantly straightens and her movements become robotic. Moreover, she becomes instantly capable of doing whatever she is commanded, even when the result flies in the face of physics; at one point, she is commanded to stop as she is leaping over a barrel. To the onlookers' and Ella's own astonishment, she freezes in midair.

Although in the book Ella is obedient, readers are well aware of her resentment and rebelliousness. She loathes being forced into obedience, and she struggles against it—but in the end, the physical distress of resistance overpowers the psychological distress of obedience, and she submits to each command. She resists obeying several times in the novel, but "each moment cost [her] dear—in breathlessness, nausea, dizziness, and other complaints" (5). She devises other ways to rebel, such as by following the letter of the command but not the spirit. When told to hold a bowl while Mandy, her fairy godmother and household cook, beats the eggs, Ella holds the bowl but moves her feet around the kitchen so the cook would have to follow; when told to bring almonds from the pantry, she returns with only two. She also resists by following the command, but destroying the results. When her future stepsister, who has discovered the curse, commands her to clean up some dirt in their carriage, Ella does so, but then she grinds it into the girl's face. She also picks a bouquet for the girl but laces it with a truth-telling herb, and she garnishes her stepmother's meal with parsley (as commanded) and a sleeping herb (as sabotage).

The curse, besides making Ella vulnerable to ill-wishers (particularly her stepsisters, who strip her of her valuables and essentially enslave her), also makes her clumsy and foolish. When her father, who does not know of the curse, says "Run off and bang into someone else" (39), Ella is forced to literally run off and bang into someone—in this case, the laundress, who spills the clean, wet clothes. Conflicting orders cause conflict in Ella's body, which wants to obey each command as it is issued. Nor do these orders magically come with the ability to comply; in finishing school, Ella has so many rules to follow that she must concentrate fiercely, instructing herself from moment to moment. At only one point in the novel does Ella become happily obedient: when Lucinda tells Ella to "Be happy to be blessed with such a lovely quality" (127). Ella runs off, glowing with joy thinking about the many commands she might be given. Mandy, dismayed and disgusted to see Ella's joy in servitude, orders her to feel as she wants. This is both a blessing and a burden to Ella; when she was told to be happy, she actually was, but when she is allowed to feel trapped, desperate and despairing, she feels that instead.

The filmic Ella is not shown to resist her curse. Her "independence and rebelliousness" are strictly of the "good causes" kind, with Ella protesting for giants' and elves' rights. (She does not protest in the novel, because these peoples' rights are not impinged upon in the book.) It appears that some-times, people command her to do what she would have enjoyed doing anyway: when a schoolyard bully tells her to "bite me," Ella does so, biting the bully's hand. As mentioned above, Ella's curse is played for laughs in the film, through the funny "magic" sound, literal interpretations of commands and sped-up camera work. When told to hold her tongue during a debate, Ella puts her fingers in her mouth to literally hold her tongue. When told to "dig in" to a cake, the film speed increases as the little-girl Ella uses both hands to literally dig in; when told to "hurry up," the film speed increases until she is just a blur racing around the room. Ella is granted improbable abilities whenever commanded to do anything outside of her natural skill set. At a giant's wedding, for instance, Ella is told to sing, which she does; then to project more loudly, and then to accompany herself by dancing. She seems amazed to find herself doing these things, since she does not know herself to be a singer or dancer.

The characterization of the human women is similar from book to film: Ella's mother, who dies when Ella is a girl, is kind and loving; Dame Olga, her stepmother, is vicious and vain. Ella's stepsisters are greedy and mean-spirited (Hattie, the elder) and mildly retarded and emotionally needy (Olive, the younger)[4]. However, the portrayals of the two female fairies, Mandy (Ella's godmother) and Lucinda (the flamboyant fairy who bestows terrible gifts), are quite different on screen from the book. In the film, Mandy is slender, young, and beautiful, a far cry from the book-Mandy's "frizzy gray hair and two chins" (24). Film-Mandy is incompetent, confined to doing small magic because she is incapable of doing large magic. For instance, she inadvertently transformed her boyfriend into a talking book while trying to trim his hair. She can be of no real help to Ella, both because of her ineptitude and because if she tries to work against Lucinda's gift, Lucinda will take away Mandy's eternal youth. Book-Mandy is practical and loving. She does not remove Ella's curse because to remove another fairy's gift would be to perform "big magic," which could have dangerous, unforeseen consequences. She is neither incompetent nor vain. She is immortal, and does not fear Lucinda taking away her eternal youth; Mandy could magically appear young, but she does not chose to do so.

Lucinda, in both the book and the film, is more flamboyant than the other fairies. She is the only one "rude enough and stupid enough" (24) to use her magic in front of others and publically declare herself a fairy. She is vain, both of her magically-enhanced looks and of her magical ability, and she recklessly performs big magic when she bestows her uniformly terrible gifts on humans. She gets her comeuppance toward the end of the novel, when Mandy convinces her to spend three months as a squirrel and three months obedient, two of her most common "gifts" to others. At the end of her six months, she vows never to bestow these gifts again, and she declares she will never again perform big magic. She does provide Ella with a carriage in which to go to the prince's balls, and she makes the traditional back-by-midnight proviso, but she does not save Ella.

In the film, Lucinda is portrayed as a clichéd sassy black woman, complete with ghetto-fabulous hands-on-hips attitude, pursed lips, and hand-and-finger shaking. Her go-go boots, fur-trimmed halter top, and "aren't I fabulous?" are cringe-worthy. More than that, she learns nothing about the true nature of her gifts. When she comes across Ella, chained to a tree in an attempt not to obey a command to kill the prince (a plot twist invented for the film), Lucinda unchains her and transforms her dress into a ball gown, sending Ella on her unhappy way.

Ella's father differs greatly from book to film. In the book, he is a cold, distant man, usually absent, present neither at Ella's birth nor at subsequent birthday celebrations. He does not know she goes by "Ella" instead of "Eleanor," and his primary interest is money. He has never been home long enough to issue many commands, and he knows nothing of Ella's curse. The two have no relationship before the death of Ella's mother, and their relationship after that lies primarily in her father seeking to use her to increase his fortunes, first by sending her to finishing school and then by finding her a rich husband. He describes himself: "They may have said I'm selfish, and I am. They may have said I'm impatient, and I am. They may have said I always have my way. And I do" (35). He is a cold man, a dangerous man, and Ella fears him. She spends little time with him, and on the one occasion Ella writes to him for help, he takes six months to send his reply: "no."

In the film, Ella and her father have a warm relationship. He assures her that his new wife will be a good mother to Ella, and they sadly embrace when he leaves to go work as a traveling watch salesman. He tilts up her chin and kisses her forehead as he takes his leave. Much later, at the prince's ball, he berates Dame Olga for being so self-involved that they have lost track of Ella. Because Ella and her father have such a close, loving relationship, his thoughtless marriage and essential abandonment of Ella seems more of a betrayal in the film than in the book. He brings the horrible stepfamily into the house and then leaves Ella alone with them. He marries for money, as he did in the novel, but it seems that he should have told Ella about the impending match prior to the wedding, and that she would have encouraged him to sell the house instead of marrying poorly. If they are as close as they seem, how can he be so oblivious, not to know of Ella's curse and not to know what life Dame Olga is creating for her?

Ella's relationship with Prince Charming, "Char," is also quite different when translated to the screen. In the book, the two first meet at her mother's funeral. Char knows all about Ella, because their cooks gossip, and he liked her mother, whom he knew from formal functions. They meet periodically through the novel, and their friendship grows. Ella impresses Char with her ability with languages, and she goes out of her way to make him laugh. They play together, sneaking off to slide down castle banisters. When Char spends a year in a neighboring country, they become pen-pals. They share their personal histories, their faults and foibles, and their relationship deepens. Ella's ultimate sacrifice comes as Char declares his love to her; she realizes she cannot marry him, because her curse makes her a real threat to him and to the country. She writes to him in Hattie's voice, telling Char that Ella has been leading him on and that she has just run off to marry a rich old man. Char, heartbroken, determines to forget her and never to marry.

Ella, determined though she is neither to marry Char nor to hurt him further, cannot resist going to the royal ball. It is a masque, and Ella disguises herself both her appearance and her voice. Her humor and warmth win Char's favor, and he dances with her night after night, explaining that although he will not marry he would appreciate her friendship. On the last night of the ball, Hattie unmasks Ella, who, aghast, runs home and prepares to leave town. Char and her stepfamily are in close pursuit, and the final struggle for control of Ella begins. Char proposes; Hattie countermands it; Dame Olga reminds Hattie that with Ella in the castle they would all gain. Ella is conflicted, happy at the proposal but horrified that she would be a weapon against her husband and her country. Char proposes again, and Ella is torn.

> But I had to obey—wanted to obey—hated to harm him—wanted to marry him. I would destroy my love and my land. They were in danger, and no one could rescue them. We were doomed.
>
> Char was too precious to hurt, too precious to lose, too precious to betray, too precious to marry, too precious to kill, too precious to obey. (225)

Ella struggles. She wants to open her mouth to accept Char's proposal, but she swallows the words. She bites her tongue; she feels the bile rise in her throat; she puts her hands over her mouth in the attempt to remain silent, to disobey the command "marry me." She concentrates on saving Char and her country. "In that moment I found a power beyond any I'd had before, a will and a determination I would never have needed if not for Lucinda, a fortitude I hadn't been able to find for a lesser cause. And I found my voice" (226). Ella says no. She refuses to marry Char, refuses to be forced. She shouts it to the world. She is free, the curse broken by her determination to save her realm and her beloved. She turns to Char and accepts his proposal, asking him to marry her. The epilogue shows the two married, and they and their friends living happily ever after, with Ella refusing the title of princess but adopting the titles of Court Linguist and Cook's Helper. The story of Ella's struggle for freedom has been at the center, aided and supplemented by the romance.

In the Disney film, Char and Ella "meet cute." He is being chased by his screaming fans, and he literally runs into Ella; they fall to the ground together. She has nothing but scorn for him because of the political practices of his uncle, the prince regent; she is snide and sarcastic. Their typical bickering banter leads him to declare Ella "the first maiden I've met who hasn't swooned at the sight of me," and when Ella suggests she has done him some good by not adoring him, he posits, "Perhaps that's why I find your obvious disdain for me so refreshing." He rescues her almost immediately upon meeting her, tackling her out from under the wheels of an oncoming carriage (she has been frozen in spot by his "wait here" while he retrieves her forgotten purse). The two land together on the side of the road, thus embracing twice in the very first few minutes of their acquaintance.

They meet up again while Ella is travelling to find Lucinda; Char saves her from the ogres who are about to eat her. She is mute and still, first as she is lowered into a pot of boiling water and again as Char cuts her down and lands (again) holding her on the ground. In the book, she saves herself through her facility with languages; in the film, the ogres have rendered her silent and helpless, needing male rescue. Her prickly defensiveness about Char's help leaves her looking not only helpless, but ungracious about receiving help. "I see the score currently stands at chivalry two, gratitude zero," Char tallies, and indeed Ella is nothing but hostile and defensive. Then she apologizes, and it appears that Char has taught her manners. Ella's group (Ella, Slannen and Benny the book) joins Char's company at his insistence—"It makes it so much easier rescuing you if I don't have to commute," he quips—and although she tries to demur, she complies (as she must) when Slannen tells her "Tell him to come with us." The couple bonds over their shared dislike of following orders as they ride.

The central portion of the book involves Ella's adventures as she seeks Lucinda to plead with her to remove the curse. Ella initially sets out because Hattie has ordered her to abandon her friendship with Arieda, Ella's one school friend. Rather than destroy their friendship and hurt the only girl with whom she has a close relationship, Ella leaves school. She sets off on her own to find Lucinda, in the hopes of getting her to remove the curse; she takes only a few provisions and her native skill in languages. Ella is captured by ogres, creatures who can see their victims' dreams and secrets and use them as weapons. Ogres are also extremely persuasive; their magic is in their language and their voices, and they convince their captives to surrender themselves through their words. Ella, captured, briefly despairs—but she uses the ogres' own weapon against them, practicing her command of Ogrese until her words are as magically convincing as theirs. She convinces them that they are too tired and full to eat her. Char, who has been on an ogre-hunting mission, stumbles across the scene of Ella taming the ogres and is wholly impressed. He sends her on her way with one of his men, who escorts her to her next destination.

In the film, Ella leaves home after crying to Mandy about breaking off her friendship with Arieda; Dame Olga has commanded Ella to end their friendship. Ella does so, tearfully, and tearfully tells Mandy that this is the worst thing the curse has made her do. She is inspired to seek out Lucinda, and Mandy encourages her in this quest. Mandy also gives her a magic book, as did Mandy in the novel, but this book is actually Mandy's enchanted boyfriend; the book's cover is his talking face. Ella is therefore not alone as she sets out; she is accompanied by a man. She is joined by another man: Slannen the elf, whom she finds being tormented by a gang of men. She tries to bluff, declaring herself a "master of the ancient art of origami," but the men are undeterred. Slannen, however, calls to Ella: "don't let them scare you, sweetheart. Kick his butt!" Ella, hearing the command, does so. As Slannen calls out fighting moves, Ella becomes his puppet, responding to his orders and fighting the men. She wins—or Slannen wins—and he joins her on her quest. She is thus accompanied by two men, and when Char comes along to save the group from ogres (Ella unable save herself), the party joins him. Ella's adventures in the film are not her own; she is not demonstrably capable of doing anything except magically following orders. Char goes to the giant wedding with Ella, where they kiss for the first time, and then takes her to his castle to marry her. The plot veers to focus on the prince regent at this point.

Much of the plot of the film version revolves around Char's Uncle Edgar, a character invented for the film, who plots to kill Char and assume the throne. Edgar commands Ella to kill Char, but to thwart the command, she first has Slannen tie her to a tree, as mentioned above. Once she is at the ball, Char proposes to her in the hall of mirrors; she looks at her reflection and tells herself "you will no longer be obedient." This effectively breaks the curse, or at least countermands Edgar's directive, but Ella is thrown into the dungeon for this attempt on Char's life. Moreover, this breaking of the spell—the main point of the novel—and Ella's realization that she is free are overshadowed by Ella being thrown in a dungeon for her assassination attempt (this was perhaps meant as an ironic juxtaposition, being imprisoned at the moment she's freed, but if so, it does not work). Char's emotional turmoil at his beloved's attempt on his life and Edgar's plan to kill Char at the upcoming coronation become the focus of the film. This focus on Char may be intended to make him more fully developed, but the letters he and Ella exchange (and his journal entries, which Ella's magic book allows her to read) do a far better job in the novel, giving him emotional depth instead of simply "screen" time.

Meanwhile, Benny, Slannen and the ogres rescue Ella from the dungeon. She leads them to the coronation, where Edgar has poisoned the crown which is about to be placed on Char's head. Ella and her band of men burst into the hall, and a melee ensues. Char swoops to Ella's side, protesting, "I can't believe I'm saving you, after you tried to kill me." Char has thus rescued Ella thrice, and while Ella managed not to kill him she does not actually save him. While she explains her curse, Char fends off their attackers. Ella kicks Edgar's snake when it tries to bite Char, but it is the screaming fangirls (members of the Prince Char fanclub) who dispatch him. Edgar inadvertently neutralizes himself by donning the poisoned crown, at which point Edgar declares that Ella has saved his life. Their kiss dissolves to their wedding, and the film ends with much singing and dancing. The story of the romance has taken center stage from the start of the film, with Char's near-death at the hands of his uncle the second-most important plot thread. Ella's struggle for freedom is of tertiary importance.

The novel's smart, rebellious, tormented heroine who liberates herself has been subsumed by the film's smart-mouthed, eyeball-rolling damsel in distress. Char saves Ella thrice in the film, instances not only invented for the movie but which replace instances when Ella saved herself in the novel. Ella's political stances and her disdain for the prince are supposed to make her attractive, but they are a poor alternative to the humor and intelligence of the novel's Ella. The filmmakers added many storylines (elvish freedom, Uncle Edgar, giants' rights) to the plot provided in the novel, but these serve to make Ella's own story almost irrelevant. What had been a third-wave feminist princess story has become a cluttered, clichéd romance—*Ella Enchanted* has become *Sleeping Beauty*, a princess story in which the heroine takes a backseat to the prince, and the secondary, comic characters take over the screen.

Conclusion

As for the argument that movies are by nature different from films, and that adaptations always take liberties—yes, that is correct. However, it was not necessary to weaken Mia and Ella so. Other princess story films were made during this period, and they all feature strong, independent heroines. None of these films, however, were made by Disney. *Ever After: A Cinderella Story* (Twentieth Century Fox, 1998), *A Cinderella Story* (Warner Brothers, 2004) and *The Prince & Me* (Lions Gate, 2004) all feature intelligent, self-reliant girls who look out for themselves, who have goals and desires, and who just happen to end up with princes (two real princes and one figurative one). These stories were not simply about the romance; the romance was an added intrigue but not the girls' sole purpose. They are not saddled with male sidekicks, and their fathers are not unduly important. Their feminist messages are not subverted. Seen in the larger context of these contemporaneous princess films, the choices made by the Disney corporation seem less necessary and more pointedly, intentionally anti-feminist.

❖ CONCLUSION ❖

Romance and the Princess's Continuing Relevance

PRINCESS STORIES continue to have a readership even when those readers reach adulthood. Novel-length adaptations of princess stories can be found for an adult audience, most commonly in the genres of romance and science fiction/fantasy. In both genres, authors of princess stories wrestle with feminist issues. It is unsurprising that these issues arise in the science fiction and fantasy adaptations, as science fiction has always had feminist ties. According to Merja Makinen, in fact, no genre has been more feminist-friendly than science fiction. The speculative nature of the genre opens it to thought experiments and innovations not found elsewhere in literature. All of the major feminist debates are found in science fiction, "from the explorations of phallocentric language, to strong action-women agency; from ideal feminine communities, to the phallocentric dystopias; from explorations of the alien 'other' to questions of identity with the cyborg" (129). Women in science fiction and fantasy often have more agency, more financial or magical wherewithal, than female characters in any other genre and often more than the male characters populating their stories. Romance, on the other hand, has no such theoretical connection or tradition of feminism. Romance novels are most often simply dismissed as not being worth reading, and rarely are they examined for feminist issues and viewpoints.

One of the fairy tales most likely to be adapted for an adult audience is that of Sleeping Beauty, which might seem to pose unique difficulties for the author as its heroine spends much of her time in a magical coma. However, the passive nature of the princess leads to discussion of women's roles: how is that passivity changed or remarked upon in an adult protagonist, written for an adult audience? Science fiction and fantasy adaptations of the Sleeping Beauty story[1] offer strongly feminist musings on the tale and on women's roles in society, and their examination would certainly be interesting. Yet because this genre remains such a niche market[2], and because its audience is far from strictly female, the discussion would take us far afield from the actual topic of this study. Instead, I want to focus my attention briefly on Sleeping Beauty adaptations in the genre most strongly linked to adult women: romance.

There are many novel-length, romance-genre Sleeping Beauty adaptations for adults, both traditional romances (Judith Michael's *Sleeping Beauty* [1991], Judith Ivory's *Sleeping Beauty* [1998], and Dallas Schulze's *Sleeping Beauty* [1999]) and chick lit versions, younger, hipper romances. Although there has been some argument that chick lit is not romance[3], the ties between the genres cannot be denied. Each is written for a female audience, usually by female authors. Each has been the object of critical scorn and derision, which touches not just the novels but the readers of those novels. And some chick lit imprints were created by romance houses (Red Dress Ink is Harlequin's; Zebra Contemporary Romance belongs to Kensington). Moreover, Louise Burke, publisher of Simon & Schuster's Pocket Books division (which specializes in romance and suspense), says "I think chick lit is really a subgenre of romance" (qtd. in Wyatt). In addition to examining Sleeping Beauty in traditional romance novels, I will also discuss three chick-lit adaptations of Sleeping Beauty, all of which comment on the story: Kristine Grayson's two-book series *Utterly Charming* (2000) and *Thoroughly Kissed* (2001); Donna Kaufman's *Sleeping with Beauty* (2005); and Sarah Strohmeyer's *The Sleeping Beauty Proposal* (2007).

Romance

Much has been written about the romance genre, which generated $1.358 billion in sales in 2010, the greatest market share of any genre. Romance accounts for nearly 50 per cent of the paperback book trade (*Romance Writers*), but romance and its readers are not held in high critical esteem. "It has become part of contemporary 'common sense' that romantic fiction is a 'formulaic' 'trivial' and 'escapist' form read by 'addicted' women" (Hollows 70); many romance readers hide their books in plain cloth covers (or now, simply use e-books) for public consumption without public scorn. Yet romances have power. Tania Modleski writes that romance novels' "enormous and continuing popularity... suggests that they speak to very real problems and tensions in women's lives" (15). Janice Radway claims that "the ideal romance offers the opportunity to escape from a world characterized by the excesses of male power and into a utopian world in which heterosexual relationships can work" (79). Writers of romance agree that the genre offers its readers escape. According to Susan Phillips, a reader and writer of romance, "the fantasy these novels offered me was one of command and control over the harum scarum events of my life—a fantasy of female empowerment" (55). Similarly, Diana Palmer writes that romance novels allow their readers to explore any variety of lives, without risk. Readers may want "...to be virgins again. To be career women. To be debutantes. To be princesses. To live in luxury and even, sometimes, in decadence. [Romance] novels allow them to escape the normal cares and woes of life by returning in dreams to a time less filled with responsibilities" (156). Surely there is some truth in all of these readings: women may read fairy tales featuring princesses as a means of escape or stress relief or to safely try on different identities. But these motivations may become more difficult to ascribe to readers when considering the Sleeping Beauty story, with its most passive of all princesses.

Romance writer Stella Cameron offers another reason women read her books even in the face of ridicule: "In romance novels love is portrayed as an adventure embarked upon by free, bold women who know that their true power lies in their own heroic qualities" (144). But her argument is based on the heroine's control of the hero, and upon her teaching him to love—a storyline usually turned upside down by the Sleeping Beauty adaptations, in which the heroine is usually taught to love by the hero, who awakens her from emotional and sexual slumber. The romances discussed below are no different. No matter how empowered the heroine is in other parts of her life—a respected lawyer, a wealthy woman of leisure, or a thirty-six-year-old well aware of cultural sexism—it takes a heterosexual love relationship to "awaken" her. The situations are unrealistic. The happy ending is often crammed into the final pages. Surely no thinking woman would find these appealing—yet many do.

The demographics of romance readership suggest one other factor which may account for women reading romance genre princess stories: gender intensification, the same concept that explains why little girls and adolescents are drawn to princess stories. 41% of readers of romance are between the ages of 25–44 (*Romance Writers*). This time of life, 25–44, is when most American readers of romance are becoming married and becoming mothers, often a period of gender intensification, a time when, no matter their politics, many women find themselves fulfilling traditional gender roles. As 63% of romance readers are currently married or have been previously (*Romance*

Writers), it can be assumed that the majority of them are also mothers. Little girls play princess because it is comforting to reinforce their femininity at a time they are not sure they will always be girls. Young teens, developing physically and socially, read princess stories because gender roles and romance are stressful, and the concept of the princess is educational. And adult women, who have not been the focus of this project except in how they have created and used the princess story, come to romance novels—princess romance novels among them—for a variety of reasons in this stressful period of fulfilling the traditional gender roles of wife and mother.

Sleeping Beauty in Romance

Writers of these romances most often take the "sleeping" of Sleeping Beauty metaphorically; the princess's awakening is usually sexual[4]. This links the romance versions to the original tale, which had many explicitly sexual versions: one version has Sleeping Beauty raped while asleep, only to awaken when one of her children starts to suckle; others explicitly link the spindle which pricks her to a penis (Doughty 145). The transformation in the story is usually related to love and sex, with the "prince" elevating the princess to a physically exciting and emotionally nurturing love life. Traditional romance novels often include graphic sexual detail. This varies from "yearning" and "fulfillment" to discussion of the male's "fine, thick erection" (Ivory 374), to detailed depictions of cunnilingus, and it almost always includes paragraph-long descriptions of the heroine's orgasms. Chick lit versions do not include the sort of sexual detail included in many traditional romances, often ending with a kiss or a male moan of pleasure or a friend's allusion to "hours of fantastic hot sex" (Kauffman 379). The relationship, the heroine's life situation and the humor are foregrounded in chick lit novels, not the passion and sexual detail[5].

The "princesses" offered in romance Sleeping Beauty stories are rarely, if ever, actual princesses. In the versions I have chosen, none is. Each novel presents an independent, yet somehow damaged "beauty" who is sexually or romantically awakened by her "prince." Judith Michael's Anne Garnett (note the jeweled last name) was repeatedly raped by her uncle. She ran away from home, but returns to attend a funeral nearly twenty years later. As a result of her abuse, she has cut herself off to all possibility of romance and physical intimacy; specializing in divorce law makes the notion of love and romance even less appealing to her. Dallas Schulze's heroine, Anne Moore (who does indeed want "more" from life) has been hurt by the murder of her sister fifteen years ago and by her mother's overprotection ever since. At twenty-five years old, she is trapped in her childhood town, in her childhood relationships, contemplating marrying a reliable yet dull man. Love and lust have both been outside her experience, and although she longs to leave, and "dream[s] of a man with a heart strong enough to break the loving ties that bind her" (8) she feels she cannot leave her mother or her town on her own. Coco Wild (again, note the last name), Judith Ivory's heroine, is a former courtesan, now a widow. She has a grown son she is proud to send to college and, at thirty-seven, she wants to put her tumultuous past behind her and have a calm "old age." Her son's father denied the affair and the child, and Coco has been determined since then to avoid becoming truly involved with a man. She has had many lovers, but has kept herself from falling in love. The damage suffered by these heroines is unlikely to have been experienced by many (if any) readers, which makes it safer to read about and lends the readers some perspective on their own lives. On the other hand, many women have experienced lesser versions of the tribulations the heroines have suffered; there is some element of cheerleading, of empowerment-by-example, in these novels.

The chick lit heroines have problems of lesser scale, but they, too, wrestle with their pasts and others' perceptions of them. Nora Barr (a lawyer, of course, who not only passed the bar but has also set the bar high for romantic involvement), from *Utterly Enchanted*, is a lawyer who despairs of finding romance; she is blond and petite, but even those physical advantages have not helped in light of her forceful personality. "Men always found her attractive at first—so little, so cute—and then she would open her mouth. So few men appreciated her blunt style, and even fewer of them appreciated her opinions. She didn't know how many men she had scared away. The ones who liked her mouth and her brains saw her only as a friend" (28-29). Emma Lost (whose name represents her lost 1,000 years), the literal Sleeping Beauty who serves as the catalyst for the plot of *Utterly Enchanted,* takes the heroine position in *Thoroughly Kissed.* Sent into a 1,000-year coma because she kissed a boy, Emma is understandably leery of romance. Furthermore, she is coming into her own magical powers, which makes the possibility of romance even less likely. Lucy Harper (*Sleeping with Beauty*), an elementary-school teacher, has never had a relationship that combines sexual attraction and friendly compatibility. She bears the scars of her gawky, geeky childhood and adolescence, and has never allowed herself to show men her true witty and sensuous nature. Genie Michaels (*The Sleeping Beauty Proposal*), watches her live-in boyfriend propose to another woman during a nationally televised interview. These chick lit romances, with their more realistic settings and heroines (even magical Emma struggles with her boss and her fear of intimacy), offer heroines with whom it is easier to identify than those provided in traditional romance novels. The chick lit plots and their narrative commentaries impart morals in a direct manner, intentionally educating their readers about modern womanhood and learning to be happy with oneself.

These novels play on the Sleeping Beauty fairy tale with varying degrees of subtlety. Although not peopled by royalty and rarely involving magic, the novels firmly establish the plots' connection to fairy tale and the heroines' connection to princess-hood by choice of title. As Jack Zipes writes, "the writers of stories, novellas, and novels for older readers assume a deep knowledge of the traditional narrative....In fact, they depend upon this relevant knowledge as though it were part of the reading audience's material experiences, as though they were already disposed to the tale" (*Why* 120). In the more traditional novels, the Sleeping Beauty title emphasizes for the reader who the heroine "really" is; in the less traditional novels, references to the fairy tale give the heroine a way of understanding her dilemma.

The Judith Michael novel just hints at its titular fairy tale. From the moment he first saw Anne, Josh "wondered what it would take... to wake her up" (324). At the end of the novel, as they contemplate their future together, Anne credits Josh for healing her: "You woke me up" (832). He corrects her: "You woke yourself up...I helped, but it came from within you" (832). Most of the Sleeping Beauty references hearken back to nothing but the title of the novel, not its sprawling, complex plot. The title resonates, however, assuring readers that—no matter how convoluted and wide-ranging the story—there will be a romantic happy ending. The title encourages the readers to see psychologically damaged Anne as "asleep," and Josh as her rescuer, although Anne is also depicted as intelligent, competent, and self-sufficient.

Dallas Schulze's novel references the fairy tale less subtly but with elements of irony. The preface is entitled "Once Upon a Time" (7) and it closes with the comment that "this was real life, after all, and no one knew better than [Anne] that life was not a fairy tale" (8). Neill, the hero, "didn't believe in ... witches on broomsticks, fairies dancing on buttercups, or happily-ever-after" (9). These sardonic comments belie the romance at the core of the story. The wicked queen is Anne's mother, who has manipulated and controlled Anne since the death of Anne's sister; she tries to come between Anne and Neill as she has come between Anne and every other potential love interest. There is also a fairy godmother in the town's motorcycle repairman, who delays telling Neill that his motorcycle is repaired. He explains his rationale to Neill:

> "By the time she was in high school, I don't think there was a boy within thirty miles who would have even thought to get fresh with her. She didn't date, didn't go away to college. It was like she was—"
>
> "Sleeping Beauty," Neill murmured, remembering his initial impression.
>
> "Yeah...Like Sleeping Beauty. It wasn't like she was unhappy. She was just not really awake. And then I saw her laughing with you, and I just thought—hell, I don't know what I thought...So I didn't tell you the bike was fixed and—"
>
> "Hoped I'd hang around long enough to wake her up?" Neill suggested. (377)

When Anne and Neill are finally reconciled, Neill offers her "the modern-day equivalent of a white charger" and tells Anne that "no handsome prince ever got this lucky" (379). The fairy tale references are played here for chuckles, but they also suggest just the opposite—sardonic on the surface but, since they have been validated by the romance of the plot, they are also meant to reinforce the fairy-tale nature of the story.

Judith Ivory's novel plays on the fairy tale more earnestly and thoroughly than the other two traditional romances. Ivory's heroine is illustrating a translation of Perrault's *Sleeping Beauty*, and excerpts from this (fictional) translation and from the translation's (fictional) preface rather heavy-handedly precede many of the chapters. Before Coco meets James, seven years her junior, the quote reads "It must be remembered that Sleeping Beauty was a hundred years older than the prince" (1). Before the chapter describing how Coco has kept herself from romantic involvement, a quote reads "the earliest known version of The Sleeping Beauty is probably the legend of the valkyrie Brynhild. Interestingly enough, in this tale the princess sleeps in full armor—a warrior-maiden all alone on a deserted island surrounded by a wall of fire" (18). Coco herself also references the fairy tale in a letter about her illustrations:

> I shall make the forest fierce. It will all but swallow the handsome prince who comes along and, with a kiss, gives Beauty's life meaning again.
>
> Ha. What a foolish tale this is at heart, don't you think? I say, wake up there, Beauty. Who better to make your life count than yourself? (87)

James also considers Coco in terms of the fairy tale, with her "roundly questionable ability to draw princes to her. La Belle au bois dormant. The Sleeping Beauty in the Woods. They came; they mired themselves in the thorny bramble of her reputation and her oddly potent power wielded from the bedchamber. Her forest slew some, while others fled with scrapes and scratches" (310). When James realizes he wants to marry her, he finds her in a theater balcony and calls up to her "Your fairy tale ending... I want to give it to you" (364). There is no possibility of forgetting the fairy tale in this rendition; it is referenced relentlessly.

Kristine Grayson's *Utterly Charming* and *Thoroughly Kissed* take a different approach in exploring the Sleeping Beauty fairy tale. The novels work from the assumption that the magic sleep could have happened, then explore the modern-day ramifications. Nora, the lawyer heroine of *Utterly Charming* is hired to help the "prince" (Blackstone, a magician) legally take possession of the glass coffin in which Emma, the sleeping beauty, is entombed. The heroine leads a mundane existence until she is drawn into a business relationship with Blackstone and a guardian/friendship with Emma. Once these relationships are established, the Sleeping Beauty's plotline is surpassed by the lawyer's; Nora becomes the sexual-metaphor Sleeping Beauty and Emma becomes the plot device to unite Nora with Emma's awakener, Blackstone. What could have been a simple modern rendition of the fairy tale (literal magical in the world today) cleverly turns to become a different type of modern retelling: the metaphorical, love-and-romance Sleeping Beauty. Throughout the novel, Nora is concerned with defending Emma, the sleeping beauty. She accurately describes the warfare between Blackstone and the wicked witch as a struggle for possession of the woman as an object, not as a human. She becomes Emma's defense against Emma's own archaic belief that she should simply acquiesce to Blackstone's demands, and she teaches Emma how to be a modern, independent woman. Nora keeps her own last name, not only through her first marriage and subsequent divorce but into her second, happy marriage with Blackstone. These feminist lessons also serve to teach the reader. The fact that Nora finds love at the end justifies being a strong woman, because only through her force of personality does Nora attract the sort of strong, interesting man who is her match.

The series' second novel, *Thoroughly Kissed*, follows Emma, who relinquishes her role as literal Sleeping Beauty to become a metaphorical one. Awakened from her 1,000-year sleep in the first novel, Emma is sexually awakened in the second novel. As in the first story, Emma's status as the magical/literal Sleeping Beauty serves as a plot catalyst (this time for her own plot, not someone else's). Leery of triggering another magical sleep, she has not been kissed since the kiss that initiated the coma. Emma describes herself to a colleague as "the original feminist" (29), happy with her work and her romance-free life. She did not stay with Blackstone because she hated the way he "tried to take over [her] life" (163). In the ten years that she has been awake, she has recreated herself as a professor, and it is another professor who becomes her "prince." Initially antagonistic colleagues, the two grow close as they travel cross-country, although Emma warns him that metaphorically and literally, "it may never be [his] turn to drive" (164). Emma, after her experiences as a sleeping pawn in a 1,000-year battle, does not believe in fairytales: "I think they sugarcoat everything. I mean, who believes in happily ever after?" (178). She learns differently, of course, falling in love and learning "what happily ever after felt like" (348). The novel ends with the two engaged to be married. There are lessons here, underneath the fanciful story: that women earn the respect of a potential romantic partner by arguing intellectually with him, and that even women who have been hurt in past relationships may find love and happiness.

Sleeping with Beauty alludes to fairy tales throughout, especially in italicized narrative commentary in the prologue and epilogue. It is also consistently a third-wave feminist princess story. The prologue, which takes place in sixth grade and which establishes the heroine's relationship with her two best friends (one female, one male), begins with the traditional "once upon a time, long, long ago..." before veering into modern-day parlance and setting. Taunted at lunchtime, Lucy is rescued by a new boy in school; she "followed her young knight-errant" (6) to the schoolyard after the altercation. She asks him why he interceded, "not sounding as much the grateful princess as she'd meant to. But then, no one had ever mistaken Lucy Harper for any kind of princess" (6). As mundane as the story seems, the use of the fairy-tale references in addition to the title leave little doubt as to what sort of ending there will be, or even with whom. Grady, the 6th-grader identified as a knight-errant, will surely be the one to ultimately awaken Lucy from her sexual sleep. When Lucy is invited to her 10-year high school reunion, she decides to go to "Beauty Queen Boot Camp" (33), an intensive makeover facility called Glass Slipper (which references Cinderella, not Sleeping Beauty, but no matter). The women at Glass Slipper act as Lucy's fairy godmothers, primping her outside: bleaching her hair, waxing her bikini line, and revamping her wardrobe. More than that, they force Lucy to examine her insides. They insist that while anyone can improve someone's appearance, their goal is to help "people find the best within themselves" (81). The concept of working on one's self-esteem and personal satisfaction is crucial to the story, a message meant for the reader; Lucy is not made over from the outside until she has begun the inner process. Lucy is praised for taking her destiny into her own hands, another lesson for the reader. To gain her ultimate goal (winning the attention of the object of her high school fantasies), the Glass Slipper women teach her, "You have to go into this as his equal...There can't be even a whiff of inferiority in your mind" (111). They use fairy-tale language to discuss her transformation, but they credit Lucy, not the man that Lucy had previously fantasized would "awaken" her, discussing "the power of [her] own magic" (145). The epilogue highlights the link to the fairy tale in one more italicized passage: "And so it came to pass that the knight known as Grady, his heart steadfast and true, swept his lady love Lucy off her feet (and frankly, those four-inch spikes were killing her anyway) and carried her into the sunset of their everlasting love (which looked a lot like his apartment in Alexandria)" (383). This takes the agency from Lucy for almost the first time in the novel—she not only remade herself, she also broke the nose of Mr. Wrong herself—but its flippant tone does not undercut the novel's message of female empowerment too much, and it falls in line with the Sleeping Beauty source material.

The Sleeping Beauty Proposal references the fairy tale repeatedly, but the relationship between the novel and the fairy tale is ambivalent and uneasy. The novel begins with Genie, the narrator-protagonist, dismissing the modern fairy tale:

> If you ask me, the best part about the Sleeping Beauty fairy tale is that she didn't have to do anything to get a man. She just lay around for a hundred years. And one day a cute guy ... hacked through a bunch of brambles, ran upstairs, and kissed her.
>
> Voila, instant husband.
>
> .... I'd like a husband in theory, but I don't want to have to work for one.... You know, keep my legs shaved and my figure trim. Dress well for all occasions. Learn how to grill a steak, twice-bake a potato, check my teeth for spinach, say no to desserts, look stunning in a bikini, bat my eyes, suck in my stomach, never burp, fetch beer, giggle at his every joke, wear thongs that ride up my butt, make nice to his sister, and play those games. (1-2)

Genie has nothing but scorn for women who play games, such as setting a timer for phone calls with men. Yet, ultimately, Genie does many of the activities she initially dismisses. When her boyfriend, Hugh, proposes to someone else on national television, then tells her she has always been sexually unappealing, Genie is devastated. Patty, Genie's best friend, convinces her to pretend to everyone that she and Hugh are engaged. Patty outlines all the ways Genie's life has been on hold with Hugh: Genie hasn't bought a house or changed her job because of how those decisions might impact their relationship. Patty sees Genie as "that idiot Sleeping Beauty, lying around like a zoned-out zombie waiting for your prince. Well, guess what, he rode right past your castle tonight and now you have a choice—you can either go back to bed or you can wake up" (22). Genie finally acquiesces, rationalizing, "If my prince wasn't going to come, then maybe the next best thing was pretending he had" (23). Once on the fast track to a (pretend) wedding, Genie begins all of those transformative behaviors that make her ready to meet her real prince, although that is never a stated purpose of the transformation. She hires a personal trainer, buys fancy underwear, and adds highlights to her hair. More importantly, she also does those things necessary to improve her life on her own. She buys her own house, speaks her mind at work, and earns a promotion; her life is improved in every way without Hugh. She does ultimately find a fulfilling relationship and is engaged by the end of the novel, but that romantic storyline shares the story equally with the revenge storyline of living better without Hugh. In case the reader did not deduce the moral, the novel's final lines provide one: "Like they say, good things come to those who wait. But, if you ask me, better things come to women who don't" (309). Genie calls herself and Patty feminists, although they fall on different points of the feminist spectrum, modeling for women the ways in which one can be a feminist and still enjoy men, still enjoy sex, still marry. The educative commentary given by the first-person narrator makes this more than a romance or a fairy tale for adults; *The Sleeping Beauty Proposal* is an educative third-wave feminist princess story.

The lessons offered by the traditional romance princess stories work in much the same way as those found in the Disney oeuvre. Read repeatedly or in multiples, the romance novels function as princess stories by teaching the same lessons: be beautiful, make yourself vulnerable to a man, and you will be rewarded with a lover who brings you to multiple orgasms and proposes marriage. The chick lit versions offer different, more feminist lessons: flaunt your intelligence, take care of yourself, and speak your mind. The immediate reward is to be happier about yourself, more confident and free—and that will bring a man into your life who is worthy of you. Women readers are still being taught by the princess stories they read, even in adulthood, even at the start of the twenty-first century.

Conclusion

The princess story thrives. "In spite of criticism and ridicule, mockery and disdain, artificial insemination notwithstanding and critics taken into consideration....Cinderella, Beauty and the Beast, and Sleeping Beauty are as eternal as life itself, impervious to reality" (Palmer 156-7). It is not quite 'impervious to reality,' however, as this century-spanning survey demonstrates. The princess story changes, reflecting the moment of the culture that produced it. As I hope this study has shown, the princess story can serve as a useful way of exploring the ways in which the waves of feminism altered the expectations of American girls and women. Princess stories may seem silly, inconsequential. We may believe we outgrow them. But—as do other fairy tales—they "provide a unique window into our most central concerns, our sense of social and cultural identity, who we think we are (or should be)— and how we change" (Orenstein 8). Princess stories in particular provide this sort of window into the central concerns of women and children. Perhaps as the culture becomes more comfortable with feminism and as women find the balance between work, romance, and carving their own identities, more princess stories will feature princesses who are unabashed, and unremarkable, feminists. That certainly seems to be the trend, even in the most traditional of romances. Although the images of the ideal princess have changed, the princess story maintains its influence and relevance in the lives of American girls and women at the start of the twenty-first century.

❖NOTES❖

Introduction

1. See Barbara Ehrenreich ("Bonfire of the Princesses"), Peggy Orenstein ("What's Wrong with Cinderella?"), Martin Goodman ("Dr. Toon: Growing Up Princess"), Gretchen McKay ("Makeovers Turn Little Girls into Disney Princesses"), and Melissa Fletcher Stoeltje ("Little Girls Carried Away on a Pink Wave of Princess Products"), to start.

2. Analysis of the Disney princesses is often along the lines of calling them "a sorry bunch of wusses" (Ehrenrich) or lauding Mulan and Pocahontas as "more can-do" girls (Stoeltje). While there is some truth to these assessments, these are not very useful, in-depth readings.

Chapter One

1. Because she was called so many names in her lifetime, modern biographers (Thwaite, Carpenter and Shirley, and most recently Gerzina, all of whose work has been consulted for this section) consistently call her "Frances" in their writing; I will do the same for this biographical section.

2. Frances described her marriage in a letter to Katharine Thomas as "so grotesquely hideous – it is like some wild nightmare which I surely must waken from presently" (qtd. in Gerzina 217).

3. See: Bixler; Cadogan and Craig; Connell; and Murray.

4. Critics often do not recognize how long it takes Sara to begin her project of identifying with a princess, characterizing it as the role she takes "first and always" (Gruner 166). Bixler (1984) sees Sara as a Cinderella, a princess in the beginning and then enchanted away from the role. She writes, "Burnett's stories do not emphasize a change within the main character but rather in the recognition of that character's true nature." I disagree with that assessment. As a princess story, *A Little Princess* is very much concerned with the transformation from regular (albeit bright and generous) little girl to princess.

5. This passage echoes one which Burnett wrote years earlier, about living with her brothers: "If you call names and stamp your feet they will tease you more; if you burst out crying they will laugh and say that is always the way with girls, so upon the whole it seems better to try not to look in a rage and keep your fury inside the little bodice of your frock" (Carpenter 15). It seems to have worked well enough

against real-life adversaries that Burnett gave the technique to her fictional alter-ego.

6. In fact, this was Shirley Temple's fourth Pickford remake, a terrible business decision on Pickford's part. (Pickford, one of the most powerful people in Hollywood, owned the rights to her films.) According to Elaina B. Archer, manager of the Mary Pickford library, "Shirley Temple remade a lot of Mary's films. If a grown woman can pull off playing a little girl, it's because she's such a talented actress. A little girl playing that role is just too darn cute and sickly sweet. I think Shirley Temple ruined Mary's name because it pinpointed her then as the sickly sweet little girl. It was the worst business decision of her life'" (qtd. in Lybarger). Other Temple remakes of Pickford films include *The Poor Little Rich Girl*, *Curly Top* (a remake of *Daddy Long Legs*) and *Rebecca of Sunnybrook Farm*.

7. Oddly, Lavinia and Sara are reconciled by the film's end, hugging each other and grinning as Sara says her final farewells. There is no hint given as to what reconciles Sara and the spiteful, insulting, unnecessarily cruel Lavinia. Certainly, in the novel there is no rapprochement; Burnett's Sara does not just forgive people simply from her general amiability. Perhaps the filmmakers thought it would be nicer, more winsome, if Sara forgave Lavinia and if Lavinia loved Sara. It is certainly less realistic.

Chapter Two

1. I will avoid the word "waves" in my discussion so as not to confuse them with the waves of feminism.

2. Two other animated princess films, *The Princess and the Frog* and *Tangled*, have since been released; their princesses are marketed with the twentieth century group. They are presently purported to be the last of the Disney princesses; the company has decided to stop animating fairy tales, as they are difficult to market to boys. (*Tangled* was originally titled *Rapunzel Unbraided*, but the company shifted the emphasis off the princess and onto her prince-to-be in an effort to boost male interest.)

3. Compared to the other terrifying plot elements and visuals, however, this seems a less-than-convincing justification. Indeed, one possibly apocryphal story about the film's initial theater run suggests that what remained in the story was so terrifying that Radio City Music Hall (which ran the film for a remarkable five weeks [Maltin 31]) had to re-upholster the seats because so many children had wet them in fear while watching the movie (Schickel 220). Certainly, many children had to be removed in tears from theaters all over the country.

4. M. Thomas Inge dismisses this change in the source material, saying it "had to do with dramatic engagement—that is creating more interest in the characters or plot through audience sympathy or involvement...(the sight of a princess throwing up would not be very appealing)" (8). Scenes of resuscitation and revival are a staple in thrilling, life-or-death screen situations, which leads to dramatic engagement, but they are not particularly romantic.

5. Disney would be the show's host from its inception in 1954 until his death in 1966, although the name went through a number of permutations, eventually becoming "The Wonderful World of Disney."

6. Princess ethnicity will become more inclusive in the second wave of Disney princess films, with Pocahontas (Native American), Mulan (Chinese), and Jasmine (Arabic) joining the group; Princess Tiana, the first African-American princess, will come along in 2009.

7. Although Disney's second group of princesses will include a more multicultural spectrum, there is a remarkable similarity between these more modern, more "exotic" princesses and their white antecedents, as well as a striking similarity among themselves. This will be further developed in Chapter Four.

8. While screen time alone does not necessarily correlate to the character's agency and importance (Snow White's prince has little actual time on screen), the princesses' lack of both does correlate to their diminishing screen time.

9. "Oh, no!" she exclaims in dismay at Maleficent's arrival. Later in that scene, she hopefully asks of Maleficent: "You're not offended, Your Excellency?" She can react, but not act—and she is concerned with etiquette and avoiding offense, all very feminine traits, but not important to the plot.

10. Both *Cinderella* and *Sleeping Beauty* have moments in the final scenes where the willowy princess lightly kisses her blustering, rotund father-in-law. Cinderella's father-in-law, in an oddly remove-the-garter motion, puts her slipper back on her foot after she loses it running to her honeymoon carriage. She kisses him, and he flushes. Aurora silences her father-in-law with a kiss as he asks, confused, how Phillip and Aurora came to be together. He, too, flushes deeply. Flushing, stammering silence is a very strange reaction from a father figure upon receiving a chaste kiss from his daughter in law. Snow White's motherly kisses also cause the dwarfs to blush, but at least those bachelors have no experience and no filial relationship to confuse the issue.

11. Although I remembered the godmother causing the glass slipper to magically turn Cinderella's work clothes into a princess gown the moment it was slipped on, that in fact does not happen; the shoe-fitting scene cuts to the wedding day, and Cinderella is shown in her wedding gown. The godmother neither effects the transformation nor appears in the wedding scene.

Chapter Three

1. She would revisit this introductory essay in the introduction to 1995's *Wonder Woman: Featuring over Five Decades of Great Covers*. Much of her second essay simply rehashes the 1972 essay, albeit in a somewhat less florid manner and with the successes of the second wave of feminism behind her.

2. This was the third attempt at a *Wonder Woman* television project. The first was Stan Hart and Larry Siegel's 1967 *Wonder Woman*, a campy disaster; the filmed product was less than 5 minutes long. The second was a "resolutely low concept" (Daniels

136) made-for-TV movie starring Cathy Lee Crosby as a blond "Diana Prince" era Wonder Woman, with no actual superpowers and modern, Emma Peel-style gear.

3. On the album and in the television special, this is a particularly glorious moment, with Alan Alda and Marlo Thomas reciting the lines in triumphant unison.

4. See also "Women who do and women who don't join the women's movement: Issues for conflict and collaboration" (R. Rowland, 1986); "A study of feminist identity development in women" (A. Bargad, and J.S. Hyde, 1991); "Predictors of feminist self-labeling" (G. Cowan, M. Mestlin, and J. Masek, 1992); "'I'm Not a Feminist, But...': Understanding Feminism" (J. Pilcher, 1993); "Fear of feminism" (L. M. Hogeland, 1994); *Who stole feminism? How women have betrayed women* (C.H. Sommers, 1994), and "'I Don't See Feminists as You See Feminists': Young Women Negotiating Feminism in Contemporary Britain" (M. Jowett, 2004) among many others.

5. An article by Jeannette Kavanagh reports that according to the Programme for International Student Assessment, "there is a significant gender gap in reading and writing. Girls performed significantly better than boys on the reading and writing tests in all countries" (*Literacy Gap Between Boys and Girls*).

Chapter Four

1. This is why the princess Jasmine, from the movie *Aladdin* [1992], is not under discussion here. A Disney princess story is signified by the princess as titular main character, not supporting love interest for the protagonist. While Jasmine is indeed marketed as a Disney Princess, the story in which she appears is not a princess story.

Chapter Five

1. Both *Elizabeth: Red Rose of the House of Tudor* and *Marie Antoinette: Princess of Versailles* mention women disfigured by smallpox and the havoc that disfiguration wreaked on their lives, but their commentary is fairly brief.

2. Disney also produced 2008's *Enchanted*, but this is a tongue-in-cheek almost-spoof of traditional princess stories, more along the lines of Dreamwork's *Shrek* than *Cinderella, The Little Mermaid*, et al.

3. The inclusion of Sara Crewe is interesting, as each Princess Diaries novel uses a quote from *A Little Princess* as its prefatory epigraph. These quotes link Cabot's princess story to Burnett's, both in terms of being modern princess stories and in terms of being didactic.

4. The filmic stepsisters are also members of the "Prince Char Fan Club," invented for the film and meant to lend a cheeky, modern air to the piece, but their personalities are unvarying in both depictions.

Chapter Six

1. Adaptations include but are certainly not limited to Orson Scott Card's *Enchantment* (1999), Mercedes Lackey's *The Gates of Sleep* (2002), Robin McKinley's *Spindle's*

End (2000), Sheri S. Tepper's *Beauty* (1991), and Deborah Ward's *The Wizard's Ward* (2004).

2. Science Fiction/fantasy comprises a mere 6.4% of all books sold and generates about half the revenue generated by romance.

3. Stephanie Harzewski (2006) argues that chick lit is not romance because of chick lit's first-person narratives, its use of humor, and because (she says) the one woman-one man romantic connection is not the central plot of the chick lit novel.

4. Anne Rice, writing as A.N.Roquelaure, has written a three-volume sadistic/pornographic version of the story which while not discussed here does firmly illustrate the connection between the fairy tale and sex.

5. Reader reviews of chick lit princess stories often express disappointment that, although they are romances, they contain little "romance," i.e., sex.

❖ BIBLIOGRAPHY ❖

Primary Texts

Baker, E. D. *The Frog Princess.* New York: Bloomsbury, U.S.A., 2002. *Tales of the Frog Princess.* Print.

Beauty and the Beast. Dir. Gary Trousdale and Kirk Wise. Perf. Robby Benson, Paige O'Hara. 1991. Buena Vista Home Entertainment, 2002. DVD.

Beauty and the Beast: Belle's Magical World. Dir. Cullen Blaine and Daniel de la Vega. Perf. Robby Benson, Paige O'Hara. Buena Vista Home Entertainment, 1998. DVD.

Binchy, Maeve. "Cinderella Re-Examined." 1985. Reprint. *Ride on Rapunzel: Fairytales for Feminists.* Dublin: Attic Press, 1992. Print.

Burnett, Frances Hodgson. *A Little Princess.* 1905. Ed. U.C. Knoepflmacher. New York: Penguin, 2002. Print.

———. *The One I Knew the Best of All.* New York: Scribner's, 1893. Print.

———. "Sara Crewe; or, What Happened at Miss Minchin's." *Sara Crewe, Little Saint Elizabeth, and Other Stories.* 1888. Reprint. New York: Charles Scribner's Sons, 1900. Print.

Cabot, Meg. *Perfect Princess.* New York: HarperCollins, 2004. *The Princess Diaries.* Print.

———. *The Princess Diaries.* 2000. New York: HarperTrophy, 2001. *The Princess Diaries.* Print.

———. *Princess Lessons.* New York: HarperCollins, 2003. *The Princess Diaries.* Print.

———. *Princess in Love.* New York: HarperCollins, 2002. *The Princess Diaries.* Print.

———. *Princess in the Spotlight.* New York: HarperTrophy, 2001. *The Princess Diaries.* Print.

———. *Princess in Waiting.* New York: HarperTrophy, 2003. *The Princess Diaries.* Print.

Card, Orson Scott. *Enchantment.* New York: Ballentine Publishing Group, 1999. Print.

Cinderella. Prod. Walt Disney. Dir.Wilfred Jackson, Hamilton Luske, and Clyde Geronimi. Voices by Ilene Woods, Eleanor Audrey, Verna Felton, Claire Dubrey, Helene Stanley, etc. Buena Vista Home Entertainment. 2005. DVD.

Dokey, Cameron. *Beauty Sleep.* New York: Simon Pulse, 2002. Print.

———. *Before Midnight: A Retelling of 'Cinderella'.* New York: Simon Pulse, 2007. Print..

Ella Enchanted. Dir. Tommy O'Haver. Perf. Anne Hathaway, Hugh Dancy. 2004. Buena Vista Home Entertainment, 2004. DVD.

Foreman, Michael. *All the King's Horses.* Scarsdale, NY: Bradbury Press, 1976. Print.

Friesner, Esther. *Nobody's Princess.* New York: Random House, 2007. Print.

Gibson, Mia. "Atalanta." Created 3 March 1997; last modified 11 March 2006 (Revision 3). *Encyclopedia Mythica™.* Web. 30 Apr. 2008.

Grayson, Kristine. *Thoroughly Kissed.* New York: Zebra Contemporary Romance, 2001. Print.

———. *Utterly Enchanted*. New York: Zebra Contemporary Romance, 2000. Print.

Gregory, Kristiana. *Cleopatra VII: Daughter of the Nile, Egypt, 57 B.C.* New York: Scholastic, 1999. The Royal Diaries. Print.

———. *Eleanor: Crown Jewel of Aquitaine, France 1136.* New York: Scholastic, 2002. The Royal Diaries. Print.

Hale, Deborah. *The Wizard's Ward*. New York: Luna Books, 2004. Print.

Hale, Shannon. *The Goose Girl*. New York: Bloomsbury, U.S.A., 2003. Print.

———. *Princess Academy*. 2005. Reprint. New York: Bloomsbury, U.S.A., 2007. Print.

Healy, Gráinne. "Snow-Fight Defeats Patri-Arky." Reprint. *Ride on Rapunzel: Fairytales for Feminists*. Dublin: Attic Press, 1992. Print.

Herman, Harriet. *The Forest Princess*. Berkeley, CA: Over the Rainbow Press, 1974. Print.

Ivory, Judith. *Sleeping Beauty*. New York: Avon Books, 1998. Print.

Kauffman, Donna. *Sleeping with Beauty*. New York: Bantam Books, 2005. Print.

Kavanagh, Linda. "The Princesses' Forum." 1985. Reprint. *Ride on Rapunzel: Fairytales for Feminists*. Dublin: Attic Press, 1992. Print.

Kaye, M.M. *The Ordinary Princess*. 1980. Reprint. New York: Puffin, 2002. Print.

Lackey, Mercedes. *The Gates of Sleep*. New York: Daw Books, Inc., 2002. Print.

Lasky, Kathryn. *Elizabeth I: Red Rose of the House of Tudor, England, 1544.* New York: Scholastic, 2002. The royal Diaries. Print.

———. *Marie Antoinette: Princess of Versailles*. New York: Scholastic, 2000. The Royal Diaries. Print.

Lau, Jaime. Trans. "Ode to Mulan.'"Yellowbridge: Your Literary Bridge to China." Web. 9 July 2008.

Lee, Tanith. "Princess Sansu." *Princess Hynchatti and Some Other Surprises*. New York: Farrar, Straus and Giroux: 1973. Print.

Levine, Gail Carson. *Ella Enchanted*. 1997. Reprint. New York: HarperTrophy, 1998. Print.

———. *The Fairy's Return*. 2002. Reprint. *The Fairy's Return*. New York: HarperCollins, 2006. Print.

———. *Princess Sonora and the Long Sleep*. 1999. Reprint. *The Fairy's Return*. New York: HarperCollins, 2006. Print.

———. *The Princess Test*. 1999. Reprint. *The Fairy's Return*. New York: HarperCollins, 2006. Print.

———. *The Two Princesses of Bamarre*. 2001. Reprint. New York: Scholastic, Inc., 2002. Print.

The Little Mermaid. Prod. Howard Ashman and John Musker. Dir.John Musker and Ron Clements. Perf. Jodi Benson, Pat Carroll, Rene Aberjonois. 1989. Buena Vista Home Entertainment, 1999. DVD.

The Little Mermaid II: Return to the Sea. Dir. Jim Kammerud and Brian Smith. Perf. Jodi Benson, Pat Carroll, Rene Aberjonois. Buena Vista Home Entertainment, 2000. DVD.

A Little Princess. Dir. Alfonso Cuarón. With Liam Cunningham, Liesel Matthews. 1995. Warner Home Video, 1997. DVD.

The Little Princess. Dir. Walter Lang. With Shirley Temple, Arthur Treacher. 1939. DVD. GoodTimes DVD, 2000.

The Little Princess. Dir. Marshall Neilan. With Mary Pickford, ZaSu Pitts. 1917. Nostalgia Family Video, 1996. Videocassette.

Lynn, Tracy. *Snow: A Retelling of 'Snow White and the Seven Dwarfs'*. Copyright 2003 by Elizabeth Braswell. New York: Simon Pulse, 2006. Print.

McKinley, Robin. *Spindle's End*. New York: Ace Books, 2000. Print.

Meyer, Carolyn. *Kristina: The Girl King, Sweden, 1638*. New York: Scholastic, 2003. The Royal Diaries. Print.

Michael, Judith. *Sleeping Beauty*. Large Print Book Club Edition. New York: Poseidon Press, 1991. Print.

Morenus, David. "The Real Pocahontas." N.d. Web. 9 July 2008.

Mulan. Dir. Tony Bancroft and Barry Cook. Perf. Eddie Murphy, Ming-Na Wen, B.D. Wong. 1998. Buena Vista Home Entertainment, 1998. DVD.

Munsch, Robert and Michael Martchenko. *The Paper Bag Princess 25th Anniversary Edition: the Story Behind the Story*. New York: Annick Press, 2005. Print.

Owens, Lily, ed. *The Complete Brothers Grimm Fairy Tales*. New York: Gramercy Books, 1996. Print.

Pocahontas. Dir. Mike Gabriel and Eric Goldberg. Perf. Irene Bedard, Mel Gibson. 1995. Buena Vista Home Entertainment, 1995. DVD.

The Princess Diaries. 2001. Dir. Garry Marshall. Perf. Julie Andrews, Hector Elizondo, Anne Hathaway. Buena Vista Home Entertainment, 2004. DVD.

The Princess Diaries II: Royal Engagement. 2004. Dir. Garry Marshall. Perf. Julie Andrews, Hector Elizondo, Anne Hathaway. DVD. Buena Vista Home Entertainment, 2004. DVD.

Schulze, Dallas. *Sleeping Beauty*. Ontario, Canada: Mira, 1999. Print.

Sleeping Beauty. Prod. Walt Disney. Dir. Clyde Geronimi. Voices by Barbara Jo Allen, Eleanor Audley, Mary Costa, etc. 1959. Buena Vista Home Entertainment, 2003. DVD.

Smith, Sherwood. *A Posse of Princesses*. Winnetka, CA: Norilana, 2008. Print.

Snow White and the Seven Dwarfs. Prod. Walt Disney. Dir. Davis Hand. Voices by Andriana Caselotti, Lucille la Verne, Pinto Colvig, etc. 1937. Buena Vista Home Entertainment, 2001. DVD.

Strohmeyer, Sarah. *The Sleeping Beauty Proposal*. New York: Dutton, 2007. Print.

Tepper, Sheri S. *Beauty*. New York: Bantam Books, 1991. Print.

Tompert, Ann. *The Clever Princess*. Chapel Hill, NC: Lollipop Power, Inc., 1977. Print.

Wrede, Patricia C. *Dealing with Dragons*. San Diego: Harcourt, Inc, 1990. The Enchanted Forest Chronicles. Print.

Yolen, Jane and Heidi E. Y. Stemple. *Mirror, Mirror: Forty Folktales for Mothers and Daughters to Share*. New York: Penguin, 2000. Print.

Secondary Sources

Aidman, Amy. "Disney's *Pocahontas*: Conversations with Native American and Euro-American Girls." *Growing Up Girls: Popular Culture and the Construction of Identity*. Ed. Sharon R. Mozzarella and Norma Odom Pecora. New York: Peter Lang Publishing, Inc., 1999. Print.

Allan, Robin. *Walt Disney and Europe*. Bloomington: Indiana University Press, 1999. Print.

Applebaum, Susan Rae. "The Little Princess Onstage in 1903: Its Historical Significance." *Theatre History Studies* 18 71-87 Je '98. Web. 11/8/2007.

"Author Q & A: Samuel R. Delany on *Dhalgren.*" *Random House, Inc. Academic Resources.* March 2001. Website. 22 Apr. 2008.

Bacchilega, Christina. *Postmodern Fairy Tales: Gender and Narrative Strategies.* Philadelphia: University of Pennsylvania Press, 1997. Print.

Bargad, A., and J.S. Hyde. "A study of feminist identity development in women." *Psychology of Women Quarterly,* 15, 181-201, 1991. Print.

Baumgardner, Jennifer and Amy Richards. "Feminism and Femininity: Or How We Learned to Stop Worrying and Love the Thong." *All About the Girl: Culture, Power, and Identity.* Ed. Anita Harris. New York: Routledge, 2004. Print.

———. *Manifesta: Young Women, Feminism, and the Future.* New York: Farrar, Straus, and Giroux, 2000.

Bell, Elizabeth. "Somatexts at the Disney Shop: Constructing the Pentimentos of Women's Animated Bodies." *From Mouse to Mermaid: the Politics of Film, Gender, and Culture.* Ed. Elizabeth Bell, Lynda Haas, and Laura Sells. Bloomington: Indiana University Press, 1995. Print.

Bernard, Jami. "HAIL 'MULAN'! SHE'S A KNIGHT TO REMEMBER DISNEY'S LATEST TEEN HEROINE DEFENDS CHINA FROM THE HUNS & WINS THE BATTLE OF THE SEXES." *New York Daily News.* 19 June 1998, 61. Web. 7 July 2008.

Bernheimer, Kate, ed. *Mirror, Mirror on the Wall: Women Writers Explore Their Favorite Fairy Tales.* 1998. 2nd edition. New York: Anchor Books, 2002. Print.

"Beyond Tiger Lily." Review. Newsweek. June 19, 1995. Web. 7 July 2008.

"Biography of Shirley Temple Black." The Kennedy Center. Web. Copyright 1990-2008. 7 April 2008.

Bixler, Phyllis. *Frances Hodgson Burnett.* Boston: Twayne Publishers, 1984. Print.

———. "Tradition and the Individual Talent of Frances Hodgson Burnett: A Generic Analysis of *Little Lord Fauntleroy, A Little Princess,* and *The Secret Garden.*" *Children's Literature* 7 (1978): 191-207. Print.

Bixler, Phyllis and Lucien Agosta. "Formula fiction and children's literature: Thorton Waldo Burgess and Frances Hodgson Burnett." *Children's Literature in Education.* Vol. 15, no. 2 June 1984. Print.

Brown, Marian E. "Three Versions of *A Little Princess*: How the Story Developed." *Children's Literature in Education.* Vol. 19, No. 4. 1988. 199-210. Print.

Brownlow, Kevin. "On Mary Pickford." *The Parade's Gone By.* New York: Alfred A. Knopf, 1968. Excerpt. *Milestonefilms.* The Mary Pickford Institute, Timeline Films, and Milestone Film & Video. Web. 19 March 2008.

Brownstein, Rachel. "Sarah Rothchild [sic] prospectus, 8/8/07." Email to Meghan Mehta. 16 Aug. 2007.

Burr, Ty. "The Beast Goes On." *Entertainment Weekly.* November 14, 1997. Web. 10 July 2008.

Cadogan, Mary and Patricia Craig. *You're a Brick, Angela! A New Look at Girls' Fiction from 1839 – 1975.* London: Trinity Press, 1976. Print.

Cameron, Stella. "Moments of Power." *Dangerous Men and Adventurous Women: Romance Writers on the Appeal of the Romance.* Ed. Jayne Ann Krentz. Philadelphia: University of Pennsylvania Press, 1992. Print.

Carpenter, Angelica Shirley. "Lady of the Manor." *In the Garden: Essays in Honor of Frances Hodgson Burnett.* Ed. Angelica Shirley Carpenter. Lanham, Maryland: The Scarecrow Press, 2006. Print.

Carpenter, Angelica Shirley and Jean Shirley. *Frances Hodgson Burnett: Beyond the Secret Garden.* Minneapolis: Lerner Publications Co., 1990. Print.

Carvel, John. "Cinderella Said To Be a Poor Role Model for Later Life." *Guardian.* 23 Apr. 2005. Web. 18 Feb. 2009.

Cashdan, Sheldon. *The Witch Must Die: The Hidden Meaning of Fairy Tales.* New York: Basic Books, 1999. Print.

Chandler, Daniel. 'Notes on "The Gaze"' 1998. Web. 2 Feb 2007.

Chmielewski, Dawn C. "Disney seeks high-end cachet; It's expanding its merchandising into couture fashion and furniture lines." Los Angeles Times. Jun 19, 2007. Web. 8/28/08.

Connell, Eileen. "Playing House: Frances Hodgson Burnett's Victorian Fairy Tale." *Keeping the Victorian House: A Collection of Essays.* Ed. Vanessa D. Dickerson. New York: Garland Publishing, 1995. Print.

"A Conversation with Shannon Hale." *The Goose Girl.* New York: Bloomsbury, U.S.A., 2003. Print.

Cowan, G., M. Mestlin, and J. Masek. "Predictors of feminist self-labeling." *Sex Roles: A Journal of Research:* 27, 321-330, 1992. Print.

Cowden, Tami. "The Women We Want to Be: The Eight Female Archetypes." *All About Romance.* 15 Aug. 1999. Web. 25 Aug. 2008.

Crawford, Philip Charles. "The Legacy of Wonder Woman." *School Library Journal.* 1 Mar. 2007. Web. 16 May 2008.

Cruea, Susan M. "Changing ideals of Womanhood During the Nineteenth-Century Woman Movement." *ATQ* ns 19 no3 187-204 S 2005. Web. 8 Nov. 2007.

Cupaiuolo, Christine. "Catherine Orenstein on Stepford Wives and the Culture of Reinvention." *Ms. Magazine.* July 2, 2004. Web. 8 Aug. 2008.

Daniels, Les. *Wonder Woman: The Complete History.* San Francisco: Chronicle Books, 2000.

Davies, Bronwyn. *Frogs and Snails and Feminist Tales: Preschool Children and Gender.* Revised Edition. Cresskill, NJ: Hampton Press, Inc., 2003. Print.

Davis, Amy M. *Good Girls and Wicked Witches: Women in Disney's Feature Animation.* Eastleigh, UK: John Libbey Publishing, 2006. Print.

Delahoyde, Michael. "Archetypal Criticism." Web. 25 Aug. 2008.

"Disney Princess." *Disney Consumer Products.* Jan 2008. Web. 20 Mar. 2008.

Doughty, Amie A. *Folktales Retold: A Critical Overview of Stories Updated for Children.* Jefferson, NC: McFarland, 2006. Print.

Douglass, Susan J. *Where the Girls Are: Growing Up Female with the Mass Media.* New York: Three Rivers Press, 1994. Print.

Druley, Deborah. "The Changing Mothering Roles in *Little Lord Fauntleroy, A Little Princess,* and *The Secret Garden.*" *In the Garden: Essays in Honor of Frances Hodgson*

Burnett. Ed. Angelica Shirley Carpenter. Lanham, Maryland: The Scarecrow Press, 2006. Print.

Durbin, Karen. "A New, if Not Improved, Use of Stereotypes." *New York Times*. 21 June 1998: 13. Web. 7 Jul. 2008.

Ebert, Roger. "Cinderella." Review. *Chicago Sun-Times*. Nov 20, 1987. Web. 26 Nov. 2007.

———."The Little Mermaid." Review. *Chicago Sun-Times*. November 17, 1989. Web. 5 July 2008.

———. "A Little Princess." Review. May 19, 1995. *Chicago Sun-Times*. Web. 8 Apr. 2008.

———. "Pocahontas." Review. June 16, 1995. *Chicago Sun-Times*. Web. 5 July 2008.

EDBakerBooks. Bloomsbury USA. N.d. Web. 12 July 2008.

Edgerton, Gary, and Kathy Merlock Jackson. "Redesigning Pocahontas: Disney, the "white man's Indian," and the marketing of dreams." *Journal of Popular Film & Television* Vol. 24.2 (1996): 90. Web. 5 July 2008

Edidin, Rachel. "Less Than Wonderful." *Inside Out*. 11 Feb. 2008. Web. 5/16/2008.

Ehrenreich, Barbara. "Bonfire of the Princesses." *The Huffington Post*. 11 Dec. 2007. Web. 8/25/08.

Evans, Meredith A. and Chris Bobel. "I Am a Contradiction: Feminism and Feminist Identity in the Third Wave." *New England Journal of Public Policy*. 207-222. Print.

Farrell, Amy Erdman. *Yours in Sisterhood: Ms. Magazine and the Promise of Popular Feminism*. Chapel Hill: University of North Carolina Press, 1998. Print.

Flinn, John C. "Snow White and the Seven Dwarfs." Review. *Variety*. Wed, Dec 29, 1937. Web. 26 Nov. 2007.

Foreman, Michael. *All the King's Horses*. Scarsdale, NY: Bradbury Press, 1976. Print.

Free to Be Foundation. N.d. Web. 22 Apr. 2008.

Gerzina, Gretchen Holbrook. *Frances Hodgson Burnett: the Unexpected Life of the Author of The Secret Garden*. New Brunswick, NJ: Rutgers University Press, 2004. Print.

———. "The Life and Legacy of Frances Hodgson Burnett." *In the Garden: Essays in Honor of Frances Hodgson Burnett*. Ed. Angelica Shirley Carpenter. Lanham, Maryland: The Scarecrow Press, 2006. Print.

Gibson, Mia. "Atalanta." Created 3 March 1997; last modified 11 March 2006 (Revision 3). *Encyclopedia Mythica™*. Web. 30 Apr. 2008.

Gleiberman, Owen. "Pocahontas." Review. *Entertainment Weekly*. June 16, 1995. Web. 5 July 2008.

Glenn, Joshua. "Wonder-working power." *The Boston Globe*. April 4, 2004. Web. 16 May 2008.

Goodman, Martin. "Dr. Toon: Growing Up Princess." *Animation World Magazine*. Jan 04, 2008. Web. 27 Aug. 2008.

Grant, John. *Encyclopedia of Walt Disney's Animated Characters*. 2nd ed. New York: Hyperion, 1993. Print.

Greene, Sheila. *The Psychological Development of Girls and Women: Rethinking Change in Time*. New York: Routledge, 2003. Print.

Greydanus, Steven D. "Cinderella (1950)." Review. *Decent Films Guide*. N.d. Web. 26 Nov. 2007.

Griffin, Sean. *Tinker Belles and Evil Queens: The Walt Disney Company from the Inside Out.* New York: New York University Press, 2000. Print.

Gruner, Elisabeth Rose. "Cinderella, Marie Antoinette, and Sara: Roles and Role Models in *A Little Princess.*" *Lion and the Unicorn: A Critical Journal of Children's Literature.* 19998 Apr; 22 (2): 163-87. Print.

Haase, Donald. "Feminist Fairy-Tale Scholarship." 2000. Reprint. *Fairy Tales and Feminism.* Ed. Donald Haase. Detroit: Wayne State University Press, 2004. Print.

Hanlon, Tina L. "To Sleep, Perchance to Dream": Sleeping beauties and wide-awake plain janes in the stories of Jane Yolen." *Children's Literature.* Storrs: 1998. Vol. 26 pg 140, 28 pgs. Web. 14 Apr. 2008.

Harries, Elizabeth Wanning. "The Mirror Broken: Women's Autobiography and Fairytales." *Marvels & Tales: Journal of Fairy-Tale Studies.* Vol 14, No 1. Detroit: Wayne State University Press, 2000. Print.

———. *Twice Upon a Time: Women Writers and the History of the Fairy Tale.* Princeton, NJ: Princeton University Press, 2000. Print.

Harzewski, Stephanie. "Tradition and Displacement in the New Novel of Manners." *Chick Lit: The New Woman's Fiction.* Ed. Suzanne Ferriss and Mallory Young. New York: Routledge, 2006. Print.

Hogeland, L. M. "Fear of Feminism." *Ms. Magazine.* 1994: November-December, 18-21. Print.

Hollows, Joanne. *Feminism, Femininity and Popular Culture.* New York: Manchester University Press, 2000. Print.

Howe, Desson. "Beast's' Beauty Only Skin-Deep." *The Washington Post.* Nov. 1991, n51. Web. 7 July 2008.

Inge, M. Thomas. "Art, Adaptations and Ideology: Walt Disney's Snow White and the Seven Dwarfs." *Journal of Popular Film and Television.* Fall 2004. Web. 28 Apr. 2005.

Jackson, Kathy Merlock. Introduction. *Walt Disney: Conversations.* Jackson: University Press of Mississippi, 2006. Print.

Jeffords, Susan. "The Curse of Masculinity: Disney's Beauty and the Beast." *From Mouse to Mermaid: the Politics of Film, Gender, and Culture.* Ed. Elizabeth Bell, Lynda Haas, and Laura Sells. Bloomington: Indiana University Press, 1995. Print.

Joosen, Vanessa. "Fairy-tale Retellings between Art and Pedagogy." *Children's Literature in Education.* Vol 36, No. 2 June 2005. Print.

Jowett, Madeleine. "'I Don't See Feminists as You See Feminists': Young Women Negotiating Feminism in Contemporary Britain." *All About the Girl: Culture, Power, and Identity.* Ed. Anita Harris. New York: Routeledge, 2004. Print.

Kamen, Paula. *Feminist Fatale: Voices from the "twentysomething" generation explore the future of the "Women's Movement".* New York: Donald I. Fine, 1991. Print.

Kamiya, Gary. "Not the book, but a lovely 'Princess'." *San Francisco Examiner.* Friday, May 19. 1995. Web. 8 Apr. 2008.

Kanfer, Stefan. *Serious Business: The Art and Commerce of Animation in America from Betty Boop to "Toy Story."* New York: Scribner, 1997. 1st paperback edition. Cambridge, MA: Da Capo Press, 2000. Print.

Kaufman, Joanne. "A Little Princess (review)." *People Weekly*. V 43 p17 May 22 1995. Web. 8 Nov. 2007.

Kavanagh, Jeannette. "Literacy Gap Between Boys and Girls." April 12, 2007. *Suite101.com*. Web. 3 June 2008.

Kehr, Dave. "'All Dogs,' 'Little Mermaid' a winning animated pair." *Chicago Tribune*. 17 Nov. 1989. Web. 7 July 2008.

Keyser, Elizabeth Lennox. "'The Whole of the Story': Frances Hodgson Burnett's "A Little Princess"." *Triumphs of the Spirit in Children's Literature*. Ed. Francelia Butler and Richard Rotert. Hamden, Connecticut: Library Professionals Publications, 1986. Print.

Kibler, M. Alison. *Rank Ladies: Gender and Cultural Hierarchy in American Vaudeville*. Chapel Hill: UNC Press, 1999. Print.

Kirkland, Janice. "Frances Hodgson Burnett's Sara Crewe through 110 Years." *Children's Literature in Education*, Vol 28. No 4, 1997. Print.

Knoepflmacher, U.C. Introduction. *A Little Princess*. Frances Hodgson Burnett. New York: Penguin, 2002. Print.

Kuykendal, Leslee Farish and Brian W. Sturm. "We Said Feminist Fairy Tales, Not Fractured Fairy Tales! The Construction of the Feminist Fairy Tale: Female Agency over Role Reversal. " *Children and Libraries*. Vol 5, No 3. Winter 2007. 38-41. Print.

Lamb, Sharon and Lyn Mikel Brown. *Packaging Girlhood: Rescuing Our Daughters from Marketers' Schemes*. New York: St. Martin's Griffin, 2007. Print.

Langer, Cassandra L. *A Feminist Critique: How Feminism Has Changed American Society, Culture, and How We Live from the 1940's to the Present*. New York: Icon Editions, 1996. Print.

Laski, Marghanita. *Mrs. Ewing, Mrs. Molesworth and Mrs. Hodgson Burnett*. London: Arthur Barker, 1950. Print.

Lewis, Barbara. "Fairy Tale Princes Turn into Beasts." 19 June 2005. Web. 17 Feb. 2009.

Lieberman, Marcia K. "Some Day My Prince Will Come: Female Acculturation through the Fairy Tale." 1972. Reprint. *Don't Bet on the Prince: Contemporary Feminist Fairy Tales in North America and England*. 1986. Jack Zipes, ed. Reprint. New York: Routledge, 1989. Print.

"A LITTLE PRINCESS starring Mary Pickford and ZaSu Pitts." Review. *PHOTOPLAY JOURNAL*. December, 1917. Web. 12 Mar. 2008.

Lott, Bernice and Diane Maluso. "The Social Learning of Gender." *The Psychology of Gender*. Ed. Anne E. Beall and Robert J. Steinberg. New York: The Guilford Press, 1993. Print.

Lurie, Alison. "The Making of a Marchioness." *In the Garden: Essays in Honor of Frances Hodgson Burnett*. Ed. Angelica Shirley Carpenter. Lanham, Maryland: The Scarecrow Press, 2006. Print.

Lybarger, Dan. "Something About Mary Pickford." *Pitch Weekly*. November 18, 1999. Web. 7 Apr. 2008.

Makinen, Merja. *Feminist Popular Fiction*. New York: Palgrave, 2001. Print.

Maltin, Leonard. *The Disney Films*. 4th edition. New York: Disney Editions, 2000. Print.

Mangan, Lucy. "Happily Never After." *Guardian*. 2 May 2005. Web. 18 Feb. 2009.

Marmion, Shelly and Paula Lundberg-Love. "Learning Masculinity and Femininity: Gender Socialization from Parents and Peers across the Life Span." *Praeger Guide to the Psychology of Gender.* Ed. Michele A. Paludi. Westport, CT: Greenwood Publishing Group, 2004. Print.

Maselin, Janet. "Fairy Tale doing a Child's Job: Reveling in Exuberant Play." *New York Times.* May 10, 1995. Web. 8 Apr. 2008.

Mazzarella, Sharon R. and Norma Odom Pecora, eds. *Growing Up Girls: Popular Culture and the Construction of Identity.* New York: Peter Lang, 1999. Print.

McGillis, Roderick. *A Little Princess: Gender and Empire.* New York: Twayne Publishers, 1996. Print.

McKelvie, Martha. "Interview with Mary Pickford." *Motion Picture Classic.* July 1918. "Eleven Contemporary Interviews with Mary Pickford." *Taylorology: A Continuing Exploration of the Life and Death of William Desmond Taylor.* Issue 55: July 1997. Ed. Bruce Long. Web. 7 Apr. 2008.

Millard, Rosie. "The People's Princesses." *TimesOnline.* June 17, 2006. Web. 114 Jan. 2008.

Modleski, Tania. *Loving with a Vengeance: Mass-Produced Fantasies for Women.* New York: Routledge, 1984. Print.

Mondello, Bob. "MULAN." *All Things Considered.* 21 June 1998. Web. 7 July 2008.

Mulan. Dir. Tony Bancroft and Barry Cook. Perf. Eddie Murphy, Ming-Na Wen, B.D. Wong. 1998. Buena Vista Home Entertainment, 1998. DVD.

Mulvey, Laura. "Visual Pleasure and Narrative Cinema." 1975. *Feminisms: an Anthology of Literary Theory and Criticism.* Ed. Robyn R. Warhol and Diane Price Herndl. New Brunswick, NJ: Rutgers University Press, 1997. Print.

Murray, Gail Schmunk. *American Children's Literature and the Construction of Childhood.* New York: Twayne, 1998. Print.

Nugent, Frank S. "Snow White." Review. *New York Times.* January 14, 1938. Web. 26 Nov. 2007.

O'Keefe, Deborah. *Good Girl Messages: How Young Women Were Misled By Their Favorite Books.* New York: Continuum International Publishing Group, 2000. Print.

Orenstein, Catharine. *Little Red Riding Hood Uncloaked: Sex, Morality, and the Evolution of the Fairy Tale.* New York: Basic Books, 2002. Print.

Orenstein, Peggy. "What's Wrong with Cinderella?" *New York Times Magazine.* December 24, 2006. Web. 8 Aug. 2008.

Palmer, Diana. "Let Me Tell You About My Readers." *Dangerous Men and Adventurous Women: Romance Writers on the Appeal of the Romance.* Ed. Jayne Ann Krentz. Philadelphia: University of Pennsylvania Press, 1992. Print.

Pecora, Norma Odom. "Identity by Design: The Corporate Construction of Teen Romance Novels." *Growing Up Girls: Popular Culture and the Construction of Identity.* Ed. Sharon R. Mazzarella and Norma Odom Pecora. New York: Peter Lang, 1999. Print.

Phillips, Susan Elizabeth. "The Romance and the Empowerment of Women." *Dangerous Men and Adventurous Women: Romance Writers on the Appeal of the Romance.* Ed. Jayne Ann Krentz. Philadelphia: University of Pennsylvania Press, 1992. Print.

Pilcher, J. "'I'm Not a Feminist, But…': Understanding Feminism." *Sociology Review.* 3 (2): 2-6, 1993.

Pogrebin, Letty Cottin. "A Note to Parents and Other Grown-Up Friends." *Free to Be...You and Me*. Marlo Thomas & Friends. Philadelphia: Running Press, 1974. Print.

———. Editor's Introduction. *Stories for Free Children*. New York: McGraw-Hill, 1982. Print.

Poniewozik, James, with Lina Lofaro and Desa Philadelphia. "The Princess Paradox: Hollywood's Newest Cinderella Stories Seek to Inject Some Feminist Messages into the Age-old Fantasy." *Time*. April 5, 2004. Web. 18 Apr. 2008.

Quong, Andrea. "MULAN'S WONDERFUL WORLD OF DISNEY ASIAN FEMINISM, WITH (UNBOUND) FOOTNOTE." *Chicago Tribune*. 23 Aug. 1998, 9. *Chicago Tribune*. 7 July 2008.

Rasky, Frank. "80 Million a Year from Fantasy." 1964. *Walt Disney: Conversations*. Ed. Kathy Merlock Jackson. Jackson: University Press of Mississippi, 2006. Print.

Regel, Jody. "The subversive value of feminist fairy tales: overthrowing some Grimm stereotypes." *Inter Action 4. Proceedings of the Fourth Postgraduate Conference*. Ed. Gabeba Baderoon, Chris Roper, Hermann Wittenberg. 1996. Bellville: UWC Press, pages 51-57. Web. 1 May 2008.

Reimer, Mavis. "Making Princesses, Re-Making *A Little Princess*." *Voices of the Other: Children's Literature and the Postcolonial Context*. Ed. Roderick McGillis. New York: Routledge, 2000. Print.

Ringel, Eleanor. "On Screen POCAHONTAS Disney's American tale of love in the New World is one of its best ever." *The Atlanta Constitution*. 23 June 1995, P/1. 5 July 2008.

———. "THE WONDERFUL WORLD OF 'MULAN' Disney redefines 'heroine,' refines animation in a tale of legendary China." Rev. of: *Mulan. The Atlanta Journal the Atlanta Constitution*. 19 June 1998, P/01. 7 July 2008 .

Robinson, Lillian S. *Wonder Women: Feminisms and Superheroes*. New York: Routledge, 2004. Print.

Romance Writers of America, Inc. *Romance Writers of America*. Web. 18 Sept. 2008.

Rosario, Rebecca-Anne. "The Princess and the Magic Kingdom: Beyond Nostalgia, the Function of the Disney Princess." *Contemporary Women's Issues Database*. 1 Mar 2004. Web. 4 Apr 2007.

Rowland, R. "Women who do and women who don't join the women's movement: Issues for conflict and collaboration." *Sex Roles: A Journal of Research*, Vol 14, 1986, pp 679-692. Print.

Rowe, Karen E. "Feminism and Fairy Tales." 1979. Reprint. *Don't Bet on the Prince: Contemporary Feminist Fairy Tales in North America and England*. 1986. Jack Zipes, ed. Reprint. New York: Routledge, 1989. Print.

Schickel, Richard. *The Disney Version*. 3rd edition. Chicago, Elephant Paperback: 1997. Print.

Schwartz, Lynne Sharon. Afterward. *A Little Princess*. Frances Hodgson Burnett. New York: Signet Classics, 1990. Print.

Schwartzbaum, Lisa. "A Little Princess." May 26, 1995. *Entertainment Weekly*. Web. 8 April 2008.

Scrimshaw, Diana. "Killing Dragons: Does This Turn a Princess into a Feminist?" *Talespinner*. #10 September 2000. Print.

Solomon, Charles. *The History of Animation: Enchanted Drawings.* 2nd ed. New York: Random House, 1994. Print.

Sommers, C. H. *Who Stole Feminism? How Women Have Betrayed Women.* New York: Simon & Schuster, 1994. Print.

Steinem, Gloria. Introduction. *Wonder Woman.* New York: Holt, Rinehart and Winston, 1972. Print.

———. Introduction. *Wonder Woman: Featuring over Five Decades of Great Covers.* New York: Abbeville Press, 1995. Print.

———. "What Buying This Book Will Do." *Free to Be...You and Me.* Marlo Thomas & Friends. Philadelphia: Running Press, 1974. Print.

Steinle, Diane. "'The Little Mermaid' has a disturbing message." *St. Petersburg Times.* 18 Dec. 1989,2. 7 July 2008.

Stone, Kay F. "Feminist Approaches to the Interpretations of Fairy Tales." *Fairy Tales and Society: Illusion, Allusion, and Paradigm.* Philadelphia: University of Pennsylvania Press, 1986.

Strickland, Carol A. "All-time worst panel: Wonder Woman #203." Web. 16 May 2008.

———. "The Diana Prince Era." August 2001. Web. 16 May 2008.

Stuever, Hank. "Wonder Woman's Powers: As the Superheroine Turns 60, She Maintains Her Grip on the Psyche." *The Washington Post.* Apr 18, 2001. Pg C01. Web. 14 Apr. 2008.

Tartar, Maria. Introduction. *The Classic Fairy Tales.* Ed. Maria Tartar. New York: W.W. Norton & Co., Inc., 1999. Print.

Tibbets, John C. "Mary Pickford and the American 'Growing Girl'." *Contemporary Women's Issues Database*: 06-01-2001. Web. 9 Nov. 2007.

Thomas, Frank and Ollie Johnson. *The Illusion of Life: Disney Animation.* Popular ed. New York: Hyperion, 1984. Print.

Thomas, Marlo. "This Is the Forward..." *Free to Be...You and Me.* Marlo Thomas & Friends. Philadelphia: Running Press, 1974. Print.

Threadgold, Rosemary. "The Secret Garden: an appreciation of Frances Hodgson Burnett as a novelist for children." *Children's Literature in Education,* Vol. 10, No. 3. Sept 1979. Print.

Thwaite, Ann. "A Biographer Looks Back." *In the Garden: Essays in Honor of Frances Hodgson Burnett.* Ed. Angelica Shirley Carpenter. Lanham, Maryland: The Scarecrow Press, 2006. Print.

———. *Waiting for the Party: The Life of Frances Hodgson Burnett.* 1974. Reprint Boston: Nonpareil, 1991. Print.

Triece, Mary E. "Rhetoric and Social Change: Women's Struggles for Economic and Political Equality, 1900-1917." *Women's Studies in Communication* 23 no 2 238-60 Spring 2000. Web. 8 Nov. 2007.

Trites, Roberta. "Disney's Sub/version of Andersen's The Little Mermaid." *Journal of Popular Film & Television.* 18.4 (1991): 145. Web. 7 July 2008.

Trousdale, Ann M. "I'd Rather Be Normal: A Young Girl's Responses to 'Feminist' Fairy Tales." *The New Advocate.* Volume 8, Number 3, Summer 1995. Print.

Trousdale, Ann M. and Sally McMillan. "'Cinderella Was a Wuss': A Young Girl's Responses to Feminist and Patriarchal Folktales." *Children's Literature in Education.* Vol 34, No. 1 March 2003.

Turan, Kenneth. "'A Little Princess' Casts an Enchanting, Magical Spell." April 6, 1995. *Los Angeles Times.* Web. 8 April 2008.

U.S. Department of Labor Bureau of Labor Statistics. "Women in the Labor Force: A Databook (2007 Edition)." Web. 3 June 2008.

U.S. Department of Labor Women's Bureau. "Women in the Labor Force 2007." Web. 3 June 2008.

Von Franz, Marie-Louise. *The Interpretations of Fairy Tales.* 1970. Revised Edition. Shambhala: Boston, 1996.

Warner, Marina. *From the Beast to the Blonde: On Fairy Tales and Their Tellers.* New York: Farrar, Straus and Giroux, 1994. Print.

Watts, Steven. *The Magic Kingdom: Walt Disney and the American Way of Life.* New York: Houghton Mifflin, 2001. Print.

"The Wide World of Walt Disney." *Newsweek.* Dec 31, 1962. *Walt Disney: Conversations.* Ed. Kathy Merlock Jackson. Jackson: University Press of Mississippi, 2006. Print.

Williams, Rachel and Michele Andrisin Wittig. "'I'm not a feminist, but...' Factors contributing to the discrepancy between pro-feminist orientation and feminist social identity." *Sex Roles: A Journal of Research.* Dec, 1997. Web. 8 Sept. 2008.

Womack, Sarah. "Fairy-tale Girls 'Don't Have Happy Endings'." *Telegraph.* 22 Apr. 2005. Web. 18 Feb. 2009.

Wyatt, Edward. "Chick lit is the romance novel's newest home wrecker." *New York Times.* August 18, 2004. Web. 18 Sept. 2008.

Zipes, Jack. *Breaking the Magic Spell: Radical Theories of Folk & Fairy Tales.* 2nd edition. Lexington: The University Press of Kentucky, 2002. Print.

———. *Fairy Tale and the Art of Subversion: the Classical Genre for Children and the Process of Civilization.* 2nd edition. New York: Routledge, 2006. Print.

———. *Fairy Tale as Myth/Myth as Fairy Tale.* Lexington: The University of Kentucky Press, 1994. Print.

———. Introduction. *Don't Bet on the Prince: Contemporary Feminist Fairy Tales in North America and England.* 1986. Jack Zipes, ed. Reprint. New York: Routledge, 1989. Print.

———. *Why Fairy Tales Stick: The Evolution and Relevance of a Genre.* New York: Routledge, 2006. Print.

❖ INDEX ❖

MODERN AMERICAN LITERATURE
New Approaches

Yoshinobu Hakutani, *General Editor*

The books in this series deal with many of the major writers known as American realists, modernists, and post-modernists from 1880 to the present. This category of writers will also include less known ethnic and minority writers, a majority of whom are African American, some are Native American, Mexican American, Japanese American, Chinese American, and others. The series might also include studies on well-known contemporary writers, such as James Dickey, Allen Ginsberg, Gary Snyder, John Barth, John Updike, and Joyce Carol Oates. In general, the series will reflect new critical approaches such as deconstructionism, new historicism, psychoanalytical criticism, gender criticism/feminism, and cultural criticism.

For additional information about this series or for the submission of manuscripts, please contact:

Peter Lang Publishing
P.O. Box 1246
Bel Air, MD 21014-1246

To order other books in this series, please contact our Customer Service Department at:

800-770-LANG (within the U.S.)
(212) 647-7706 (outside the U.S.)
(212) 647-7707 FAX

Or browse online by series at:

www.peterlang.com